Letters to a
Law Student

'This is a splendid book. It is well written, readable and wholly absorbing . . . a "must have" for every student of the law.'

from the Foreword by Lord Grabiner Q.C.

'I would strongly recommend this book to current students, as it raises issues which are not dealt with in other texts and has many sterling qualities. It could potentially become a classic text for law students.'

Roger Thomas
Undergraduate Pathway Leader (Cambridge) and Senior Lecturer, Anglia Law School, Anglia Ruskin University

'An excellent and comprehensive guide for all students who are considering doing a law degree or are already in the midst of one.'

Rajvir Thakore
first year law student, Middlesex University

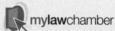 **mylaw**chamber

Visit the *Letters to a Law Student, second edition* mylawchamber site at **www.mylawchamber.co.uk/letters** to find more information on studying law at university.

- Get detailed guidance for using online resources in applying to university, studying law, and considering a legal career
- Read the author's responses to readers' questions in the regularly-updated 'Dear Nick' column
- Submit your own questions for the author to dearnick@pearson.com

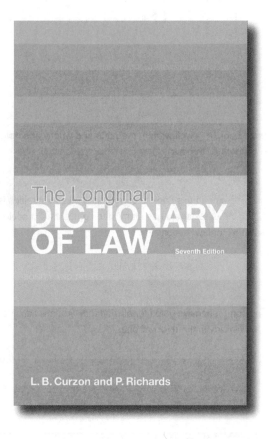

Letters to a Law Student

A guide to studying law at university

Second Edition

Nicholas J. McBride

Fellow in Law,
Pembroke College,
University of Cambridge

**Longman
is an imprint of**

Harlow, England • London • New York • Boston • San Francisco • Toronto • Sydney • Singapore • Hong Kong
Tokyo • Seoul • Taipei • New Delhi • Cape Town • Madrid • Mexico City • Amsterdam • Munich • Paris • Milan

Pearson Education Limited

Edinburgh Gate
Harlow
Essex CM20 2JE
England

and Associated Companies throughout the world

Visit us on the World Wide Web at:
www.pearsoned.co.uk

First published 2007
Second edition published 2010

© Pearson Education Limited 2007, 2010

ISBN: 978-1-4082-1880-8

British Library Cataloguing-in-Publication Data
A catalogue record for this book is available from the British Library

Library of Congress Cataloging-in-Publication Data
McBride, Nicholas J.
    Letters to a law student : a guide to studying law at university /
Nicholas J. McBride. —2nd ed.
        p. cm.
    Includes bibliographical references and index.
    ISBN 978-1-4082-1880-8 (pbk. : alk. paper) 1. Law students—
England—Handbooks, manuals, etc. 2.   Law—Study and teaching—England.
I. Title.
    KD442.M36 2010
    340.071'142—dc22

                                                                                2009048613

10   9   8   7   6   5   4   3   2
14   13   12   11   10

Typeset in 10.5/14 pt Minion by 75
Printed in Great Britain by Henry Ling Limited, at the Dorset Press, Dorchester, DT1 1HD

To Isabel and Ines

você está na minha cabeça o tempo todo

Contents

PART 4 Preparing for Your Exams 253

PART 5 Thinking About the Future 341

 mylaw**chamber**

Visit the *Letters to a Law Student, second edition* mylawchamber site at **www.mylawchamber.co.uk/letters** to find more information on studying law at university.

Companion Website for students

- Get detailed guidance for using online resources in applying to university, studying law, and considering a legal career
- Read the author's responses to readers' questions in the regularly-updated 'Dear Nick' column
- Submit your own questions for the author to dearnick@pearson.com

Also: The Companion Website provides the following features:

- Search tool to help locate specific items of content
- Online help and support to assist with website usage and troubleshooting

For more information please contact your local Pearson Education sales representative or visit **www.mylawchamber.co.uk/letters**

Foreword

This book is primarily aimed at law students, including aspirant ones. It takes the highly original form of letters written by a law teacher to Jo, an A-Level student who goes on to become an undergraduate law student.

Some of the letters or parts of them will be invaluable also to non-law students. There is shrewd guidance on how to go about one's studies; developing and applying an exam technique, planning and writing an essay; making and storing notes so as to maximise their value and to justify the time spent accumulating them; and, of course, revising for the inevitable exam. The guidance and advice in the letters should be followed: they will enable the student better to realise her or his full potential.

As an undergraduate law student, one of my first year courses was called 'English Legal System'. The textbooks were 'black letter' and, frankly, a bit tedious. As I read through Nick McBride's book, I became more and more convinced that this was the ideal educational tool and a 'must have' for every student of the law. The letters are stuffed with common sense and the wisdom and experience of an outstanding law teacher.

Time and again, the letters identify and elaborate upon some great legal issue: What is the rule of law? What is the relationship between law and morality? What should be the test of intention in the law of murder? There is an incisive essay on this subject which bravely, and rightly on the particular point, includes the sentence 'Glanville Williams is wrong'. The reader must understand that the late Professor Williams was one of the most outstanding legal scholars of the 20th century. Nick McBride's observation brings home to the student the critical importance of challenging fundamental assumptions (including those which may have been set down by distinguished commentators) with rational and logical analysis, concisely expressed.

At all times the reader is encouraged in the learning process to think about issues in a sensible, flexible and intelligent way: to apply reasoning and common sense rather than mechanically to invoke the principle enunciated in some recent well-known case which may only have some general relevance to the subject. The purpose of all the letters is to teach the student how to think for himself or herself, how to get to the heart of the problem and how to solve it.

This is a splendid book. It is well written, readable and wholly absorbing. The problem examples which are littered throughout are modern and realistic. The student will swiftly come to realise that the study and practice of law is an exciting and living thing which enables solutions to be found to what, at first sight, may seem to be quite intractable and brand new problems.

My only regret is that this book of letters was not available to me when I was a student.

Lord Grabiner Q.C.

Preface

This book has been written for anyone who is doing, or thinking about doing, a law degree at university. The book comprises a series of letters to a law student, Jo. The first letter is sent to Jo while Jo is doing A-Levels and thinking about doing a law degree at university. The final letter finds Jo studying law at university. It gives Jo some advice as to what sort of career Jo might pursue after leaving university. The 23 letters in between track Jo's progress from school to university, giving advice to Jo on various issues such as how to study law, how to write legal essays, and how to revise for exams.

Jo does not exist, but if you are thinking about studying law or actually studying law you will share some of the concerns that prompt the letters to Jo which are set out in this book. Some letters will be of more relevance than others. If you are thinking about whether law is the 'right' choice for you as a degree subject, you should definitely read Part I of this book. You may also find it useful to read letters 4 and 5, and then 10–14, and also letter 16 to get some idea of what you'd actually be doing if you studied law at university. I've made a start at doing this in the first letter in this book, but the later letters will give you a much better idea of what is involved in studying law at university. If you decide to apply to university to study law, then you should read letter 6; and if you are applying to a university that requires you to come for interview, then letters 7 and 8 are for you (and it would be a good idea to go back over letters 4 and 5).

If you have already secured a place to study law at university, then Part I of this book will be of limited relevance to you – though you may find some parts of the first and second letters useful. If you have yet to take up your place at university, you should read letters 4 and 5, and then letters 8 to 22. You should read the final three letters later, when you need to.

If you have already started studying law at university, read letters 4, 5 and 8, and then letters 11–22; again leaving the final three letters to later, when you need to. You may find some aspects of letter 10 useful for your studies; and it might be an idea to read letter 9 just before your next summer holiday.

One of the themes of this book is that to remember information, it is not enough to read it; you have to use it as well. Anyone who reads letters 12–21 just the once is likely to forget quite quickly what they have to say about how to study law and how to write well as a lawyer, and as a result their studies and their legal writing will not benefit at all from the advice contained in those letters. Aim instead to re-read constantly letters 12–21 in the early stages of your legal studies, to ensure that you are putting the lessons of those letters into practice. If you do this, you'll soon find that you'll never have to read those letters again to remember what they say; the habits of study and writing that they seek to inculcate will have become completely natural to you.

Because Jo doesn't exist, it was necessary to give Jo an identity – to make certain assumptions about Jo. I've assumed that Jo is doing a normal three-year law degree. So Jo is not doing a mixed law degree, such as a degree in Law and Politics or Law and Criminology; and Jo is not doing a degree that involves going somewhere on the Continent for one or two years to find out what the law says over there. I've also assumed that Jo is studying law at an English or Welsh university, and not a university in Northern Ireland or Scotland. Finally, I've assumed that Jo takes *exams* and that how Jo does in those exams will determine what class of law degree Jo will get. So, Jo's law degree does not involve doing coursework or a dissertation.

Making these assumptions has, of course, made the focus of this book a little narrower than some might like. For example, there is no advice in this book for students as to how best to approach the job of doing course-work, or how best to write a dissertation. But I'm not unduly concerned by this. One of the themes of the later letters in this book is the need for students to stop being so passive in the way they study law and adopt a much more active approach to their studies. Those who are capable of rising to this challenge will be more than capable of adapting the lessons taught in this book to their individual circumstances.

Another criticism that might be made of this book in some quarters is that it is too 'prescriptive' – it gives law students detailed guidance as to how they should study law instead of leaving it up to them to decide for themselves how best to approach the job of 'learning the law'. Not surprisingly, I would reject this criticism. In theory, the idea of allowing everyone to find their own way of studying law and letting 'a thousand flowers bloom' sounds very appealing. But in practice, giving law students no or little guidance as to how they should approach their studies leaves them in a wasteland, feeling confused, upset and very lonely. It is better, surely, to provide students with a model for studying law that they can all adopt, and then allow them to make *improvements* to that model in the light of their own individual circumstances. That is what I have tried to do in this book, among other things.

There are only a handful of books in this world that are incapable of being improved and this book is definitely not one of them. Students or teachers who have read this book and have constructive suggestions as to how it might be changed for the better shouldn't hesitate to get in touch with me at njm33@cam.ac.uk. I would very much welcome hearing from you.

Nick McBride
Pembroke College, Cambridge
1 August 2009

Acknowledgements

Thanks must go first to Christine Statham, the Commissioning Editor at Pearson Education, both for the initial suggestion that I write a second edition of *Letters to a Law Student*, and for all the efforts she put into guiding this edition to publication. I would also like to thank everyone at Pearson Education who contributed to the production of this edition, in particular Kevin Ancient, Andrea Bannuscher, Mary Lince and Caterina Pellegrino.

As always, I'm extremely grateful to my family, and especially my mother, for all their support and encouragement.

This book is dedicated to two of the most special people in my life: my best friend, Isabel Haskey, for always being there for me, and her daughter, Ines, for just being there. I simply couldn't function without their love and example.

Much love and thanks also go to Natalie Wilkins, for whom a lot of the letters in the original edition of *Letters to a Law Student* were written. Anyone who gets anything out of this book owes her a huge debt of gratitude, as do I.

I'd also like to thank Gabi Rutherford, Amanda Perreau-Saussine, and Amanda's family, for being such a huge source of encouragement and joy in my life. I also owe Gabi, Amanda, and Sean Butler, many, many thanks for taking the time to read a lot of the letters in this book and provide me with invaluable suggestions for how they could be improved.

This book could not have been written without the endless stimulation provided by my students – both in asking me for help and advice with particular aspects of their studies, and in showing me the traps that students can fall into and need to be warned against. I'd like in particular to thank Anastasia Bykova, Ashleigh Reid, Andrew Young and Charlie Brearley for providing me with feedback on some of the chapters in this book.

The final chapter of the book was rewritten to take into account the hugely helpful advice that two of my ex-students, Alex Robson and Siobhan Sparkes McNamara, gave at a careers evening that they helped to put on for my students at Pembroke College, Cambridge.

Finally, I'd like to thank my father for all the help he gave me with the writing of this book.

PART 1

Thinking About Studying Law

Why Law?

- From: Nicholas J. McBride [dearnick@pearson.com]
- To: Brown, Jo
- Subject: Why Law?

Dear Jo,

Thanks for your e-mail. So, you're thinking about what to study at university, and you are thinking about whether or not you should do a law degree. Well, the issue isn't so much whether you *should* study law at university but do you *want* to study law? The worst thing you could do is apply to study law at university and, once you are there, find that you have no basic interest in the subject. Anyone doing a law degree needs to work hard and think hard to do well, and the hours and hours you will need to put in to be successful as a law student will seem very long indeed unless you have a spark inside you that makes you really enthusiastic about studying law. So, what I'll try to do in this letter is set out some reasons why someone *might* want to study law at university. If these reasons make you want to study law, then that's great. But if they don't make you want to study law, I'll also be happy – at least you'll know that law probably isn't for you, and be able to start thinking about doing some other subject at university.

● Thinking skills

This is my number one reason why someone might want to study law at university: it teaches you how to think properly. I don't know of any other degree that does a better job of teaching people how to:

1 be logical in their reasoning;
2 discriminate between what is important and unimportant;
3 identify the key issues that affect a particular problem or situation that needs resolving.

This is because a lot of your time in studying law will be spent **reading cases** and **analysing problem questions to determine what the law says in those situations.**

Let me explain first how **analysing problem questions** helps you acquire the thinking skills listed above. For example, suppose in the course of your studies, you are given this legal problem to answer:

A was at a dinner party at B's house. On his way out, A noticed that it was raining outside. As he had no umbrella, he took an umbrella from the umbrella stand by B's door, intending to return it when he next saw B. A did not ask anyone's permission to do this as he thought no one would miss the umbrella: it was quite dusty and had clearly not been used for a while. A then walked to the nearest train station and took a train home. Unfortunately, he left the umbrella on the train. Is A guilty of theft?

You are told that A will be guilty of theft if he 'dishonestly takes property belonging to another with the intention of permanently depriving that other of the property'.

To answer the question, you first of all have to employ thinking skill (3) – you have to identify the key issues that are relevant to whether A is guilty of theft. You already know that A took the umbrella, and it's obvious that the umbrella belonged to someone else – so those aren't the issue here. The key issues are: (i) whether A was dishonest in taking the umbrella; and (ii) whether A had an intention permanently to deprive the owner of the umbrella of the umbrella.

Having identified these issues, you now have to employ thinking skill (2) – determine which of the facts of A's case are relevant to the issues that you have identified, and which facts are irrelevant. So, on issue (i), the fact that A needed an umbrella to avoid getting wet is irrelevant to the issue of whether he was dishonest: plenty of people steal because they need what they are stealing. On the other hand, the fact that A thought no one would mind that he had taken the umbrella might well be relevant to issue (i). And – on issue (ii) – the fact that the umbrella's owner has now lost the umbrella for good is irrelevant to whether A intended, when he took the umbrella, permanently to deprive the umbrella's owner of the umbrella: what happened to the umbrella after A took it has no bearing on what A's mental state was when he took the umbrella. But, of course, the fact that A intended to return the umbrella when he next saw B is highly relevant to issue (ii).

Now that you have identified what facts are relevant to the key issues on which A's guilt depends, you have to employ thinking skill (1) – reach a conclusion as to whether A is guilty of theft that follows logically from the definition of the offence of theft that you have been given, any information you have been given about the meaning of the particular terms used in the definition, and the facts of A's case.

So you can't answer a legal problem question properly without employing all of the thinking skills identified above. And if you work hard and study hard as a law student, you will invariably pick up all of these thinking skills because so much of your time as a law student will be spent reading cases. Let me explain: 'a **case**' consists in a set of facts that have given rise to a legal issue, which the courts have been asked to resolve. The decision of the court in that case is delivered in one or more **judgments**, delivered by the judge or judges who have been assigned the task of deciding what the law says on the issue in question. When you read a case, you read the report of that case, which will normally consist in a short summary (called a 'headnote') of the facts of the case and the decision of the judge or judges in that case, followed by a full report of the judgment(s) or the judge(s) who decided that case.

Lawyers read cases for two reasons. First, if a lawyer has a client who wants some advice as to what the law says on a particular issue ('Am I guilty of theft?', 'Can I sue X for what he did to me?', 'Am I entitled to that piece of property?', 'Did the government act illegally in closing my business down – and if so, what I can do about it?'), the lawyer can look up the relevant cases on that issue and in the light of those cases, advise the client as to what view the courts are likely to take on that issue, if that issue ever came to court.

Secondly, if a lawyer is representing a client in court, and is arguing that the court should decide the case in a particular way that favours the lawyer's client, the lawyer can win the day for her client by drawing the court's attention to statements or decisions made by the courts in previous cases which indicate that the client's case should be decided in a particular way. The courts are deeply committed to the principle that they should not be seen to be acting in an arbitrary or unpredictable manner when deciding cases. So suppose the courts have, in a number of cases decided in the past, said that, 'It is not theft if you borrow someone else's property, intending to return it in a useable state.' If a case now arises where Joe Bloggs has done precisely that, the court that has to decide whether or not he is guilty of theft may well feel itself bound – because of the statements in those previous cases – to declare that Bloggs is not guilty of theft. If they did anything else, he would have good ground for thinking that he was the victim of an injustice, and that if his case had been decided by some other judges, at some other time, he would have been acquitted. So if Bloggs' lawyer can find some statements in previous cases that indicate that he should be acquitted of theft, then she may well swing the verdict in his favour.

Students read cases for the same reason that fully fledged lawyers do – so that they can get a better understanding of how the courts are likely to decide a particular issue if that issue ever came to court. But in reading cases, they pick up all three of the thinking skills that I have listed above. That is because when a judge decides a case, he does precisely the same thing that a law student does in answering a legal problem. He identifies the key question relevant to the legal outcome of the case. He identifies the key facts relevant to that question. And having done both of those things, he reaches a conclusion as to the outcome of the case that follows logically from a combination of that key question and those key facts. Every time a law student reads a judgment, she get a practical demonstration of those thinking skills in action, and almost by osmosis picks up these skills herself.

It's not just lawyers who need to have these kinds of thinking skills: anyone involved in the sort of work that requires them to analyse information, and reach conclusions on the basis of that information has to have these skills if they are to do their job properly. So people involved in business, journalism, administration, or the civil service all need the sort of thinking skills that doing a law degree can give you.

● Rhetoric

In Ancient Greece and Ancient Rome, young men from privileged families used to be taught rhetoric: the art of speaking and writing effectively. A law degree is the closest thing you can get nowadays to a course in rhetoric.

Doing a law degree teaches you how to write effectively. This is for two reasons. First, anyone who does a law degree will be asked to read a lot of **articles**. These articles will discuss what the law says on a particular issue, or criticise the law on a particular issue, and call for the law on that issue to be reformed. Reading these articles will help you pick up the skills required to make out an argument in favour of a particular point of view ('The law says . . .', 'The law should say . . .') in a very clear and convincing fashion. Of course, not everything you read will present a particularly good example of good writing, but even a bad example can, through its badness, teach you some good lessons about what not to do. Secondly, as a law student you will be asked on a regular basis by your teachers to write essays or submit coursework on particular legal issues. If you do them properly, writing essays and doing coursework will help you hone your skills at putting together clear, convincing arguments in favour of a particular point of view. And if you don't turn in a very good essay, you will be soon told in what respects it fell short and shown how you could have done it better.

As for learning how to speak effectively, if you do a law degree at university, your university will usually hold regular mooting competitions. A moot is a hypothetical case giving rise to a couple of legal issues that students have to argue over in front of a 'judge' (normally a student studying law at postgraduate level, or a legal academic, or occasionally a proper judge who has come to the university especially to hear the moot). There are normally two students on each side, each student arguing their client's side of a particular issue. Mooting is a very effective way of enhancing your public speaking skills, and I recommend it to anyone who is doing a law degree.

I know some would say that other degrees, such as degrees in History or English, are just as good as a law degree in teaching you how to write effectively. I admit that taking a degree in English or History may well help improve your writing skills, but I don't believe that your writing skills will be improved as much as they would be if you did a law degree. Take the following passage, which I believe is representative of the sort of thing you might read if you did an English degree:

> Both Pound's 'Portrait [d'une Femme]' and Eliot's ['Portrait of a Lady'] constitute a kind of *epyllion* which, as we shall see, is a pattern they used a great deal – the parallel actions function as a plot and counterplot which enrich each other by their interplay. Poe's 'Descent into the Maelstrom' has structurally much in common with the vortices of the *Cantos*. Similarly, the 'Sargasso Sea' is a vortex that attracts multitudinous objects but which also tosses things up again in recognisable patterns which serve for survival.

I don't believe spending three years reading this sort of thing will help you learn how to write effectively.

Contrast the above with the following passage, which is taken from Lord Denning MR's judgment in *George Mitchell* v *Finney Lock Seeds* [1983] 1 QB 284. The facts of the case are made completely clear in the first section of Lord Denning's judgment:

> ### In outline
>
> Some farmers, called George Mitchell (Chesterhall) Ltd, ordered 30 lbs of cabbage seed. It was supplied. It looked just like cabbage seed. No one could say it was not. The farmers planted it over 63 acres. Six months later there appeared out of the ground a lot of
>
> >

loose green leaves. They looked like cabbage leaves but they never turned in. They had no hearts. They were not 'cabbages' in our common parlance because they had no hearts. The crop was useless for human consumption. Sheep or cattle might eat it if hungry enough. It was commercially useless. The price of the seed was £192. The loss to the farmers was over £61,000. They claimed damages from the seed merchants. The judge awarded them that sum with interest. The total comes to nearly £100,000.

The seed merchants appeal to this court. They say that they supplied the seed on a printed clause by which their liability was limited to the cost of the seed, that is, £192.

The heyday of freedom of contract

None of you nowadays will remember the trouble we had – when I was called to the Bar – with exemption clauses. They were printed in small print on the back of tickets and order forms and invoices. They were contained in catalogues or timetables. They were held to be binding on any person who took them without objection. No one ever did object. He never read them or knew what was in them. No matter how unreasonable they were, he was bound. All this was done in the name of 'freedom of contract.' But the freedom was all on the side of the big concern which had the use of the printing press. No freedom for the little man who took the ticket or order form or invoice. The big concern said, 'Take it or leave it.' The little man had no option but to take it. The big concern could and did exempt itself from liability in its own interest without regard to the little man. It got away with it time after time. When the courts said to the big concern, 'You must put it in clear words,' the big concern had no hesitation in doing so. It knew well that the little man would never read the exemption clauses or understand them.

It was a bleak winter for our law of contract. It is illustrated by two cases, *Thompson* v *London, Midland and Scottish Railway Co.* [1930] 1 K.B. 41 (in which there was exemption from liability, not on the ticket, but only in small print at the back of the timetable, and the company were held not liable) and *L'Estrange* v *F. Graucob Ltd.* [1934] 2 K.B. 394 (in which there was complete exemption in small print at the bottom of the order form, and the company were held not liable).

>

The secret weapon

Faced with this abuse of power – by the strong against the weak, by the use of the small print of the conditions – the judges did what they could to put a curb upon it. They still had before them the idol, 'freedom of contract.' They still knelt down and worshipped it, but they concealed under their cloaks a secret weapon. They used it to stab the idol in the back. This weapon was called 'the true construction of the contract.' They used it with great skill and ingenuity. They used it so as to depart from the natural meaning of the words of the exemption clause and to put upon them a strained and unnatural construction. In case after case, they said that the words were not strong enough to give the big concern exemption from liability; or that in the circumstances the big concern was not entitled to rely on the exemption clause. If a ship deviated from the contractual voyage, the owner could not rely on the exemption clause. If a warehouseman stored the goods in the wrong warehouse, he could not pray in aid the limitation clause. If the seller supplied goods different in kind from those contracted for, he could not rely on any exemption from liability. In short, whenever the wide words – in their natural meaning – would give rise to an unreasonable result, the judges either rejected them as repugnant to the main purpose of the contract, or else cut them down to size in order to produce a reasonable result.

Or look at this passage, from Brandeis J's dissenting judgment in the American Supreme Court case of *Liggett* v *Lee*, 288 U.S. 517 (1933) – containing observations that still have a great deal of relevance and power today:

Through size, corporations, once merely an efficient tool employed by individuals in the conduct of private business have become an institution – an institution which has brought such concentration of economic power that so-called private corporations are sometimes able to dominate the state. The typical business corporation of the last century, owned by a small group of individuals, managed by their owners, and limited in size by their private wealth, is being supplanted by huge

>

concerns in which the lives of tens or hundreds of thousands of employees and the property of tens of hundreds of thousands of investors are subjected, through the corporate mechanism, to the control of a few men. Ownership has been separated from control; and this separation has removed many of the checks which formerly operated to curb the misuse of wealth and power. And, as ownership of the shares is becoming continually more dispersed, the power which formerly accompanied ownership is becoming increasingly concentrated in the hands of a few . . . [and] coincident with the growth of these giant corporations, there has occurred a marked concentration of individual wealth; and . . . the resulting disparity in incomes is a major cause of the existing depression.

Both passages are very clear, very forceful – excellent examples of good, effective writing. It is no accident that so many of the greatest orators of all time – such as Demosthenes, Cicero, Daniel Webster, Henry Clay, Abraham Lincoln, William Jennings Bryan (and even Barack Obama, in our own time) – were all lawyers before going on to achieve fame as great speech-makers. It's no accident either that the speech for which Abraham Lincoln is most famous – the Gettysburg Address – is only 272 words long. Lawyers are past masters at learning how to express themselves succinctly and to the point. (In contrast, the Professor of Greek Literature who spoke before Lincoln at the Dedication Ceremony at Gettysburg spoke for two hours.)

It follows then that if you are interested in doing any kind of job which requires you to be able to express yourself effectively – and that would include any job that involves some sort of leadership role, as well as jobs in journalism, or politics, or the civil service – then you should be very interested in doing a law degree. No other degree is as effective in helping someone to acquire the skills they need to write and speak clearly, convincingly and forcefully.

○ Training to be a lawyer

Of course, if you become a lawyer after you leave university, you will definitely need the kind of thinking and rhetorical skills that I've been talking about. So doing a law degree at university is a great way of acquiring the sort of skills that someone needs to possess if they want to become a lawyer after leaving university. So if you want to become a lawyer after you leave university, then do a law degree. But do you want to be a lawyer?

You may have your doubts about that. Many people think that you have to sell your soul to become a lawyer. I understand why people might think that way. Anyone who has the power to argue convincingly on either side of a case will always attract suspicion. (The first philosopher in history, Socrates, was executed in Athens in 399 BC. One of the charges in the indictment against him was that he had the power to make the weaker case seem stronger.) The lawyer's ability to take either side of a case seems to indicate an unprincipled indifference to right and wrong. Lawyers – it is suspected – sell out their consciences and simply seek to represent whichever side in a dispute is willing to pay them the most for their services.

Let me act like a typical lawyer and put the other side of the case. Deciding to become a lawyer is just as morally worthwhile as choosing to become a doctor, or a teacher. This is because you can't have a functioning legal system without lawyers, and a society's legal system is as vitally important to the flourishing of the people living in that society as are that society's health or education systems. We tend to forget this in Western societies because we take our legal systems – and the benefits we obtain from living under our legal systems – for granted. To appreciate how important our legal systems are, I want you to do two things.

First of all, imagine what it would be like to live in a society where *everything is permitted*. We don't have to try too hard to do this: we just have to watch or read the news from other parts of the world to see examples of societies that have no legal systems worth speaking of – where there are no effective limits on what the State may do to its citizens, or what its citizens may do to each other. Life in such societies is 'solitary, poor, nasty, brutish, and short', in the words of the philosopher Thomas Hobbes, who lived through the breakdown of social order triggered by the English Civil War. People who live in such societies are condemned to live in chaos and disorder and to experience all the evils that flourish in conditions of chaos and disorder: murder, rape, arson, theft, starvation, despair, suicide. The fact that we don't live in such a society is due to the fact that we live under the **rule of law**. That is, we live under a legal system that sets strict limits on what the State may do to us ('no one may be deprived of their liberty by the State without due process of law') and what we may do to each other ('if it is reasonably foreseeable that your acting in a particular way will expose another to an unreasonable risk of harm, you must take care not to act in that way'), and those limits are – by and large – observed.

Secondly, imagine what it would be like to live in a society where *there is no trade*. In other words, imagine a society where each of us has to grow, or make, everything we need for ourselves and our families. Again, it's not too hard to do this – thinking about what life is like in the poorest areas of the world should give you some idea of what this sort of existence would be like. There would be no shops, no buildings bigger than those that could be built by a few pairs of hands, no guaranteed water supply, no food other than what you and your family could grow on land that you are lucky enough to have inherited, no tools to grow food other than those a single person could make for him or herself, no books, and no retirement in old age. Life in such a society would not necessarily be marked by chaos and disorder, but it would still involve a desperate and continuous struggle to stay alive. Again, the fact that we don't live in such a society is due to the fact that we live under a legal system that helps people to trade with each other, by doing two things in particular. First of all, it gives people something to trade by granting them legally enforceable rights over such things as their bodies, land, things and ideas. Secondly, our legal system allows people to enter into binding contracts with each other under which contracts their legal rights can be transferred to other people. Almost everything around you owes its existence to the fact that our legal system helps people trade with each other. Just think, for example, of the immense network of transactions that was required simply to produce the computer on which I am typing this letter.

So we in the West owe *everything* to the legal systems under which we live. Without them, our lives would be unimaginably different, and unbelievably difficult. And as you can't have a legal system without lawyers to run it, it follows that we should regard the lawyers who help to keep our legal system running as public heroes, in the same way that we regard doctors and nurses and teachers as heroic for the work they do. That, then, is my positive argument for thinking that becoming a lawyer is a morally worthwhile thing to do. But like any good lawyer, I won't close my argument without first considering, and dismissing, three arguments that might be made on the other side.

Defending evil

A question criminal lawyers are often asked is, 'How can you defend someone you know is guilty?' And a question corporate lawyers are often asked is, 'How can you work for a company that pollutes the environment/pays its workers so little/does as much as it can to avoid paying taxes?' The implication of both questions is that the work that the lawyer does is, at least on occasions, morally disreputable. The implication is unjustified. The short answer to both questions is that our legal system simply won't work properly if people are denied access to its benefits by lawyers who stand in judgment on them and refuse to work for them on the ground that they are not entitled to those benefits, or don't deserve them. The rule of law would be fatally undermined if the mere fact that you *looked* guilty ensured that you *were* found guilty without a proper trial. Freedom to trade under the law would be similarly undermined if the mere fact that people disapproved of the way you ran your business meant that you could not find adequate representation. If our legal system is going to work properly, and provide us with the benefits set out above, then lawyers have to be willing to represent unpopular or unpleasant clients, and do their best for them.

Irrelevance

It might be argued that the UK is no longer a country that lives under the rule of law. Whatever limits UK law does place on what the State can do to us, and what we may do to each other, these limits are purely theoretical. In practice, nothing usually happens when those limits are violated.

For example, police officers shoot an innocent man in a Tube station. And what happens? Nothing – other than that the police authority that was in charge of the officers is prosecuted for a trivial health and safety offence. No one of any consequence is prosecuted. Again, someone breaks into your house and makes off with all your

>

belongings. And what happens? Usually, nothing – the police give you an incident number so that you can claim for the break-in on your insurance, and do very little to track down the offenders. Again, someone is almost killed by an *e.coli* bug that was in some food that they bought in a shop. What happens? If the shop is unwilling to admit liability, usually nothing. If the person affected is very rich, then they may have the money to be able to afford to fund a legal action to obtain compensation from the shop; but if they aren't, and aren't eligible for legal aid to fund an action against the shop, then they may be advised to forget all about it – the chances of suing and losing are too great to make it worth the risk of litigation.

On this view, then, the games lawyers play are largely irrelevant to the vast majority of society and make little or no contribution to ensuring that we don't slide into living in a society where everything is permitted. To borrow the legal philosopher Roberto Mangabeira Unger's striking language, lawyers are 'like a priesthood that [has] lost [its] faith and kept [its] jobs . . . [standing] in tedious embarrassment before cold altars.' I don't think this is true. But even if it were, then you have even more of a reason to want to become a lawyer. If it is true that the UK cannot be said at the moment to live under the rule of law, and it's only morality or custom that currently stands between us and our living in a society where everything is permitted, then your generation can turn things around and start rebuilding the rule of law in the UK. If the rule of law is as important as I say it is – and it is – then no enterprise could be more valuable, or more urgent, or make more of a contribution to people's welfare. But to get involved in this great enterprise, you have to become a lawyer.

Corruption

The third argument against the view that becoming a lawyer is a morally worthwhile thing to do goes as follows:

'Becoming a lawyer is morally dangerous. In theory, you could do a lot of good as a lawyer in exactly the ways Nick McBride describes – you could help to uphold (or rebuild) the rule of law in the UK by becoming a criminal lawyer or a tort lawyer, or you could help foster commerce within the UK by becoming a commercial lawyer, or a corporate

>

lawyer, or a land lawyer. But lawyers also have the potential to do great evil. They can use their position to help destroy the rule of law in the UK, for example, by telling lies to the courts to ensure that guilty clients go free. And they can use their position to damage commerce, for example, by threatening their clients' competitors with expensive and potentially ruinous legal actions if they attempt to market a new invention that would transform the lives of millions. Unfortunately, the likelihood is that someone who becomes a lawyer will end up doing evil, rather than good. The power of money is too great to resist – a client who offers a lot of money to a lawyer in return for their doing something wrong or unethical will usually not be turned away. So whatever good you could do as a lawyer, it's better to do something else where you could do an equivalent amount of good (if not more), and not be exposed to the temptations to do evil that lawyers are routinely exposed to, and to which many lawyers succumb.'

This argument fails, at two levels. First of all, it's simply not true that lawyers are more likely than not to end up acting immorally. If that were true, decent lawyers would be extremely hard to come by. That is not my experience: most lawyers I come across are decent people, who haven't been corrupted by money, but instead seek to fulfil their professional responsibilities as best they can. Secondly, even if the factual basis of this argument were correct, and if this argument were accepted, it would mean that no one should become a lawyer, which – as we have seen – would be ruinous for our society. A society without lawyers is one without any kind of future. If it is true that lawyers are very susceptible to being tempted to do the wrong thing, the proper response to that fact is not for people to stop becoming lawyers, but for us to strengthen the sanctions against lawyers who do the wrong thing, so as to encourage them to resist temptation.

So far as morality is concerned, then, there is absolutely nothing wrong with becoming a lawyer. Quite the opposite: lawyers are just as important to the functioning of society as teachers or doctors.

And life as a lawyer can be much more interesting (not to mention more lucrative financially) than life in most other professions. This is because there is no aspect of social life that is left untouched by our legal system, and the impulse to guide people's conduct by laying down rules for them to obey that lies at the heart of our legal system. There are, then, as many different areas of law as there are different areas of social life: criminal law, private law (the law governing how we treat each other), personal injury law, medical law, professional negligence law, commercial law, sales law, competition law, copyright law, media law, entertainment law, sports law, animals law, land law, construction law, wills and probate law, trusts law, family law, labour law, company law, public law (the law governing how the government conducts itself), health and safety law, social services law, education law, tax law, international law (the law governing what nation states may do to each other, and how they should conduct themselves), immigration law, European law (made up of the law governing the UK's responsibilities as a member of the European Union, and the domestic law that results from those responsibilities). Given this huge range of different areas of law, it is open to practising lawyers either to specialise in one area of law that they find absolutely fascinating, or to enjoy working in a variety of different areas of law which ensures that they will always be meeting new challenges and issues over the years.

However, I should sound a warning note here. Precisely because the idea of becoming a lawyer is so attractive to a lot of people, the market for jobs as lawyers – particularly to become a solicitor in a top city law firm, or a barrister in a good set of chambers – is becoming increasingly competitive. So if you think you might want to become a lawyer, you have to be realistic about what the chances are of your achieving that ambition after you leave university. A useful website to look at for this purpose is:

http://www.unistats.com/

This will give you some information about what percentage of law graduates from particular universities obtain jobs once leaving university, and general levels of student satisfaction with the courses they receive. Look at the universities you are likely to be applying to and see how they rate for law. (Also ask the universities themselves for any statistics that they might have on this.)

If they don't rate so highly, don't despair! Just be careful – think about what other careers you might be interested in, and what sort of skills and qualifications they would require, and think about whether a law degree would put you in a good position to pursue those other careers, if a career as a lawyer doesn't happen to work out for you. If the other careers you are interested in (I am thinking in particular here of teaching) require you to have done a degree other than a law degree at university, remember it is always open to you to do a non-law degree at university and then qualify to practise as a lawyer by doing a one year Graduate Diploma in Law (GDL) – essentially a crash course in the core legal subjects – at a College of Law before then going on to do a one-year course to qualify to practise as a solicitor or a barrister. (Someone who does a law degree is exempt from the need to do a GDL and can go straight on to the one-year course to qualify to practise as a solicitor or a barrister.) So *if* you are not confident of your chances of making it as a lawyer once you leave university, given the universities you are likely to be applying to, *and* there are other careers you might be interested in *and* doing a non-law degree at university would be a better preparation for those careers, it *might* be an idea to hedge your bets by doing a non-law degree at university and then spend a year after that doing a GDL, and then see whether you can get a job as a lawyer on the basis of that, and the degree you obtained at university.

So – to sum up this letter:

> You don't have to want to become a lawyer to do a law degree. The analytical and rhetorical skills you will acquire in doing a law degree means that doing a law degree can provide excellent training for working in politics, or journalism, or business, or public service. But you shouldn't let all the lawyer jokes we both know and the caricatures of lawyers projected in the media put you off the idea of becoming a lawyer after you leave university. Lawyers perform an extremely important role in society, and they enjoy a very good quality of life in terms of how interesting and fulfilling they find their work. If you do want to become a lawyer, then doing a law degree would obviously provide you with everything you needed to become a very good and successful lawyer. However, you should be aware of how competitive it is now to become a lawyer, and you should think carefully about how likely it is that your law degree will provide you with a
>
> >

reliable launchpad for entering the legal profession, and how useful
a law degree would be to you for other careers you might be interested in pursuing if it turned out that you weren't able to pursue a career in law.

If you haven't made up your mind whether or not you want to become a
lawyer, you should read a book by a journalist called Jonathan Harr. The
book is called *A Civil Action* (Vintage Books, 1998). It may well inspire
you to become a lawyer. The book was made into a film – but try and read
the book: it's much better than the film. If you want to watch some really
great films about the law, get hold of *To Kill A Mocking Bird*, *The Verdict*,
True Believer, *Indictment: The McMartin Trial*, *The Rainmaker*, *Erin
Brockovich*, *Black and White*, and *Flash of Genius*. If those films don't
make you want to become a lawyer, then nothing will.

If you want to get a bit of a taste of what it is like to study law, and get a
better idea of how important law is to our daily lives, then I recommend
that you have a look at two books produced by my colleagues here in
Cambridge. The first is edited by Sean Butler, and is called *Discovering the
Law* (Law Matters Publishing, 2006). Each chapter deals with a different
area of law, explains what it's about, and focuses on a particular issue relating to that area of law, exploring it in some depth. I contributed three
of the chapters in the book. The second is edited by Catherine Barnard,
Janet O'Sullivan and Graham Virgo. It's called *What About Law?* (Hart
Publishing, 2007). Each chapter introduces you to a different area of law
by focusing in great detail on a particular case that is relevant to that area
of law. Both books are really good and stimulating. If I had to choose, I
would go with *Discovering the Law*, as it covers more areas of the law than
What About Law? and tells you more about them than *What About Law?*
But both are well worth reading.

Please don't hesitate to get in touch if you have any more questions.

Best wishes,

Nick

The Right Stuff?

- From: Nicholas J. McBride [dearnick@pearson.com]
- To: Brown, Jo
- Subject: The Right Stuff?

Hey Jo,

Thank you for your letter. You're quite right: I didn't say anything in my last letter about what sort of qualities you would need to do well as a law student at university, and that is obviously an important consideration in determining whether a law degree is the right choice for you.

It seems to me that there are seven qualities that you need to have to be a successful law student. To be a successful *lawyer*, you're going to need to have other qualities in addition to these seven. For example, someone who works in the field of family law will almost certainly need to be very good at dealing with other people in difficult situations. However, there's no point in my going into those other qualities in this letter. You shouldn't be put off doing a law degree because you are temporarily lacking in one or more of the additional qualities that you will need to be a successful lawyer. By the time you leave university, you will be a very different person from the person you are now and may well have acquired those qualities. So I'll just focus on the seven qualities that I think any law student needs to have if he or she is going to make a success of his or her studies.

Study skills

You will obviously need to have good study skills. Some of these (for example, the ability to concentrate for long periods of time, the ability to work hard, a love of reading) are maybe a bit too obvious to be worth spelling out. One less obvious study skill that you will need to have is **self-reliance**. You are going to have to be able to work on your own, to puzzle things out for yourself, to look up things yourself without anyone else's assistance, to find alternative sources of information when the sources that you've been pointed to run dry. Law is the most 'self-taught' subject that you can study at university. Anyone who is uncomfortable with working on their own, who prefers to be 'spoon fed' information, will find it hard to be a successful law student.

● Drive

Studying law is very much like flying a helicopter over certain terrain. From high altitude, the ground looks smooth and even. But as you fly in for a closer look, you can see that this is wrong: the ground has a lot of features and details that you couldn't see from higher up. Similarly, you can study law at different levels. You can 'fly high' and simply master the basic principles underlying the law. Or you can 'fly low' and come to appreciate the detailed features of the law that mark and qualify those basic principles.

Now, sometimes it's good to 'fly high' when studying law. It's good to get an understanding of the basic principles underlying some area of the law before flying in for a closer look. But someone who is content in his studies to 'fly high' *all the time* is flirting with disaster. He will come to think that the law is very simple and easy to understand – but this is an illusion created by the fact that he hasn't pushed himself to come to grips with the details of the law. Such a person is not likely to do well. To be successful as a law student, you have to **push** yourself to make the effort to 'fly low' and get a better view of the details of the law. A good law student will constantly ask herself: Is there anything more to learn here? Am I missing anything? Too often law students fail to do this. They are content to 'fly high', and learn their law from books that present the law in an oversimplified, 'nutshell' form. As a result, they lack the detailed knowledge of the law that they need in order to do well in their exams.

● Logic

A successful law student will be able to think **logically**. To explain what I mean by this, suppose that a law student is supplied with a couple of pieces of information that support a particular conclusion. If he or she can't see the conclusion that is supported by those pieces of information, then he or she isn't thinking logically. Take this problem:

> Someone will commit the crime of murder if his or her actions cause another to die and he or she performed those actions intending to kill someone or to cause someone to suffer serious bodily harm and he or she had no lawful justification or excuse for acting as he or she did.
>
> D sent his enemy, A, a parcel bomb, which was designed to explode and kill A when A opened it. Shortly after he posted the bomb, D repented of his plans and telephoned the police to warn them of what he had done. He gave the police detailed instructions as to how to disarm the bomb. B, a member of the Bomb Squad, was given the job of defusing the bomb but in doing so he accidentally cut the wrong wire. As a result, the bomb blew up and B was killed.
>
> Is D guilty of murder?

Here you are supplied with two pieces of information: (1) a definition of when someone will be guilty of murder; and (2) some facts. You are asked to reach a conclusion as to whether D is guilty of murder. Reaching the conclusion should be very simple if you think logically.

All we have to do is apply the facts to the definition of when someone will be guilty of murder. Analysing the definition, it is in three parts, so we need to consider whether each part is satisfied by the facts of this case.

> First: *Did D's actions cause another to die?* (Note that the definition merely says that D's actions must have caused 'another' to die – not that they must have caused the death of the person he was trying to
>
> >

kill.) Of course D's actions caused B to die: had D not sent A a parcel bomb through the post, B would not have died.

Secondly: *Did D perform those actions with the intention of killing 'someone' or of causing 'someone' to suffer serious bodily harm*? The answer is 'yes'. We've seen from our answer to our first question that what D did to cause B's death was send a parcel bomb through the post – had he not done that, B would not have died. Now, when D sent the parcel bomb through the post, he had an intention to kill someone or to cause someone to suffer serious bodily harm.

Thirdly: *Did D have any lawful justification or excuse for acting as he did*? Of course he didn't.

So the conclusion that is supported by the two pieces of information we have been given is that D *is* guilty of murder. If you think logically, you would see that. But when I try this problem out on students seeking a place to study law at my college, the vast majority tend not to think logically about the problem. They normally conclude that D is *not* guilty of murder because D was trying to kill A and not B, or because D no longer had an intention to kill anyone at the time B died. These are completely irrelevant considerations. What's gone wrong in their reasoning is that instead of determining whether the information they have been given supports the conclusion that D is guilty of murder, they consult their 'feelings' and ask themselves whether it would be 'fair' to find D guilty of murder and if those 'feelings' indicate that it wouldn't be 'fair' to find D guilty of murder (because, for example, he never intended to kill B; or because he had a change of heart and didn't want to kill anyone at the time B died) then they conclude that D is *not* guilty of murder. If you are going to do well as a law student, you've got to resist the temptation to think in this way and instead cultivate the habit of thinking logically.

Here's a little test you can take to see how logical you are. Consider this problem:

Someone will commit the crime of theft if he or she dishonestly appropriates property belonging to another with the intention of permanently depriving that other of it.

>

D paid for a 40p chocolate bar at a corner shop with a £5 note. A – who served D – was working in the shop while she finished a psychology degree. She was doing a dissertation on people's levels of honesty and decided to test D's honesty by giving him £9.60 in change. She wanted to see whether he would correct her and tell her that he had paid for the bar using a £5 note, not a £10 note. When A gave him his change, D thought that he must have paid for the bar using a £10 note. He therefore put the change in his wallet and walked out of the shop. It was only when he checked his wallet again just outside the shop that he realised A's 'error'. D decided to keep the excess change.

Has D committed the crime of theft?

There are three possible answers: 'yes', 'no' or 'we don't know'. What do you think the answer is? I'll give you the answer at the end of this letter.

○ Meticulousness

A successful law student will be **meticulous**. By this I mean two things.

1 **Rigour.** A successful law student will be rigorous in applying the legal rules that he or she is supplied with. So, for example, suppose that the law says that 'If a defendant does *x* in circumstances *ABC*, he will be guilty of theft unless either *Y* or *Z* are true'. And suppose you are asked to determine whether a defendant has committed the offence of theft in a particular situation. If you're rigorous about applying the above legal rule to determine whether the defendant has committed theft, then you'll ask yourself:

1 Did the defendant do *x*?
2 If so, did he do *x* in circumstances *ABC*?
3 If so, are either *Y* or *Z* true?

You won't fail to consider *any* of these questions.

2 **Detail.** A successful law student will have a **good eye for detail**. Suppose, for example, in deciding the case of *Fox* v *Swan*, the court said that, 'If A uses B's property, then A will be held liable to pay B a

reasonable sum for the use he has made of B's property'. Then, ten pages later in its judgment the court suggested that, 'It may be that A will incur no liability to B if he uses B's property to avert an emergency, but we defer consideration of that point to a later date.' A successful law student will take note of this suggestion as possibly qualifying the rule laid down by the court in its judgment ten pages earlier. She will not overlook it and blindly assume that the case of *Fox* v *Swan* held that if A uses B's property, A will *always* be held liable to pay B a reasonable sum for the use he's made of B's property.

One easy way of testing out how meticulous you are (as well as logical) is to do some sudoku puzzles. You'll find them in any newspaper. You can also buy books of them in the shops. And you can also do them online.[1] Here's one you can try right now:

	5		1	3			8	6
	4							
6			8		9	1		
			2			4	1	
	6						2	
	9	2			3			
		3	4		8			2
							4	
4	8			1	2		3	

The rules for completing the puzzle are: (1) each line and column should feature all of the numbers 1–9, with each number appearing no more than once in each line and column; and (2) each thick shaded box should feature all of the numbers 1–9, with each number appearing no more than once in each thick shaded box. Again, I'll give you the answer at the end of this letter.

---

[1] See the notes at the end of this book.

○ Flexibility

A successful law student will be **flexible** – he or she will be able to see both sides of an argument. Which is not to say that a successful law student will be incapable of coming to a conclusion as to which side of an argument is stronger – but he or she won't fall into the trap of thinking that only one side of the argument has any merit at all. Consider, for example, the following question:

> D and his family were kidnapped by terrorists. The terrorists threatened to kill D's family unless D assassinated the Prime Minister the next day using a gun which the terrorists gave to D. D duly shot the Prime Minister dead the following day, and the terrorists released D's family.
>
> Do you think D should be punished for what he has done?

A successful law student will be able to set out the pros *and* cons of the case of punishing D in this situation. He or she would be able to write the lines for *both* sides in the following debate over whether it would be right to punish D for killing the Prime Minister:

> **Pro-punishment**: Punishing D for killing the PM would make it more difficult for terrorists to force people to do the sort of thing D did.
>
> **Anti-punishment**: But why? Even if D knew that he was going to be punished for killing the PM, he would still have acted in the same way.
>
> **Pro**: Well – it's important to punish D so as to ensure that people in D's situation only act in the way D did when it is *absolutely necessary* to do so.
>
> **Anti**: But if it's established that D *did* have to act in the way he did, what harm would be done by letting him off?
>
> **Pro**: The fundamental point is that the law should encourage people to do the right thing, and D definitely did the wrong thing by killing the PM.
>
> \>

Anti: But again I go back to the point I made earlier: even if D knew he was going to be punished for killing the PM, he would still have acted in the same way. So how would punishing D encourage people in D's position to do the right thing?

Pro: Well, maybe it wouldn't – but we don't just punish people in order to deter people from doing the wrong thing. We also punish people because they deserve to be punished for acting wickedly – and D deserves to be punished because he deliberately did the wrong thing in the situation in which he found himself.

Anti: Okay – but who's to say that D chose to do the *wrong* thing here? Killing the PM saved more lives than were lost.

Pro: You can't justify sacrificing one person's life on the ground that doing so will serve the 'greater good'.

Anti: Who says you can't? We allow cars to travel on the motorway at 70 mph even though we know that a certain number of lives would be saved each year if those cars were made to travel at 40 mph. We justify the yearly sacrifice of those lives on the basis of the 'common good'.

Pro: But we're not trying to kill the people who die on the motorway. If you set out to kill someone, the fact that you are doing it for the 'greater good' can never make it right to kill that person.

Anti: That's ridiculous – what difference does it make if, on the one hand, you are trying to kill someone and, on the other hand, you know that someone is certainly going to die as a result of your actions (for example, setting the speed limit at 70 mph rather than 40 mph)?

And so on, and so on. Here's an exercise that you can attempt in order to judge how flexible you are:

David was part of a team of policemen trying to catch a serial killer known as the 'Riverside Strangler'. One night while David was on duty he received a call from a man purporting to be the 'Riverside Strangler'.

>

The caller said: 'You police are so useless. You'll never catch me without my help. I'll tell you what – I'll tell you where and when I'm next going to strike. I'm going to kill my next victim on Ashurst Lane, sometime between midnight and 3 am next Monday. Catch me if you can.' David dismissed the call as a prank call and failed to report it to his superiors. The following Monday, at about 1 am, Sally Jones was strangled to death on Ashurst Lane. David confessed to his superiors that he had been given prior warning that the 'Riverside Strangler' would strike when and where he did. David was immediately sacked. The story of David's dismissal got into the newspapers. Sally Jones' husband – Carl Jones – wants to sue David for compensation for the death of his wife.

Can you write out three arguments in favour of *allowing* Carl's claim *and* three arguments in favour of *dismissing* his claim? I'll set out my answer at the end of this letter.

● Judgment

It's important for a law student to have **good judgment** if he or she is going to be successful in his or her studies. If you have good judgment, two things will be true of you. First, you will be able to tell the difference between what's important and what's not important. In other words, you will have good **evaluation skills.** Secondly, you will be able to see what's going to help you and what's not going to help you achieve your goals. In other words, you will be blessed with **practical wisdom.** So someone who has got good judgment will have good evaluation skills and will be blessed with practical wisdom.

It is crucial that you have good evaluation skills if you are to be a successful law student. When taking notes on the materials you are told to read, it's vitally important that you be able to discriminate between what's important to remember and what's not. The same point applies when you are taking notes in lectures. In order to test your evaluation skills, consider the following passage, which is taken from Frederic Bastiat's pamphlet, *The Law* (published in 1850):

/?

s law? It is the collective organization of the individual right to lawful defense.

Each of us has a natural right – from God – to defend his person, his liberty, and his property. These are the three basic requirements of life, and the preservation of any one of them is completely dependent upon the preservation of the other two. For what are our faculties but the extension of our individuality? And what is property but an extension of our faculties? If every person has the right to defend even by force – his person, his liberty, and his property, then it follows that a group of men have the right to organize and support a common force to protect these rights constantly. Thus the principle of collective right – its reason for existing, its lawfulness – is based on individual right. And the common force that protects this collective right cannot logically have any other purpose or any other mission than that for which it acts as a substitute. Thus, since an individual cannot lawfully use force against the person, liberty, or property of another individual, then the common force – for the same reason – cannot lawfully be used to destroy the person, liberty, or property of individuals or groups.

Such a perversion of force would be, in both cases, contrary to our premise. Force has been given to us to defend our own individual rights. Who will dare to say that force has been given to us to destroy the equal rights of our brothers? Since no individual acting separately can lawfully use force to destroy the rights of others, does it not logically follow that the same principle also applies to the common force that is nothing more than the organized combination of the individual forces?

If this is true, then nothing can be more evident than this: The law is the organization of the natural right of lawful defense. It is the substitution of a common force for individual forces. And this common force is to do only what the individual forces have a natural and lawful right to do: to protect persons, liberties, and properties; to maintain the right of each, and to cause *justice* to reign over us all.

>

A just and enduring government

If a nation were founded on this basis, it seems to me that order would prevail among the people, in thought as well as in deed. It seems to me that such a nation would have the most simple, easy to accept, economical, limited, nonoppressive, just, and enduring government imaginable – whatever its political form might be.

Under such an administration, everyone would understand that he possessed all the privileges as well as all the responsibilities of his existence. No one would have any argument with government, provided that his person was respected, his labor was free, and the fruits of his labor were protected against all unjust attack. When successful, we would not have to thank the state for our success. And, conversely, when unsuccessful, we would no more think of blaming the state for our misfortune than would the farmers blame the state because of hail or frost. The state would be felt only by the invaluable blessings of safety provided by this concept of government.

It can be further stated that, thanks to the non-intervention of the state in private affairs, our wants and their satisfactions would develop themselves in a logical manner. We would not see poor families seeking literary instruction before they have bread. We would not see cities populated at the expense of rural districts, nor rural districts at the expense of cities. We would not see the great displacements of capital, labor, and population that are caused by legislative decisions.

The sources of our existence are made uncertain and precarious by these state-created displacements. And, furthermore, these acts burden the government with increased responsibilities.

The complete perversion of the law

But, unfortunately, law by no means confines itself to its proper functions. And when it has exceeded its proper functions, it has not done so merely in some inconsequential and debatable matters. The law has gone further than this; it has acted in direct opposition to its own purpose. The law has been used to destroy its own objective: It has

>

been applied to annihilating the justice that it was supposed to maintain; to limiting and destroying rights which its real purpose was to respect. The law has placed the collective force at the disposal of the unscrupulous who wish, without risk, to exploit the person, liberty, and property of others. It has converted plunder into a right, in order to protect plunder. And it has converted lawful defense into a crime, in order to punish lawful defense.

How has this perversion of the law been accomplished? And what have been the results?

The law has been perverted by the influence of two entirely different causes: stupid greed and false philanthropy. Let us speak of the first.

A fatal tendency of mankind

Self-preservation and self-development are common aspirations among all people. And if everyone enjoyed the unrestricted use of his faculties and the free disposition of the fruits of his labor, social progress would be ceaseless, uninterrupted, and unfailing.

But there is also another tendency that is common among people. When they can, they wish to live and prosper at the expense of others. This is no rash accusation. Nor does it come from a gloomy and uncharitable spirit. The annals of history bear witness to the truth of it: the incessant wars, mass migrations, religious persecutions, universal slavery, dishonesty in commerce, and monopolies. This fatal desire has its origin in the very nature of man – in that primitive, universal, and insuppressible instinct that impels him to satisfy his desires with the least possible pain.

Property and plunder

Man can live and satisfy his wants only by ceaseless labor; by the ceaseless application of his faculties to natural resources. This process is the origin of property.

But it is also true that a man may live and satisfy his wants by seizing and consuming the products of the labor of others. This process is the origin of plunder.

>

Now since man is naturally inclined to avoid pain – and since labor is pain in itself – it follows that men will resort to plunder whenever plunder is easier than work. History shows this quite clearly. And under these conditions, neither religion nor morality can stop it.

When, then, does plunder stop? It stops when it becomes more painful and more dangerous than labor.

It is evident, then, that the proper purpose of law is to use the power of its collective force to stop this fatal tendency to plunder instead of to work. All the measures of the law should protect property and punish plunder.

But, generally, the law is made by one man or one class of men. And since law cannot operate without the sanction and support of a dominating force, this force must be entrusted to those who make the laws.

This fact, combined with the fatal tendency that exists in the heart of man to satisfy his wants with the least possible effort, explains the almost universal perversion of the law. Thus it is easy to understand how law, instead of checking injustice, becomes the invincible weapon of injustice. It is easy to understand why the law is used by the legislator to destroy in varying degrees among the rest of the people, their personal independence by slavery, their liberty by oppression, and their property by plunder. This is done for the benefit of the person who makes the law, and in proportion to the power that he holds.

This passage is about 1,300 words long. Try and summarise it in about 100 words – and then compare your summary with mine, at the end of this letter.

As I've already observed, a law student needs to be blessed with practical wisdom if he or she is to do well in his or her exams. He or she needs to be able to tell what will help him or her impress the examiners, and what will not. Suppose, for example, that you are given an essay to do that asks you to suggest some reforms to the law on murder. Here are three possible essays you can write, each 96 lines long:

1 An essay suggesting 16 reforms, devoting 6 lines to each.
2 An essay suggesting 8 reforms, devoting 12 lines to each.
3 An essay suggesting 3 reforms, devoting 32 lines to each.

Other things being equal, which essay is likely to impress the examiner the most? The answer is (3). There is no way that you will be able to make out a convincing case for reforming an aspect of the law on murder in 6 or 12 lines – so essays (1) and (2) are going to strike the examiner as being lightweight. Only essay (3) has any chance of getting a high mark from the examiner. A law student who is blessed with practical wisdom will realise this and confine him or herself to suggesting three reforms and spend quite a lot of time on each one. A law student who is not so blessed may well decide to adopt a 'scattergun' approach, suggesting lots of reforms, hoping that the examiner will be amazed by his thoroughgoing critique of the law of murder. Sadly, the examiner will probably *not* be impressed.

● Interest in non-legal subjects

C.L.R. James, the West Indian writer, once observed, 'What do they of cricket know, who only cricket know?' The idea he was expressing in these lines was that cricket is a lot more than just a game – so those who view it as just a game don't really understand cricket at all. The same is true of law. As a law student, you'll be expected to criticise the law and develop views as to what it should say. In order to do either of these things, you will need to go outside the law, into the realms of **politics and economics**, and evaluate the law using the insights you've gathered from those subjects as to how society should be organised. So a successful law student will cultivate a keen interest in political and economic ideas, and use those ideas to add spice and interest to his or her essays on the law.

Those, then, are the seven qualities that I think you will need to have if you are going to be a successful law student. So – do you have those qualities or not? Don't necessarily assume that you know the answer to this question. Ask around – your teachers or your parents may know your strengths and weaknesses a lot better than you do. Now, what should you do if you conclude that you are lacking in one or more of these qualities? Should you give up on the idea of studying law? Not at all!

A tennis player with a weak backhand doesn't throw her rackets away. Either she works on her backhand until it's no longer a weakness, or she changes her game so she doesn't have to use her backhand very often. The same thinking applies here. Leaving good judgment aside for a moment, all of the qualities I've talked about can be acquired with **practice**. If you want to acquire any of the qualities I've been talking about, all you have to do is act as though you have that quality, and you will gradually come to acquire it. So, for example, if you find it hard to think logically, buy some puzzle magazines and start doing the puzzles and you will gradually find yourself thinking more and more logically. Similarly, if you find it hard to be meticulous. Buy a book of sudoku puzzles, start doing them and you will gradually become much more meticulous. If you have no interest in politics or economics, go down to your local library and borrow some books on those areas that look stimulating and start reading them – you'll soon find yourself developing an interest in those subjects.

This is, after all, how real-life law students improve their grades over time. Take a law student who did quite badly in his exams at the end of his first year because he wasn't very good at thinking logically. The same law student may well end up getting a first-class mark in his exams at the end of his third year. The improvement in his marks will be due to the fact that during the course of his second- and third-year studies, he will have had to answer a lot of problem questions – legal puzzles. Answering these questions will have helped him to think more and more logically, thus eliminating the weakness that pulled him down in his first-year exams. By the end of the third year, that weakness will have disappeared completely, allowing him to obtain a much higher mark in his third-year exams.

Now – what should you do if you lack good judgment? Unfortunately, good judgment can't be acquired through practice – it can only be acquired through **experience**, and there's nothing much you can do to ensure that you have the right kinds of experiences that will allow you to acquire good judgment. So good judgment is a very difficult thing to acquire if you don't already have it. However, lack of good judgment can be covered up, in the same way that a tennis player with a weak backhand can take steps to cover it up by changing her game so that she doesn't have to call on her backhand very often.

If you lack practical wisdom, you can learn to follow certain rules – for example, for writing essays – that will substitute for your lack of practical wisdom and help you do well in your exams. Of course, these rules won't help you in all situations and then your lack of practical wisdom may well trip you up, but they will suffice for most purposes. If you lack good evaluation skills, that's harder to cover up – but not impossible. You can learn from other people or books what are the most important points in some article you've been told to read. You can even learn to approach the article with a certain set of questions (such as – What point does this article make? What arguments does the author make in support of his point?) that will help highlight for you the important features of that article.

So, if you lack any of the qualities that I've said you'll need to become a successful law student, you certainly shouldn't rule out the idea of studying law at university. But what you should do is ask yourself – Am I willing to do the work that I will need to do in order to acquire these qualities, or to cover up for the fact that I don't have them? If the answer is 'no', then think about doing something other than law at university. But if the answer is 'yes' then nothing I've said in this letter should put you off the idea of studying law at university.

Best wishes,

Nick

PS

The answer to the problem on the law of theft that I set you earlier is 'No – D is not guilty of theft'. At the time D took the £9.60 change from A he was not dishonest. When he decided to keep the excess change, he may have been dishonest but by that stage the change belonged to D, so D could not be said to have been 'appropriating property *belonging to another*' when he decided to keep all of the change.

Here is the answer to the sudoku puzzle set out earlier:

2	5	9	1	3	4	7	8	6
8	4	1	6	7	5	2	9	3
6	3	7	8	2	9	1	5	4
3	7	8	2	9	6	4	1	5
5	6	4	7	8	1	3	2	9
1	9	2	5	4	3	6	7	8
7	1	3	4	5	8	9	6	2
9	2	5	3	6	7	8	4	1
4	8	6	9	1	2	5	3	7

Here are three arguments in favour of allowing Carl's claim against David:

1 Doing so will encourage the police to do their jobs properly.

2 Allowing Carl to sue David will allow Carl to think that some good has come out of his wife's death – he's been enabled to obtain a judgment against David that will encourage the police generally to be more careful in their investigations in future – and therefore make it easier for him to come to terms with his wife's death.

3 If Carl had employed a bodyguard to look after Sally and he had failed to protect Sally from being strangled, there's no doubt that the bodyguard would be held liable to Carl for Sally's death. Carl has – through paying taxes – employed people like David to look after people like Sally, so there is no real difference between David's case and that of our hypothetical bodyguard. If the bodyguard would be held liable, so should David.

And here are three arguments in favour of dismissing Carl's claim against David:

1 Allowing Carl's claim will only encourage the police to pursue every single call they receive – no matter how silly it might seem – in order to avoid the slightest risk of being sued; as a result police resources will be wasted and it will be much harder for the police to do their jobs effectively.

2 If the object of allowing Carl to sue David is to punish David for what he did, so as to encourage people like David to do their jobs properly in future, there is no need to allow Carl's claim against David. David has already been punished enough through the loss of his job. The prospect of being subject to disciplinary proceedings should be enough to encourage the police generally to do their jobs properly.

3 It is not clear what would have happened had David followed up the call he received. Maybe the 'Riverside Strangler' would have still managed to kill Sally Jones or maybe he would have killed someone else in some other location. So it is very difficult to tell whether any *net* harm was caused by David's inaction – and given this, it would be unjust to hold David liable for what he did or what he failed to do.

Finally, here's my summary of the passage from Bastiat's *The Law*:

The law exists to protect people's rights to life, liberty and the enjoyment of their property. If the law simply concerned itself with protecting people's rights, then no one would have any cause to blame the state for his misfortunes, and people would be free to satisfy their needs without any interference from the government. Unfortunately, the law has to be made and enforced by men, and because men are naturally greedy, those who are in charge of the law abuse it to deprive other people of their rights. (89 words)

Law Degree or GDL?

○ From: Nicholas J. McBride [dearnick@pearson.com]
○ To: Brown, Jo
○ Subject: Law Degree or GDL?

Hey Jo,

Thanks for your e-mail. So, as I understand it, you've decided you really want to become a lawyer when you leave university, but you're uncertain whether to (as I put it in my first letter) 'hedge your bets' by doing some other degree at university and then doing a one-year conversion course (the 'Graduate Diploma in Law', or GDL for short) in law which will then enable you to go on to become a lawyer.

Just to make sure you are clear about the alternative paths to qualifying as a lawyer that are available to you, I've set out on the next page a table illustrating two different students' paths into the legal profession. So, Andy and Lara both enter university at the same time. Andy does a law degree for three years; Lara does a history degree for the same period of time. After they leave university, both decide to become lawyers.

Andy takes a one-year vocational training course to become a lawyer – the Legal Practice Course ('LPC') if he wants to become a solicitor, the Bar Vocational Course ('BVC') if he wants to become a barrister. If Andy wants to be a barrister, having completed the BVC – at which point he will count as a fully-qualified barrister – he will go on to work in a set of chambers for a year doing what is called a 'pupillage' in the hope that at the end of the year he will be taken on as a permanent 'tenant' – or member – of the set of chambers. Alternatively, if Andy wants to be a solicitor, once

		Andy		**Lara**	
2010	Oct	Starts three-year law degree		Starts three-year history degree	
2011					
2012					
2013	Jun	Finishes law degree		Finishes history degree	
	Sep	Starts one-year Bar Vocational Course (training to be a barrister)	Starts one-year Legal Practice Course (training to be a solicitor)	Starts one year Graduate Diploma in Law (studying 'core' legal subjects that any lawyer has to know about)	
2014	Jun	Finishes BVC; qualifies for the Bar	Finishes LPC	Finishes GDL	
	Sep	Starts one-year pupillage at set of chambers	Starts two-year training contract with firm of solicitors	Starts BVC	Starts LPC
2015	Jun			Finishes BVC; qualifies for the Bar	Finishes LPC
	Sep	Accepted for tenancy by chambers		Starts one-year pupillage at set of chambers	Starts two-year training contract with firm of solicitors
2016	Sep		Qualifies as solicitor; taken on by firm to act as associate	Accepted for tenancy by chambers	
2017	Sep				Qualifies as solicitor; taken on by firm to act as associate

he has finished the LPC, he will enter a firm of solicitors as a trainee solicitor and work there for two years on a 'training contract' before qualifying as a fully-fledged solicitor.

Lara will take exactly the same route into the profession – but because she has not done a law degree, before she can do the LPC or the BVC, she will have to do a one-year crash course in law, the GDL. Anyone doing the GDL has to study the seven 'core' legal subjects that anyone practising as a lawyer is expected to know about. These subjects are: **criminal law**, **constitutional law**, **tort law**, **contract law**, **land law**, **Equity** (or the law of trusts), and **European Union law**. At the end of this course, Lara will have to take exams in each of these subjects to prove her proficiency in them. If she passes each of the exams, she can then go on to do the LPC or the BVC.

So, as you'll see from the table here, if Andy and Lara both become solicitors, Lara will always lag one year behind Andy; and this will also be the case if Andy and Lara both become barristers.

The issue, then, is – Which path should you follow: Andy or Lara's? My position on this remains the same as in the first letter I wrote to you. It makes sense to think about hedging your bets if you aren't confident that doing a law degree at the sort of universities to which you are likely to apply will result in you getting the sort of offers of law jobs that you're looking to get once you leave university. But if you aren't in that position, then I really think you should just get on and do a law degree. For the reasons I've already explained – I'm doubtful whether doing some other kind of degree would help you as much as doing a law degree would in developing the thinking and rhetorical skills that lawyers need to be effective. And there are lots of other reasons why – if you want to become a lawyer – you should think seriously about doing a law degree at university rather than taking the route of doing some other kind of degree and then a GDL.

● Breadth of experience

If you do a law degree, you will study a far wider range of subjects than if you do a GDL. So you will be in a much better position to decide what kind of area of law you want to specialise in if you have done a law degree than if you do a GDL.

◉ Legal skills

There's no doubt that someone who has done a law degree will find it far easier to perform a number of basic legal tasks – such as researching a particular legal point, reading cases, summarising the law in a particular area, and making arguments – than someone who has done the GDL. Law firms and sets of chambers tend to discount this in considering applications for positions with them because they think that someone who has done the GDL will pick up these skills quickly enough. But you will find your first six months at a law firm or in a set of chambers are a lot easier, and a lot less intimidating, if you have done a law degree than if you have simply done the GDL.

◉ Post-graduate study

Doing a one-year post-graduate degree in law, such as an LLM (whether here or abroad) or the Oxford Bachelor of Civil Law (BCL) degree, is an increasingly important way of impressing sets of chambers that you have the requisite intellectual ability to succeed as a barrister. While it is possible in theory to do this kind of post-graduate work in law if you have not already done a law degree, but have simply done a GDL, it will obviously be much harder to do well on such a post-graduate course without having already a law degree under your belt. (Though there are obviously exceptions: I know of one student who did a non-law degree at university, then a GDL, and then the next year achieved the second best performance in the Oxford BCL exam.)

◉ Evaluating the law

It's very important if you are going to work as a barrister – arguing cases in court on behalf of a client – that you learn how to make effective arguments as to what the law *should* say. This is because cases normally only go to court if it's *uncertain* what the law says on the issue raised by the case. If the law in a particular case were clear ('He's guilty!'; 'She has to pay him £50,000'; 'The government's order that he be deported is invalid and of no effect'), there'd be no reason for the parties to that case to go to court to get a judge to tell them what the law says on the issue raised by the case.

Now, if a judge has to decide a case where it's uncertain what the law says on the issue raised by that case, what's she going to do? The judge *can't* say, 'I don't know' or 'The law is very unclear here'. She *has* to come out with a clear answer as to what the law says on the issue raised by the case. So all she can do is simply assume that the law *says* what it *should say*, come to a view as to what the law *should* say in the case, and decide the case on that basis. So if the judge thinks that the law *should* say *x* in the particular case that she has to decide, then she will decide the case on the basis that the law *does* say *x*.

It follows from all of this that if you are one of the barristers appearing before the judge in this case, and you will win the case for your client if the judge decides the case on the basis that the law *does* say *x*, then the only way of swinging the case in favour of your client will be to convince the judge that the law *should* say *x*, so that she will decide the case on the basis that the law *does* say *x*. So in order to win the case for your client, you had better be able to make out some convincing and effective arguments in favour of the view that the law *should* say *x*.

You are far more likely to have acquired this skill if you have done a law degree rather than a GDL. This is because a crucial part of doing a law degree is reading articles and writing essays that critically evaluate the law, and discuss what it should say on various issues. In contrast, doing a GDL, which is very much focused on getting you to understand as quickly as possible what the law *does* say, will not do as good a job of equipping you to make, or engage with, arguments about what the law should say.

● Legal contacts

Doing a law degree allows you to make lots of useful contacts – with fellow students who will become lawyers in the future, with distinguished law academics, and with people who have already entered the legal profession – that will serve you well both in getting a job practising law and after you become a lawyer. (For example, it's not unheard of for former students of mine to get in touch with me for advice on particularly thorny legal questions that they have been asked to research.) Of course, people who enter the profession via the GDL lack this advantage.

◉ Impressing potential employers

In a recent survey, 'dedication to a legal career' was ranked as the third most important quality that solicitors and barristers looked out for in recruiting graduates. (The first and second most important qualities were 'intellectual ability' and 'flexibility'; 'self-confidence' came fourth.) There will obviously be no question that someone who has done a law degree is dedicated to pursuing a legal career. In contrast, there will be a question mark over the dedication of someone who is trying to enter the profession via the GDL. Are they trying to get a job as a solicitor or a barrister because their preferred career didn't pan out? Is their heart really set on becoming a lawyer, or will they flake out the first time the going gets really tough (as it will)? If you choose to enter the profession via the GDL, you will have to do a lot more work convincing recruiters that you are committed to the idea of becoming a lawyer than someone who has done a law degree ever will.

◉ The GDL is tough

The GDL is not a walk in the park by any means. It is a *very* tough course where you are expected to gain proficiency in seven very difficult subjects in just one year. In contrast, people who do a law degree study these subjects over two or three years, making it far easier to come to grips with them.

So, to sum up:

> If you've made up your mind that you want to become a lawyer when you leave university, and you are confident that the law degree that you will leave university with will equip you to get the sort of offers of law jobs that you are looking to get when you leave university, then
>
> >

my recommendation would be that you do a law degree at university. It's the most effective way of picking up the skills that you need to become a really good lawyer, and provides the easiest and quickest entry route into the profession.

I hope this has given you something to think about in making up your mind as to what you are going to do when you go to university. But I want to stress – this is your life, and you have to do what you personally think is right for you. So don't just blindly do whatever I recommend. Ask around, see what other people have to say, and finally ask yourself what feels right for you. This has to be your decision, and yours alone. That's the only kind of decision that will ultimately make you happy – and me.

Best wishes,

Nick

PART 2

Preparing to Study Law

Arguing Effectively (1):
Logical Arguments

○ From: Nicholas J. McBride [dearnick@pearson.com]
○ To: Brown, Jo
○ Subject: Arguing Effectively (1): Logical Arguments

Hi Jo,

As I've said before, probably the most important – and valuable – thing you'll have to do as a law student is learn how to argue effectively. Given that you've now decided you want to study Law at university, I thought you might appreciate a few pointers on how to make good, effective, arguments of your own – and in so doing show you how to make up your mind whether an argument that is being made to you is any good or not. This won't just come in useful for your legal studies, it's also essential that you be able to argue effectively if you are applying to a university that interviews applicants before deciding whether to offer them a place.

There are two basic kinds of argument that you'll come across in doing your law degree, and in life generally. We can call them **logical arguments** (otherwise known as arguments by **deduction**) and **speculative arguments** (otherwise known as arguments by **induction**). I'll talk about speculative arguments in another letter, but in this letter I'll just concentrate on logical arguments. These take the following form:

1 All children like chocolate.

2 Max is a child.

Therefore,

3 Max likes chocolate.

Steps (1) and (2) in the argument are called the **premises** of the argument. Step (3) is called the **conclusion**. If (1) and (2) are correct, and (3) logically follows from (1) and (2), then we *have* to accept that (3) is correct – if we don't, we're just plain stupid, or crazy. An example of a logical argument that a lawyer might make goes as follows:

1 The law says that A's promise to B is legally binding if B gives A something in return for that promise.

2 Helen promised to mow Peter's lawn if Peter bought her a drink, and he did so.

Therefore,

3 Helen is legally required to mow Peter's lawn.

I'll now make five points about logical arguments that you should always bear in mind either in making a logical argument of your own, or in making up your mind whether a logical argument that someone else has made to you is any good or not.

● Avoid circularity

The very first point about making a logical argument is that you have to ensure that it is not **circular**. A circular argument assumes in one or more of its premises the truth of its conclusion. A circular argument fails because it doesn't go anywhere: it just asserts that the conclusion is true without having done anything to establish that it is true – it never even gets off the launch pad. Here's an argument against capital punishment that is very obviously circular:

> 1 The State should not execute criminals.
>
> *Therefore,*
>
> 2 We should not have capital punishment.

(1) and (2) are basically identical statements, dressed up in different words. So (1) does not establish that (2) is true – it just assumes that (2) is true. Here's a more subtle form of circular argument:

> 1 Killing is always wrong.
>
> *Therefore,*
>
> 2 We should not have capital punishment.

(1) and (2) are not identical – but the argument is still circular because (1) assumes that (2) is true. If capital punishment were morally justified, then killing would not always be wrong. So by saying 'Killing is always wrong' the person making the above argument is already assuming that 'We should not have capital punishment'. So he is really just asserting, rather than arguing, that 'We should not have capital punishment'.

This second form of circularity sometimes creeps into lawyers' arguments. Consider, for example, the case where someone pays Norman £1,000 to beat up Emily. It is uncontroversial that after Norman beats up Emily, he will be held liable to compensate Emily for her injuries. But can Emily sue Norman for the gain he has made from beating her up – the £1,000? Those in favour of what is called 'restitution for wrongs' often argue that Emily should be able to sue Norman for this gain by saying:

> 1 No man should be allowed to profit from his wrong.
>
> *Therefore,*
>
> 2 Emily should be allowed to sue Norman for the gain that he has made by beating her up.

But this is circular. (1) assumes the truth of (2). If it would be wrong to allow Emily to sue Norman for the gain he has made, then it is not true that 'No man should be allowed to profit from his wrong' – Norman should be allowed to profit from his wrong. So by saying (1), the person making the above argument is simply assuming that (2) is true rather than making a serious argument in favour of (2) being true.

You'll notice that the above three circular arguments all just have one premise and then leap straight to a conclusion. This is a sure sign that something has gone wrong. A logical argument that works has at least *two* premises which *work together* to reach a conclusion. If a logical argument that you are making or looking at only has one premise then there is something wrong with it – and the problem will almost always be that the argument is circular.

○ You can't derive an 'ought' from an 'is'

Consider this argument in favour of capital punishment:

> 1 Reintroducing the death penalty for murder would reduce the number of murders in this country.
>
> *Therefore,*
>
> 2 We should reintroduce the death penalty for murder.

Again, this argument only has one premise before leaping straight to a conclusion, so there is something wrong with it. But this time the problem is not circularity – premise (1) does not assume the truth of conclusion (2). The problem is that the person making this argument is trying to derive an 'ought' ('We *should* reintroduce the death penalty for murder') from an 'is' ('Reintroducing the death penalty for murder *would* reduce the number of killings in this country'). This is impossible: you cannot make a value judgment about what should or should not happen based purely on a bare statement of fact about what is or is not or would be or would not be or was or was not the case. What has gone wrong with the above argument is that it is too compressed. We need to introduce a value statement into the premises of the argument to make it work.

1 Reintroducing the death penalty for murder would reduce the murder rate in this country.

2 We should do everything possible to reduce the murder rate.

Therefore,

3 We should reintroduce the death penalty for murder.

Because there is now a 'should' in the premises of the argument, it is now legitimate to have a 'should' in the argument's conclusion.

This basic principle – that you cannot derive an 'ought' from an 'is' – is not always observed as well as it should be by lawyers. For example, let's go back to the case of Norman and Emily. Should Emily be allowed to sue Norman for what are called 'exemplary damages' – damages designed to punish Norman for what he did to Emily? Those who say 'no' often argue:

1 The function of an award of damages to the victim of a wrong is to compensate the victim for the losses she has suffered as a result of that wrong.

2 Exemplary damages are punitive rather than compensatory in nature.

Therefore,

3 Emily should not be allowed to sue Norman for exemplary damages.

Here, we are deriving an 'ought' ('Emily *should not* be allowed to sue . . .') from two 'is's ('The function of an award of damages . . . *is* . . .'; 'Exemplary damages *are* . . .') – not allowed! The above argument is a particularly bad one because it is impossible to save it. If we reformulate it to introduce a 'should' statement into the premises, as follows –

1 The function of an award of damages to the victim of a wrong should be to compensate the victim for the losses she has suffered as a result of that wrong.

>

> 2 Exemplary damages are punitive rather than compensatory in nature.
>
> *Therefore,*
>
> 3 Emily should not be allowed to sue Norman for exemplary damages.

– can you see what problem the argument now suffers from? Yes, it's now circular. The argument's first premise assumes that the argument's conclusion is true. If Emily should be allowed to sue for exemplary damages, then it can't be true that the function of an award of damages to someone like Emily should just be to compensate her for the losses that she has suffered. So by saying (1), the person making this argument is assuming that (3) is true rather than arguing that (3) is true.

● In a logical argument, the conclusion must follow logically from its premises

Consider the following argument for capital punishment:

> 1 We should reintroduce the death penalty for murder if doing so would reduce the number of murders in this country.
>
> 2 Studies have shown that reintroducing the death penalty would have no effect on the murder rate in this country.
>
> *Therefore,*
>
> 3 We should reintroduce the death penalty for murder.

It is pretty obvious what is wrong with this argument: its premises do not support its conclusion. If you are being logical, you simply cannot conclude on the basis of premises (1) and (2) that we should reintroduce the death penalty for murder. You should, instead, conclude that there is no case (so far as you know) for reintroducing the death penalty for murder.

So, when you are making a logical argument, make sure that your conclusion follows logically from its premises. If you don't do this, your argument isn't logical at all – it's illogical, and doesn't give anyone any reason to accept your conclusion.

One form of illogical argument that you have to be particularly on your guard against making is one which suffers from the *post hoc ergo propter hoc* ('after this, therefore because of this') fallacy, that is, the fallacy of thinking that because B happened *after* A, that B happened *because* of A. This argument – which, I repeat, you should be on your guard *against* making – takes the form:

1 A happened.
2 After A happened, B happened.
Therefore,
3 B happened because A happened.

Even though B happened after A happened, it does not follow logically that B happened because A happened – B could have happened for any number of reasons, other than A's happening. A concrete example of an argument that suffers from the *post hoc ergo propter hoc* fallacy goes as follows:

1 The death penalty for murder was abolished in 1965.
2 After 1965, the murder rate rocketed, with more than double the murders per 100,000 of the population being committed in 2004 as compared with the rate in 1965.
Therefore,
3 The murder rate more than doubled between 1965 and 2004 because the death penalty for murder was abolished in 1965.

It is possible (3) is true – but it certainly does not follow logically from (1) and (2). There could be an **alternative explanation** of why (2) happened: maybe the social trends that resulted in the death penalty being abolished in 1965 also resulted in the murder rate doubling between 1965 and 2004.

Another very common type of illogical argument is an argument that suffers from **tunnel vision**. A very good example of this kind of argument is provided by Henry Hazlitt's excellent book, *Economics in One Lesson*, which I recommend to anyone who wants an education in how to argue effectively. The book begins with a story: a baker's window has been broken by a teenager who has hurled a brick through it. A crowd gathers and concludes that actually the breaking of the window is a good thing. The baker will now have to pay a glazier to install a new window, thus keeping the glazier in business, and the glazier will in turn spend the money he has earned from the baker, thus keeping a variety of people in business, and they in turn will spend the money they have earned from the glazier, thus keeping yet more people in business etc. So, the argument goes:

> 1 It is good for people to be employed.
> 2 The economic activity sparked by the breaking of the window will keep a number of different people in business.
>
> *Therefore,*
>
> 3 It was a good thing the window was broken.

This argument is illogical because it suffers from tunnel vision. What it leaves out of the picture is what the baker would have done with the money that he is now going to pay the glazier to replace his window. In Hazlitt's example, the baker would have used that money to pay the tailor to make a suit for him. Using the money to pay the tailor to make a suit would have sparked an *equal* amount of economic activity as that which will be sparked by paying the glazier to mend the window, thus keeping as many people in business as will be kept in business when the glazier is paid to mend the window. So had the window not been broken, the community as a whole would have had an intact window *plus* a new suit *plus* a certain amount of economic activity sparked by the buying of the new suit. But as it is – now that the window has been broken – the community as a whole will still have an intact window (once it has been mended by the glazier) *plus* a certain amount of economic activity sparked by the baker's paying to have the window mended *but it will have no new suit*. It follows that the breaking of the window has made the community worse off as a whole – so (3) is not true: it was *not* a good thing the window was broken. The crowd cannot see that because it suffers from tunnel vision. All it can see is the broken window and the economic activity that will be sparked by its replacement. It does not have the vision or imagination to see the new suit that would have been made had the window never been broken and the economic activity that would have been sparked by that new suit's being made.

So the argument above is illogical: conclusion (3) does not follow from premises (1) and (2). Someone who did not suffer from tunnel vision would argue:

1 It is good for people to be employed.

2 The economic activity sparked by the breaking of the window will keep a number of different people in business.

But,

3 Had the window not been broken, an equal amount of economic activity would have been sparked through the baker's spending the money he will now spend on replacing his window on having a new suit made for himself.

So,

4 The breaking of the window will make no difference to the level of employment in the community.

And,

5 The new suit that the baker would have paid the tailor to make for him had his window not been broken will now never be made.

So,

6 The breaking of the window has made the community worse off as a whole – instead of having one intact window *and* a new suit, it now (after the glazier has done his work) just has one intact window.

7 It is bad for the community to be made worse off as a whole.

Therefore,

8 It was a bad thing the window was broken.

Here is an argument *against* capital punishment that is illogical because it suffers from tunnel vision:

> 1 It is a bad thing for innocent people to die.
>
> 2 If we reintroduce the death penalty for murder, there is a danger that innocent people will be convicted of murder and be executed as a result.
>
> *Therefore,*
>
> 3 We should not reintroduce the death penalty for murder.

This is illogical: even though (1) and (2) are perfectly true, (3) does not follow from (1) and (2). The problem is that the person making this argument is simply focusing on the innocent people who might be killed by the *State* if the death penalty is reintroduced. What he is overlooking is that reintroducing the death penalty for murder might cut the murder rate and as a result save a lot of innocent people's lives. In order to restore some logic to the above argument against capital punishment, we need to get rid of the blinkers and take into account the possibility that innocent people's lives might be saved by reintroducing the death penalty for murder. There are two ways of doing this. We could argue that:

> 1 It is a bad thing for innocent people to die.
>
> 2 If we reintroduce the death penalty for murder, there is a danger that innocent people will be convicted of murder and be executed as a result.
>
> 3 There is also a possibility that reintroducing the death penalty for murder will reduce the murder rate and save innocent people's lives.
>
> *However,*
>
> 4 The number of people who are likely to be wrongfully executed if we reintroduce the death penalty for murder exceeds the number of people who are likely to escape being murdered if we reintroduce the death penalty for murder.
>
> *Therefore,*
>
> 5 We should not reintroduce the death penalty for murder.

or we could argue, more boldly:

1 It is better that an unlimited number of innocent people be murdered than that one innocent person be executed by the State.

2 If we reintroduce the death penalty for murder, there is a danger that an innocent person will be convicted of murder and executed by the State.

Therefore,

3 We should not reintroduce the death penalty for murder, and this is so no matter how many innocent people's lives might be saved by doing so.

A logical argument that is based on a false premise is worthless

Both of the arguments that have just been made against reintroducing capital punishment are perfectly logical. But the fact that an argument is logical does not mean we should accept it. If a logical argument is based on a false premise, it must be rejected. A logical argument that is based on a false premise doesn't give us any reason to accept its conclusion. In contrast, if the premises of a logical argument are correct (and, of course, the argument's conclusion logically follows from those premises) then that argument *must* be accepted – we would be crazy or stupid not to accept it. Consider, for example, the logical argument set out at the beginning of this letter:

1 All children like chocolate.

2 Max is a child.

Therefore,

3 Max likes chocolate.

If (1) and (2) are true, then, we *have* to accept that (3) is true (because (3) follows logically from (1) and (2)) – otherwise we're just stupid or crazy. But if *either* (1) *or* (2) are not true, then this argument gives us no reason at all to think that Max likes chocolate. If it's the case that not all children like chocolate, or it's the case that Max is 45 years old, then the argument completely collapses and should be rejected. Of course, it may still be the case that (3) is true – Max may actually like chocolate. But the point is that if *either* (1) *or* (2) are not true, the above argument gives us *no* reason to think that Max likes chocolate.

Let's look again at one of the arguments made above against capital punishment:

1 It is a bad thing for innocent people to die.
2 If we reintroduce the death penalty for murder, there is a danger that innocent people will be convicted of murder and be executed as a result.
3 There is also a possibility that reintroducing the death penalty for murder will reduce the murder rate and save innocent people's lives.
However,
4 The number of people who are likely to be wrongfully executed if we reintroduce the death penalty for murder exceeds the number of people who are likely to escape being murdered if we reintroduce the death penalty for murder.
Therefore,
5 We should not reintroduce the death penalty for murder.

This argument is perfectly logical, so whether we accept its conclusion depends on whether its premises are correct. Premises (1)–(3) seem perfectly reasonable. So whether we should accept this argument or not all depends on whether premise (4) is correct. Unfortunately, premise (4) does not seem to be correct. Some 766 people were murdered in the UK in 2005–6. It's not hard to imagine that, say, 30 of those 766 people would not have been killed if we still had the death penalty for murder. But it *is* hard to imagine that if we still had the death penalty for murder, in 2005–6 there would have been more than 30 *wrongful* convictions for murder resulting in the convicted being executed. So the above argument against capital punishment should be rejected – it rests on a false premise, and therefore doesn't give us any reason to think that we should not reintroduce the death penalty for murder.

Two common sources of false premises that you should always be on the lookout for when making your own logical arguments or examining other people's are **wishful thinking** and, again, **tunnel vision**. Consider the following argument that is often made for saying that animals do not have rights:

1 You can only have rights if you have responsibilities at the same time.

2 Animals do not have any responsibilities (for example, a responsibility not to kick their owner).

Therefore,

3 Animals do not have rights.

(1) is obviously incorrect. If (1) were correct then babies or patients in a coma would not have rights either, and obviously they do. So why do people keep on saying (1)? Either they say it because they do not wish to admit that animals have rights, and so they wish (1) were true – the idea being that if (1) were true, then that would make it easy for them to deny that animals have rights. Or they say (1) because they suffer from tunnel vision – they don't have the vision or imagination to realise that (1) cannot be true because if it were, then babies or patients in a coma would not have rights either.

Here's another example of tunnel vision producing a false premise. This time the argument is meant to establish that it is okay sometimes to lie to someone else. The argument begins by supposing that we are in Nazi Germany. A woman runs into your house and says, 'I'm a Jew on the run – some Nazi soldiers are a couple of minutes behind me: if they catch me, they will kill me. Please hide me.' You usher the woman into your cellar. The soldiers bang on your door two minutes later and ask you, 'We are

looking for an escaped prisoner who would have come by here – do you
know where she is?' The argument goes as follows:

> 1 *Either* you can tell the soldiers the truth that the woman is hiding in
>   your cellar with the result that they will kill her *or* you can save the
>   woman's life by lying to the soldiers, telling them that you saw
>   someone running away down the road a couple of minutes earlier.
> 2 It would be unacceptable to take the first option, given the con-
>   sequences of doing so.
>   *Therefore,*
> 3 You should lie to the soldiers.

But (1) is not true. Anyone not suffering from tunnel vision would realise
that there are other options available to you in this situation. You could
refuse to answer. Or you could give an answer which is literally true, 'Yes –
a woman did come by here two minutes ago looking for help. She can't be
that far away now.' Or you could remonstrate with the soldiers, thereby
changing the subject and possibly doing some positive good at the same
time, 'Yes – I saw a woman come by here a couple of minutes ago. You
should be ashamed of yourselves, hunting down a poor girl like that –
what would your mothers think if they knew?' So this particular argument
in favour of establishing that it is acceptable under certain circumstances
to lie to someone else simply does not work.

● Logical arguments that culminate in an 'ought' are often inconclusive

Consider another one of the arguments against capital punishment that
was made above:

> 1 It is better that an unlimited number of innocent people be mur-
>   dered than that one innocent person be executed by the State.
> 2 If we reintroduce the death penalty for murder, there is a danger
>   that an innocent person will be convicted of murder and executed
>   by the State.
>
> >

Therefore,

3 We should not reintroduce the death penalty for murder, and this is so no matter how many innocent people's lives might be saved by doing so.

Again, this argument is perfectly logical, so whether we accept its conclusion or not depends on whether its premises are correct. (2) is obviously true, so the crucial premise is (1). If (1) is true, then we should not reintroduce the death penalty for murder. So is (1) true?

Unfortunately, it's difficult to tell for certain. One school of thought holds that it is better to allow other people's rights to be violated than it is to violate someone else's rights oneself. On this view – what's called the **deontological** view – (1) is true: even if thousands of lives could be saved by reintroducing the death penalty for murder it would still be wrong to reintroduce it if doing so would result in the State violating someone's rights sometime in the future. (On the same view, it would be wrong to torture an innocent person to discover where terrorists are planning to explode a nuclear bomb, even though doing so would prevent millions of people being murdered.) However, there is another school of thought that says we should judge what to do by weighing up the costs and benefits of the consequences of our actions. On this view – what's called the **consequentialist** view – (1) is obviously not true: if reintroducing the death penalty for murder would do more good than harm then it is obviously better to reintroduce the death penalty. Unfortunately, there is no rational way to determine which view is correct. No logical argument can be made that would show us that the deontological view is correct and the consequentialist view wrong, or that the opposite is true. So we have no way of determining for certain whether (1) is true. It follows that this particular argument against capital punishment must be labelled '**inconclusive**'. It might be wrong or it might be right: we just don't know for certain.

This will often be the case with logical arguments that culminate in an 'ought' statement (here, 'We should not reintroduce the death penalty for murder . . .'). Because you can't derive an 'ought' from an 'is', logical arguments that conclude by saying that we should or should not do something will always have, as part of their premises, some kind of value judgment or 'should' statement. And – as we just saw – it's often very difficult to tell for certain whether that value judgment or 'should' statement is correct. So logical arguments that conclude by saying that we should or should not do something will often be inconclusive: we just won't know for certain whether we should accept them or not. But you shouldn't conclude from this that making logical arguments that culminate in an 'ought' statement is a waste of time.

First, there are some value judgments or 'should' statements that we know for certain *are* correct and can provide the basis for making conclusive logical arguments in favour of a particular 'ought' statement. It is wrong to stub out cigarettes on little babies. It is wrong to kill people for kicks or because of their political views. It is good to feed someone who is starving. We should be kind as often as possible. We know these things for certain and can sometimes use this knowledge to build conclusive arguments about what we should and should not do.

Secondly, making an inconclusive logical argument in favour of a particular 'ought' statement can be useful because doing so can help people make up their mind whether or not *they* accept that that 'ought' statement is true, and that in turn can influence their decisions about what to do or who to vote for in an election. So, for example, suppose you establish that the *only* logical argument that can be made against the reintroduction of the death penalty for murder is one which rests on the premise 'It is better that an unlimited number of innocent people be murdered than that one innocent person be executed by the State'. If this is the case, then most people will probably conclude – rightly or wrongly (we really can't tell) – that there is *no* good reason why we should not reintroduce the death penalty for murder and give their support to a political party that campaigns for the reinstatement of capital punishment.

I've now said enough to allow you to ensure that any logical arguments you make in future will stand up to scrutiny, and to help you detect any flaws in a logical argument that is being made to you. But before I sign off, I'll just point out four very common types of logical argument that you may want to use in the future when trying to establish a particular point.

● 'Kill all the alternatives' arguments

This sort of argument goes as follows:

> 1 Either A or B or C is true.
> 2 Neither A nor B are true.
> *Therefore,*
> 3 C must be true.

This sort of argument underlay Sherlock Holmes' principle (as expressed in Arthur Conan Doyle's novel *The Sign of Four*) that 'Once you have eliminated the impossible, whatever remains, however improbable, must be the truth.' The Professor in C.S. Lewis' *The Lion, The Witch and the Wardrobe* used a '**kill all the alternatives**' argument to establish that Lucy was telling the truth when she said that she had entered a magical world through the back of a wardrobe in the Professor's house:

> 1 Either Lucy is telling the truth, or she is lying, or she is mad.
> 2 We know that Lucy isn't a liar, and that she is not mad.
> *Therefore,*
> 3 Lucy must be telling the truth.

When you are examining whether a 'kill all the alternatives' argument stands up, be particularly on the lookout to see whether the first premise (which will be along the lines of 'Either A or B or C is true') suffers from tunnel vision – is there some other possibility that may also be true in this situation so that as to make it possible that A *and* B *and* C may *all* be untrue? Is it possible that Lucy is not lying, and that she is not mad – but that she is not telling the truth either? Maybe the fur coats stored in the wardrobe give off fumes that overcame Lucy and caused her to go into a trance where she dreamed that she was in a magical world. The fact that this is perfectly possible destroys the Professor's argument. It has to be adjusted so that it goes as follows:

1 Either Lucy is telling the truth, or she is lying, or she is mad, or something happened to Lucy in the wardrobe to make her think (incorrectly) that she was in a magical world.

2 We know that Lucy isn't a liar, and that she is not mad.

Therefore,

3 Either Lucy is telling the truth, or something happened to Lucy in the wardrobe to make her think (incorrectly) that she was in a magical world.

The Professor's argument no longer goes all the way to establish that Lucy must be telling the truth. For it to go that far, the only remaining alternative – that something happened to Lucy in the wardrobe to make her think (incorrectly) that she was in a magical world – has to be killed off.

● Arguments from contradiction

The Professor could have killed off this remaining alternative through another common kind of logical argument, which is an **argument from contradiction**. This argument goes as follows:

1 For A to be true, B would also have to be true.

2 But we know B is not true.

Therefore,

3 A is not true.

So had anyone countered the Professor's first argument for thinking Lucy must have been telling the truth with the objection, 'But it's possible that when she went into the wardrobe she was overcome by fumes which caused her to hallucinate and think she was in a magical land', the Professor could have argued back:

1 For that to be true, it would also have to be the case that she stayed long enough in the wardrobe to hallucinate all the experiences she said she had after she entered into the wardrobe.

>

> 2 But we know she did not stay long enough in the wardrobe for that to happen – she came out of the wardrobe a few seconds after she entered into it.
>
> *Therefore,*
>
> 3 We cannot put what happened to Lucy down to a chemically-induced trance.

When someone makes an argument from contradiction to you, again be particularly on the lookout to check that the first premise ('For A to be true, B would also have to be true') is correct: Is it really the case that B has also to be true for A to be true?

○ Cost–benefit arguments

An extremely common form of logical argument is a **cost–benefit argument**. An example is:

> 1 We should do *x* if the benefits of doing *x* outweigh the costs.
>
> 2 The benefits of doing *x* outweigh the costs.
>
> *Therefore,*
>
> 3 We should do *x*.

In examining this argument, test whether its premises are correct. If doing *x* would violate someone's rights, then it would still be wrong to do *x* even if the benefits of doing *x* outweighed the costs: it cannot be right to sacrifice people for the greater good. So if doing *x* would violate someone's rights then (1) will not be correct.

In examining whether (2) is correct, watch out for two things. First of all, watch out for **sentimentalism**. An example of sentimentalism is when someone argues in favour of some security measure (such as ID cards) by saying 'If it just saves one life, it's worth it.' No, it's not. If life *were* that infinitely precious, then we would ban cars – doing so would save thousands of lives each year, and this saving of life would more than offset the collosal sacrifice in wealth and happiness that banning cars would involve.

The second thing you need to look out for is the problem of **incommensurability**. Two things are incommensurable if there is no common standard of measurement which we can use to compare the two. For example, suppose that it is proposed that we should raise taxes to fund a nationwide programme of home care for the mentally ill. The cost of doing this would be to retard economic growth by 0.5 per cent a year. The benefit of doing this would be that the healthcare system in this country would treat the mentally ill with a greater level of respect and dignity than is currently possible. These two things cannot be weighed against each other: they are so completely different that there is no common standard of measurement that would allow us to say that the costs of raising taxes to fund this healthcare programme outweigh the benefits, or vice versa. So it's not possible to resolve the question of whether taxes should be raised to fund this programme through a cost–benefit argument. We simply have to *choose* which of these things – economic growth, and treating the mentally ill with dignity and showing them some respect – we value more.

● Arguments from analogy

Finally, a big favourite with lawyers are arguments from **analogy**. These kinds of arguments go as follows:

1 In situation A, B is true.
2 Situation C is identical to situation A in all material respects.
  Therefore,
3 In situation C, B is true.

So, for example, one of the most basic arguments that lawyers learn to make is the following argument from analogy:

1 In case A, a previous court awarded damages to the claimant.
2 The case here is identical to case A in all material respects.
3 Like cases should be decided alike.

>

> *Therefore,*
>
> 4 In this situation, the court should award damages to the claimant in this case, my client.

In making up your mind whether an argument from analogy is correct or not, the thing to look at is whether the second premise ('This situation is identical to the first situation in all material respects') is true – is it really true that there is no material difference between the situation at hand and the situation we initially considered? For example, here is a very famous argument in favour of the view that pregnant women have a right to have an abortion, based on the philosopher Judith Jarvis Thomson's article 'A defense of abortion', published in 1971, in the first volume of the journal *Philosophy and Public Affairs*.

Consider the situation where Samantha has gotten extremely drunk one night, and has ended up in hospital. The doctors treating Samantha realise that she has the same blood type as Frederick, a world famous violinist who is in the same hospital because he is in dire need of a kidney transplant. The doctors realise they have a way of saving Frederick's life. They insert a tube into the main artery leading away from Frederick's heart, and insert the other end of the tube into the renal artery leading into one of Samantha's kidneys. They then insert a tube into the renal vein leading away from the same kidney and pump the blood coming through that tube into Frederick's body. As a result, Frederick's blood is 'cleaned' by Samantha's kidney, thus removing the need for him to have an immediate kidney transplant. When Samantha wakes up, she asks why she is hooked up to the patient in the next bed in this way, and her doctors tell her, 'We've done this so he can survive until we get him a new kidney.' When Samantha protests, the doctors say, 'Look – if we disconnect you, he'll die, and he doesn't deserve that. Everyone has a right to live. Anyway, you can't complain – if you hadn't got so drunk last night, you wouldn't be in this position.' When Samantha asks how long she has to wait for Frederick to have a kidney transplant, the doctors say, 'Given his position on the waiting list, we think you'll have to stay like this for nine months.'

Now let's assume that in this situation, Samantha has a right to tell the doctors to get lost and disconnect her from Frederick, whatever the consequences for Frederick. If we accept that, then what about the case where Mandy gets extremely drunk one night, has unprotected sex, and discovers a few days later that she is pregnant? Does she have a right to have an abortion? The argument from analogy in favour of saying that she does goes as follows:

1 Samantha has a right to be disconnected from Frederick, even though Frederick will die as a result.

2 Mandy's case is identical to Samantha's in all material respects – after one drunken night, Mandy has discovered that someone else's life (the life of the foetus inside her) is dependent on her not disconnecting herself from that someone else (the foetus inside her), and that if she does not disconnect herself from that someone else, she will have to remain connected to that someone else for nine months.

   Therefore,

3 Mandy has a right to disconnect herself from the foetus inside her, that is, Mandy has a right to have an abortion.

Does this argument work? The crucial step in the argument is premise (2) – is Mandy's case really identical to Samantha's in all material respects? I'll leave you to think about that and tell you what I think in my next letter.

Be in touch soon,

Nick

Arguing Effectively (2): Speculative Arguments

5

- From: Nicholas J. McBride [dearnick@pearson.com]
- To: Brown, Jo
- Subject: Arguing Effectively (2): Speculative Arguments

Hey Jo,

As promised, here's another letter on arguing effectively. Just to finish up the point I left the last letter on, I *don't* think the argument from analogy presented at the end of that letter works to establish that Mandy has a right to an abortion. There is one big difference between Samantha's case and Mandy's case. In Samantha's case, the doctors violated her rights in hooking her up to Frederick. So requiring her to remain hooked up to Frederick would perpetuate the injustice that she initially suffered when the doctors started meddling with her body. In Mandy's case no one violated her rights in getting her pregnant. So there would be no injustice in requiring her to remain pregnant for the nine months necessary to give birth to the foetus inside her. It would be different if Mandy had been *raped* when she was drunk and that is why she is now pregnant – in that case, her situation would be very similar to Samantha's and if Samantha does indeed have a right to disconnect herself from Frederick then that would seem to establish by analogy that Mandy should have a right to have an abortion in the case where she was raped and that is why she is now pregnant.

I want to talk now about the other very common form of argument that you will make, and come across, as a lawyer and in life generally. That is, a **speculative argument**. This kind of argument takes the following kind of form:

1 Every swan I have ever seen has been white.
   Given this it is sensible to suppose that,
2 All swans are white.

Again step (1) in the argument is called the **premise** of the argument; step (2) is the **conclusion**.

There are two important differences between logical arguments and speculative arguments. First, a logical argument starts from a generality and then moves from that generality to reach a conclusion about a specific thing. In contrast, a speculative argument goes in the opposite direction: it moves from a statement about a specific thing to reach a general conclusion about that kind of thing.

Secondly, you'll note that – unlike with a logical argument – a speculative argument can have only one premise for its conclusion. (You'll recall that any logical argument must have at least two premises to support its conclusion – if it only has one, it doesn't work.) This is because the conclusion in a speculative argument does *not* follow logically from its premise or premises. It does not necessarily follow that *all* swans are white just because every swan *I* have ever seen has been white. It may be that not all swans are white and I just happen never to have seen a non-white swan. In fact, not all swans are white – black swans exist in Australia. So, as it happens, we should reject the conclusion 'All swans are white'. But, as a general rule, if the premises of a speculative argument are correct, and the conclusion of that argument seems the *most sensible* one to draw from those premises, we should accept that conclusion until we are given good reason to think that it is not true. So up until the time Australia was discovered by Europeans, it was rational for Europeans to think that all swans were white because no European had seen anything but a white swan. But as soon as black swans were observed in Australia, Europeans no longer had good reason to think that all swans were white.

Just in case you are tempted by the non-logical nature of speculative arguments to think that there is something dodgy about them, I should point out that scientists make speculative arguments all the time, and that all scientific progress depends on such arguments being made:

1 Every time we throw an object into the air, it falls back down towards the earth.
   Given this it is sensible to suppose that,
2 There exists a force (call it *gravity*) which pulls an object thrown into the air back down towards the earth.

Lawyers often reason like scientists. They will take a case or a line of cases and try and extrapolate from the results of those cases a rule or a principle which explains the results in that case or those cases – having done this, they then argue that that case or those cases establish that that particular rule or principle is part of English law. When a lawyer makes an argument like this, the argument will always be speculative in nature.

So, for example, in the case of *Spring* v *Guardian Assurance plc* [1995] 2 A.C. 296, the defendant gave the claimant, an ex-employee of his, a bad reference. The House of Lords held that if the claimant did not deserve a bad reference and the defendant had been careless in preparing the reference, then the claimant could sue the defendant. The defendant, the House of Lords held, had owed the claimant a 'duty of care' in preparing the reference, and if he breached that duty, then the claimant could sue him. Now what legal rule or principle was the House of Lords relying on – and therefore introducing into English law – in deciding this case?

One lawyer might argue that the House of Lords thought that: 'Whenever one person gives another a reference, the referee will owe the subject of the reference a duty to prepare the reference with a reasonable degree of care and skill.' Another lawyer might argue that the rule the House of Lords was actually relying on in deciding *Spring* was: 'Whenever an employer gives an ex-employee a reference, the employer will owe his ex-employee a duty to prepare the reference with a reasonable degree of care and skill.'

It makes a big difference who is right. If the first lawyer is right, then if I undeservedly and carelessly give an ex-student a bad reference, then *Spring* v *Guardian Assurance plc* establishes that my ex-student can sue me: I owed him or her a duty of care in preparing the reference. If the second lawyer is right, then *Spring* v *Guardian Assurance plc* does not establish any such thing: my ex-student was not a former employee of mine, so *Spring* v *Guardian Assurance plc* has nothing to do with my case.

Whichever argument as to what the *Spring* case establishes is correct, both arguments are speculative in nature. They both take the basic form:

> 1 In *Spring* v *Guardian Assurance plc,* the House of Lords decided that . . .
>
> *Given this it is sensible to suppose that,*
>
> 2 The House of Lords thought that an employer/referee will owe an ex-employee/the subject of the reference a duty of care in writing a reference for him or her . . .

This is not a logical argument because (2) does not follow *logically* from (1). Whatever you think was the basis of the decision of the House of Lords in the *Spring* case, there will always be other *possible* explanations of the House of Lords' decision in that case. So we can only determine what was the basis of the House of Lords' decision in the *Spring* case by asking ourselves: What is the *most sensible* explanation of the House of Lords' decision in *Spring*?

Lawyers don't just make speculative arguments when they are trying to clarify what rule or principle underlay a particular case or line of cases. They also make speculative arguments when they are called upon to clarify what a particular legal word (or concept) *means* so that they can apply a particular legal rule which contains that word. So, for example, the law says that you will violate my rights (in legal parlance, commit a *tort*) if you directly interfere with goods that are in my possession when you have no legal justification or excuse for doing so. But when can we say that goods are in my 'possession'? What if I own a flat in Glasgow – are the things inside that flat in my possession while I am typing this letter in Cambridge? What if I drop my wallet in the street – is the wallet still in my possession while it is lying in the street? If a friend of mine sees the wallet fall out of my coat and picks it up, intending to give it back, is it in my possession at that point? To answer these questions, we look at all the cases which have something to say about when goods were and were not in someone else's possession, and construct from them a definition of when we can say that goods are in someone's possession. But coming up with a definition will involve making a speculative argument. It will involve making an argument along the following lines:

> 1 Case A said that goods were in X's possession when . . .; case B said that Y lost possession of goods when . . .; case C said that Z obtained possession of goods when . . .
>
>   *Given this it is sensible to suppose that,*
>
> 2 Goods will be in someone's possession if and only if . . .

Having clarified why lawyers make speculative arguments at all, I'll now give you a bit of guidance as to what you should and shouldn't do in making speculative arguments of your own. As usual, my hope is that this guidance will help you make good, effective speculative arguments, as well as helping you spot any flaws in speculative arguments that you come across in your reading.

● A speculative argument based on a false premise is worthless

One thing that speculative arguments have in common with logical arguments is that a false premise will undermine a speculative argument just as effectively as it will a logical argument. If I argue that:

> 1 In *Spring* v *Guardian Assurance plc*, the House of Lords ruled
> that the defendant did *not* owe the claimant a duty of care in writ-
> ing a reference for him.
>
> *Given this it is sensible to suppose that,*
>
> 2 . . .

whatever conclusion I draw from premise (1) will certainly not be worth
the paper it's written on.

⊙ 'Most' *cannot* mean 'all'

Suppose that Charles is a well-travelled man who has been to Australia.
He gets into an argument one day down at the pub about whether all
swans are white. He argues:

> 1 Most of the swans I have seen in my life have been white.
>
> *Given this it is sensible to suppose that,*
>
> 2 All swans are white.

There is something wrong with this argument. If (1) is true, then (2) *cannot*
be true. If *most* of the swans Charles has seen in his life have been white,
then it follows that *some* of the swans Charles has seen have *not* been white.
And if *some* of the swans Charles has seen have *not* been white, then it
cannot be true that 'All swans are white'.

So in making a speculative argument you *cannot* infer that X is true of *all*
Ns based on the premise that X is only true of *most* Ns. In fact, the only
thing you can infer from this premise is that X is *not* true of *all* Ns. This
elementary point is quite often overlooked by academics writing about
the law.

For example, as a law student you *will* come across statements such as
'The first requisite of a contract is that the parties have reached agreement' or 'The function of tort law is to determine when one person may
justly be required to compensate another for a loss that that other has

suffered' or 'Under English law, Parliament is sovereign, which means that a law created by Parliament must be given effect to by the courts until it is repealed by Parliament'. But if you read on (and look hard at what you are reading), you'll see that the only evidence given in support of these statements is that: '*Most* contracts are based on agreement' (and it is acknowledged at the same time that some contracts can be made without the parties having reached any kind of agreement at all); '*Most* tort cases involve one person suing another for compensation' (and it is acknowledged at the same time that there are some tort cases where the person suing isn't looking for compensation at all, but for some other remedy such as an injunction); '*Most* laws created by Parliament are binding on the courts' (and it is acknowledged at the same time that laws purporting to bind what future Parliaments may do are of no effect). So in fact, what the textbooks *should* be telling you is that: 'You can make a contract with someone else *without* having reached an agreement with them'; 'Whatever the function of tort law might be, it is *not* to determine when one person may justly be required to pay compensation to someone else'; 'Under English law, Parliament is *not* sovereign: there are limits on what sort of laws created by Parliament will be binding on the courts'.

Notice that the last three statements are more 'interesting' than the first three because they contradict the bog-standard accounts of English law that are routinely trotted out in the textbooks. 'Interesting' statements about the law are much more likely to get high marks from your examiners than statements that have been lifted straight out of a textbook. (So long, that is, as you have backed up your 'interesting' statement with a good argument.) So remembering that what is acknowledged to be only true of 'most' cannot possibly be true of 'all' will not only help ensure that you get a much more accurate understanding of the current state of English law than some of your textbooks may give you – it may also help you do well in your exams!

● Don't oversimplify

A bad habit that you should avoid in advancing a speculative argument is that of **oversimplification**. Your explanations should take account of the complexities of what you are trying to explain.

So, for example, suppose there is a line of cases A–F. In cases A–D, it could be argued that the courts relied on rule R to reach their decision. So cases A–D seem to indicate that rule R is part of English law. But if rule R were part of English law, we would have expected cases E and F not to have been decided the way they were. Let's suppose that an academic, Herbert, analyses these cases in the course of an article. Let's suppose further that Herbert suffers from the bad habit of oversimplification. Herbert will probably argue that:

1 Case A says . . .; case B says . . .; case C says . . .; case D says . . .
   Given this it is sensible to suppose that,
2 Rule R is part of English law.

Cases E and F are simply ignored. If one (forcibly) brings cases E and F to Herbert's attention, he will almost always simply dismiss cases E and F as 'wrongly decided'. But they're only wrongly decided if rule R *is* part of English law, which is what we are trying to establish in the first place. It would be more honest and straightforward to argue as follows:

1 Case A says . . .; case B says . . .; case C says . . .; case D says . . .
   Given this it is sensible to suppose that,
2 In these cases, the courts took the view that rule R is part of English law.
   But
3 Case E says . . .; and case F says . . .
   Given this it is sensible to suppose that,
4 In these cases, the courts did not take the view that rule R is part of English law.
   Given (2) and (4) it is sensible to suppose that,
5 It is uncertain whether rule R is part of English law or not; a majority of cases seem to take the view that it is, but a minority seem to take the view that it is not.

This conclusion fits more of the cases than Herbert's does and therefore gives us a better account of the current state of English law than Herbert gives us. Moreover, this conclusion is more nuanced and therefore more 'interesting' than Herbert's conclusion. So someone who argues in favour of this conclusion in an exam is likely to do better than someone who adopts Herbert's line.

Academics are particularly prone to falling into the vice of oversimplification whenever they try to define a particular legal term (or concept). This is because academics tend to assume that there is a one-to-one relation between legal terms and definitions. As a result, they tend to think that a particular legal term is always used in the *same way*, to mean the *same thing*. So, for example, academics have endless debates over what it means to have a 'legal right'. Some argue that when we say Len has a 'legal right' we are saying that Len has an 'interest' which is protected by the law's imposing duties on other people not to violate that interest. Others argue that we are saying that Len has a power to do something that is either given to him by the law or is protected by the law. The possibility that when we say that Len has a 'legal right' we could mean *either* of those things, depending on the context, doesn't get a look-in.

A similar point can be made about the term 'trust'. Academics tend to assume that when we talk about a 'trust' (as in 'A holds this property on trust . . .') we are always talking about the same thing. And so they ask, 'What are the characteristics of a trust?', 'How is a trust created?', and 'Who has an interest in property that is the subject of a trust?' They never ever consider the possibility that in fact the term 'trust' does not refer to *one thing*, but in fact refers to a variety of different legal arrangements which bear a family resemblance to each other, but have nothing more in common than that. If this is the case, it simply makes no sense to ask, 'What are the characteristics of a trust?', 'How is a trust created?', and 'Who has an interest in property that is the subject of a trust?' The proper response to these questions can only be another question: 'What sort of trust are you talking about?'

You should aim higher. Always be on the lookout for definitional oversimplification, and avoid it like the plague wherever you come across it. Definitional oversimplification always involves a false economy: it just stores up trouble in the long run. Just look at how the trusts textbooks twist and turn like *Little Britain*'s Vicky Pollard over the issue of whether the beneficiary of a trust has an interest in the trust property: 'Yes, but no, but yes, but no . . .' All these difficulties could be avoided if it were honestly admitted at the start that there is no such *thing* as *a* 'trust' – instead there are a variety of legal arrangements which are all given the description 'trust' and only under *some* of these arrangements can the person who benefits from them be said to have an interest in the property that is held 'on trust'.

◎ Don't overcomplicate

Just as you shouldn't oversimplify in making a speculative argument, you also shouldn't **overcomplicate**. The most sensible explanation is usually the most simple. (This principle of argumentation is known as '**Occam's razor**'.) So, for example, consider the following argument:

1 Case A says . . .; case B says . . .; . . . case Y says . . .; case Z says . . .
   Given this, it is sensible to suppose that,
2 All judges belong to a secret society, the leaders of which dictate to them how they should decide their cases.

No – this is not sensible at all. The reason why this is not sensible is that for (2) to be true, all of these things would *also* have to be true: (i) there exists a society which has some means of contacting any judge who is appointed to the Bench; (ii) membership of this society is so attractive that every judge who is approached agrees to become a member of it; (iii) the leaders of this society are so charismatic that every judge who becomes a member of this society is happy to do whatever they say; and (iv) this society has some way of ensuring no word of its existence ever escapes into the media. So, in fact, (2) provides us with an incredibly complex explanation of how the cases in (1) were decided. And incredibly complex explanations are very unlikely to be correct.

For the same reason it is highly unlikely that judges decide cases the way they do in order to maximise the wealth of society. (Many academics, particularly in the United States, believe this. Academics who take this view belong to what is called the '**law and economics**' school of legal thought.) For this to be true, it would *also* have to be true that: (i) all judges, in making their decisions, are interested in promoting wealth-maximisation to the exclusion of all other considerations (such as promoting equality of opportunity, or helping the needy, or maximising everyone's liberty); (ii) all judges are equipped with the economic knowledge that would enable them to determine what rules they should give effect to so as to maximise the wealth of society; (iii) all judges have agreed that they should keep the fact that their only concern in deciding cases is to maximise the wealth of society completely secret and not allow a word of this to enter into their judgments; (iv) barristers – who argue cases before judges – must be taken to be unaware of this agenda of the judges because they too fail to mention wealth-maximisation in their arguments, but as soon as a barrister becomes a judge he or she suddenly becomes interested in promoting wealth-maximisation to the exclusion of all other considerations, while at the same time acknowledging the need to keep quiet about this desire. All this is just so complicated that it makes 'wealth maximisation' completely implausible as an explanation of why judges decide cases the way they do.

● Don't be dogmatic

The final point I want to make about making speculative arguments is that you should always remember that they are **speculative**. As the facts on the ground that you are trying to explain change, you must be ready to change your explanations with them.

For example, the decisions in cases A, B, C and D may have led you to conclude that rule R is part of English law. If case E comes along and seems to deny that rule R is part of English law, you can't let yourself be carried away by a sentimental attachment to rule R into denouncing case E as 'wrongly decided'. You have to be ready to concede that the decision in case E has made the law uncertain and made it difficult to tell whether rule R is part of English law or not.

A great example of this willingness to change is provided by the late academic Professor Peter Birks. A lot of his work focused on the legal rule that if A has been unjustly enriched at B's expense, then B will be entitled to bring a claim for restitution against A and recover the value of that enrichment from A, so long – of course – as A cannot raise a defence to B's claim. But what does it mean to say that A has been *unjustly enriched* at B's expense? For about 20 years Peter Birks argued – on the basis of a close analysis of the relevant cases – that A will be unjustly enriched at B's expense if A obtains wealth from B without B's consent or under circumstances which meant B's consent to A's having that wealth was flawed in some way (because it was given because of a mistake, or under duress, or in expectation of something being given in return that never came). But in 1994 a case was decided – *Westdeutsche Landesbank* v *Islington LBC* [1994] 4 All ER 890 – that did not fit Peter Birks' theory of unjust enrichment. In that case B was allowed to recover money that A had obtained from B even though B had consented to A's having that money and there were no facts in the case that allowed us to say that B's consent to A's having that money was flawed in some way. Instead, B's claim to recover the money he had paid A was allowed simply because – unknown to both A and B at the time – the contract under which B had paid A the money happened to be invalid.

So how did Peter Birks react? Well, he didn't reach for his gun and attempt to shoot down the decision in *Westdeutsche Landesbank* by denouncing it as 'wrongly decided'. Instead, he did something amazing. He junked the definition of when A will be unjustly enriched at B's expense that he had been advancing for the previous 20 years, and for the last few years of his life he argued that A will be unjustly enriched at B's expense if A obtains wealth from B and there is no *valid legal basis* for the transfer of wealth. This new definition was, he argued, superior to the old, because it accounted both for the old cases – on which his old definition was based – and it also accounted for the decision in the *Westdeutsche Landesbank* case.

I'll now briefly attempt a summary of what I've said in the last two letters:

When making a logical argument, make sure that it isn't circular (that is, that it doesn't assume what it's trying to prove), check that the conclusion follows logically from the premises (and that you haven't done something silly like try and derive an 'ought' from an 'is'), and ensure that your argument isn't based on a false premise. The last point also applies when making a speculative argument, but when you make a speculative argument, check to see that your conclusion is the most sensible one to draw from the argument's premise or premises, remembering that the simplest explanation is probably the most sensible as well.

If you are interested in exploring the subject of arguing effectively any further, the best book I've yet to read on arguing effectively is Julian Baggini's *The Duck That Won The Lottery, and 99 Other Bad Arguments* (Granta Books, 2008).

Best wishes,

Nick

Applying to University and Doing the LNAT

○ From: Nicholas J. McBride [dearnick@pearson.com]
○ To: Brown, Jo
○ Subject: Applying to University and Doing the LNAT

Hi Jo,

Thanks for your e-mail, asking me for advice on applying to university and how you should prepare to do the LNAT if it turns out that one of the universities you are applying to requires you to sit it. Let's take each of these in turn.

○ Applying to university

There are such a large number of universities you could apply to, and so many factors you should take into account in deciding which universities are right for you, I couldn't possibly hope to give you all the advice you need in a letter. I'd have to write you a book. Fortunately, someone already has: get hold of the latest edition of *Push Guide to Choosing a University* (Hodder Arnold). This book – and the companion website, www.push.co.uk – provides an excellent 'jumping off' spot for students wanting to decide which universities to apply to. It's extremely helpful in setting out what sort of things you should take into account when making up your mind and gives you a huge amount of information about other books and websites you should look at.

The factors you should be taking into account in deciding which universities you apply to can be divided into university-related factors, and law-related factors. University-related factors that you should take into account would include:

- *Entry requirements.* Pitch your choice of university according to what sort of results you can expect to get at A-Level. You can find out what sort of entry requirements you would have to satisfy to study law at a particular university by going to the UCAS website at www.ucas.com and then clicking on 'Course Search' – you should be able to find your way to the information you want from there. (The UCAS website is also a convenient gateway to websites for all the universities you might be interested in learning a bit more about. Go to: www.ucas.com/students/beforeyouapply/wheretostudy/instguide and start exploring.)

- *Location.* Do you want to study at a university that is near home, or further away? Do you want to study at a university that is near the centre of town, or are you happy with one which is some distance away from the nearest town centre? How easy is it to travel from your home to the university? How close is the nearest supermarket/bookstore to the university? What's the town or city that is closest to the university like? Would you be happy spending time there?

- *Accommodation.* Does the university promise to accommodate you throughout your time there? If not, how easy/cheap is it to secure good, alternative accommodation? What is the accommodation like? What are the kitchens, toilets and washing facilities (both bathrooms and laundry) that come with the accommodation like?

- *Facilities.* What are the facilities that the university lays on for its students like generally? What are the bars/common rooms like? How active is the Student Union? What is the library like? What are the facilities for accessing the Internet like? Is there much to do in the evenings?

- *Security.* How safe is the university campus? Is it well-lit and well populated? What measures does the university take to ensure the security of its students? If something goes wrong, what sort of support does the university provide?

- *Support.* Being at university, and being away from home for long periods of time, can be difficult for a lot of students. How much

>

> support does the university provide its students with to help them adjust to living at university, and to help those who are having problems coping either with their studies or other problems arising from spending time at university?

To find out the answers to these sorts of questions, books like the *Push Guide* can be very helpful. (Also, look out on the Internet to see if there exists a student guide to a university that you are thinking of applying to.) But to check out a university properly, you should definitely go to one of the university's open days for prospective students, so that you can have a look around, see what the university is like, and chat to some of the students who are there at the moment. (You can find out the dates for open days for a particular university by consulting its website.) Ideally, you should try to go to an open day which has been put on specifically for prospective law students (again, look at the university's website to find out if it is putting on a law-specific open day and, if so, when) but if you can't go on one of those, something is better than nothing. If you do get the chance to tour the university's law faculty and talk to some of the law students at the university, try to get some information about the following law-related factors that you should take into account in your final choice of university:

- *Teaching.* How good is the law teaching that the university provides its students? Who does the teaching? (In order to give their 'star' academics more time to do research – the quality of which plays a large part in determining how much money the university receives from the government – some universities now use graduate students (students who have done a first degree, and are now studying for a post-graduate qualification) to carry out small group teaching sessions with their students.) How much contact do the students have with their teachers? How much help does the university give students who are struggling with their studies? How many lectures do the students get each week, and in how many subjects? How many small group teaching sessions do the students have each fortnight, and in how many subjects? How

>

much written work are students required to do? (You are NOT looking for the answer, 'Not much' – the more written work you can do, the better; though, obviously, there are limits.) Do students get good feedback on their written work? How much assistance do the students get in preparing them for the exams?

● *Law Library.* How good is the university's law library? Are the text-books up to date? How many areas of law, and how many juris-dictions (countries) does the law library cover? Are there good computer facilities? If you have a laptop, is it easy to hook up to the Internet at the law library? What are the law library's opening hours? Is it easy to get something to eat and drink if you're work-ing there? Is it easy to get to from where you would be living?

● *Opportunities to polish your cv.* How much scope would you have to engage in law-related activities that would enhance your legal skills and your attractiveness to potential employers? For exam-ple, would you get the opportunity to work in a free legal advice clinic? Does the university regularly hold mooting competitions, where law students get to act like barristers and argue legal points before a judge (usually an academic)? Is there a university student law review that is run by the university's law students, and to which the university law students can contribute articles? Is there any scope to work as a (paid or unpaid) research assistant to one of the university's law academics during the holidays?

● *Prospects after leaving university.* What do law students who gradu-ate from the university tend to do after they leave? Do those who are predicted to get firsts or 2.1s in law from that university find it easy to land a training contract (a two-year stint at a law firm, after which you will qualify as a fully-fledged solicitor) or pupillage (a one-year stint at a barrister's chambers, after which – if they like you – you'll be offered a tenancy and allowed to practise out of that chambers)?

Oxford or Cambridge?

If your school is predicting that you will get three As at A-Level and you achieved a good number of As at GCSE (with some A*s), then

>

you should definitely think about applying to study law at either Oxford or Cambridge. The two universities are actually very different in their approach to teaching law, and you should bear this in mind in making a choice between the two universities.

First, an Oxford law student does exams ('Moderations') in three subjects at the end of his first two terms, and then he will have no exams at all until the end of his third year, when he sits 'Finals', that is, exams in nine different subjects. A Cambridge law student will sit exams ('Tripos exams') at the end of each of the three years she studies law at Cambridge, and she'll end up taking exams in about fourteen different subjects. So studying law at Oxford tends to be a less stressful affair – at least until the time to sit Finals comes around – and affords greater opportunities to think about the law and develop some interesting views about it than is the case with studying law at Cambridge. But at the same time, a Cambridge law student will study more subjects than an Oxford law student. As a result, a Cambridge law student will have greater scope to choose what subjects she is going to study than her Oxford counterpart. Moreover, she'll leave university with a wider (though not deeper) knowledge of the law than someone with a law degree from Oxford.

Second, students in both Oxford and Cambridge are taught through a mixture of lectures and small group teaching sessions (called 'tutorials' in Oxford; 'supervisions' in Cambridge) with an academic. However, in Oxford the main way you are taught law is through tutorials – lectures are an optional add-on, meant to supplement the teaching that you get in tutorials, and there's no real pressure to attend them. Lectures are also optional in Cambridge, but they are regarded as the main vehicle for teaching students law, and it's the supervisions that are regarded as supplementary (though they are most definitely compulsory): supervisions in Cambridge are designed to make sure that students are doing okay and not falling behind, and give students the opportunity to get help with resolving any problems that they are having with their studies.

Third, I think it's fair to say that the Cambridge law degree places a lot of emphasis on ensuring that the students develop a detailed

>

knowledge of the law, while the Oxford law degree is a lot more interested in ensuring that students understand the principles and ideas that underlie different areas of the law, and are able to talk intelligently about how the law should be developed, rather than worrying about whether the students are completely up to date with the most recent developments and cases. This is reflected by the fact that Cambridge law exams are very heavy on problem questions, which usually test your knowledge of the details of the law. In contrast, Oxford law exams contain plenty of essays, which invite the students to show how much they understand about why the law says what it does, and talk about what the law should say on various issues.

⊙ The LNAT

You will have to do a special 'legal aptitude test' called the LNAT (the 'National Admissions Test for Law') if you are applying to any of the following universities: Birmingham, Bristol, Durham, Glasgow, Kings College London, Leeds, Nottingham, Oxford, University College London. (Though check on the LNAT site what the current position is: the list of universities that require and do not require you to have done the LNAT changes over time.) Applicants to Cambridge aren't required to do the LNAT, but will – on coming up to interview – be set a legal aptitude test set by the Cambridge Law Faculty. It's not clear at the time I'm writing what form this test will take, but if you end up applying to Cambridge, it might be worth reading the following advice on taking the LNAT just in case any of it is helpful for taking the Cambridge legal aptitude test.

If you're going to be taking the LNAT, you should definitely have a look at the website that has been set up to assist people who are going to take the LNAT. You can find it at:

www.lnat.ac.uk

This website provides a lot of helpful information, as well as a practice paper. The practice paper is especially helpful because students taking the LNAT will do so on computer, at test centres up and down the country.

So if you download the practice paper onto a computer, you can get a bit of experience of exactly what it will be like to take the LNAT.

As you'll see from the website, the point of the LNAT is to test students' aptitude to study law. Now, this *doesn't* mean that if you do badly on the LNAT, no one will accept you for a place to study law. Your performance on the LNAT is only *one* of the things that admissions tutors at the above universities will take into account in deciding whether or not to offer you a place. By the same token, if you do really well on the LNAT, that does not necessarily mean you are guaranteed a place to study law at whatever universities you are applying to.

Having said that, a poor performance on the LNAT won't help your case for admission to a place at university to study law; and a good performance could catch the selectors' eye and win you a place that you might not have obtained otherwise. So if you are applying to a university that requires you to take the LNAT, it is important that you do as well as you can on it – and to do well, you have to prepare for it.

The LNAT is made up of two parts. There is a multiple choice section where you are given a passage to read and asked two or three multiple choice questions about that passage. For example:

What point has **not** been made so far in Nick's letter to Jo about the LNAT?

A The LNAT test is very difficult.

B Some universities require law applicants to take the LNAT.

C Admissions tutors take the LNAT results into acccount in making admissions decisions.

D The official website about the LNAT is very helpful.

E It is important to prepare for the LNAT if you are applying to do Law at one of the universities that require its applicants to have done the LNAT.

The answer is, of course, A – I haven't said anything so far about how difficult the LNAT is.

You will be asked questions on ten different passages. The total number of multiple choice questions you will be asked to answer is 30, and you will have 80 minutes to answer them. This doesn't sound like very much time. However, it should, in fact, be ample. I completed the multiple choice section of the LNAT practice paper on the LNAT website in only 15 minutes, and still obtained a very respectable mark of 25/30.

The second part of the LNAT is an essay section. You will be required to write one essay in 40 minutes. You will be given the choice of five different topics or quotes to write about. For example:

1 Many people argue that admissions tests to gain places at university discriminate against students who are educationally disadvantaged. Others argue that such tests help such students by detecting in them abilities that would otherwise go unnoticed. Which side do you agree with?

2 'Efforts to protect the environment are misplaced. Why should we care about preserving the world for generations that are as yet unborn?' Discuss.

3 'Driving different countries into a political union is simply a recipe for trouble.' Do you agree?

4 'Giving aid to Third World countries is still the best way of helping the poor of those countries.' Discuss.

5 'It would have been better had the Internet never been invented.' What do you think?

The LNAT website says that your essay should be about 500–600 words and not more than 750 words. Unlike the multiple choice section of the LNAT, your essay will not be marked centrally by the people who run the LNAT. Instead, it will be forwarded to the admissions tutors at any universities to which you are applying that require their applicants to do the LNAT. It will then be up to those admissions tutors to assess the quality of your essay.

If you are going to do the LNAT, you should have a look at the 'Preparation' section of the LNAT website, which contains a 'hints and tips' section. The multiple choice section of the LNAT has a great deal in common with 'critical thinking' tests, so in theory it might be worth having a look at some books on critical thinking as preparation for the LNAT. However, in practice I'm not that impressed by the books on critical thinking that I've seen – so I can't recommend a specific book for you to read. But have a look in the bookshops yourself, and if there is a book on critical thinking that appeals to you, then use that. There are a couple of books that have been specifically written to advise people on how to do well on the LNAT: *Mastering the National Admissions Test for Law* by Mark Shepherd (published by Cavendish Publishing) and *Passing the National Admissions Test for Law* by Rosalie Hutton, Glenn Hutton and Fraser Sampson (published by Law Matters Publishing). They go into far more detail about how best to approach the LNAT test than I can here and I would recommend that you buy at least one of these books, read it and try the practice tests at the back of the book. Which one would I recommend? Annoyingly, the Shepherd book is stronger than the Hutton/Sampson book on giving advice on doing the essay section of the LNAT; while the Hutton/Sampson book is stronger than the Shepherd book on giving advice on doing the multiple choice section. If I had to choose, I would go for the Shepherd book: it's much more readable and better presented than the Hutton/Sampson book, and contains five practice tests compared with only one in the Hutton/Sampson book. If you can afford both, then buy both – but if you have to go for one, then the Shepherd book is a clear first choice.

That's enough plugging other people's books. I'll now get on with giving you some advice on doing the LNAT. (*Very* strong disclaimer at this point: my publisher owns the company (Pearson VUE) that currently runs the LNAT test. However, what follows definitely does not at all represent any 'inside knowledge' on my part on how to do well on the LNAT. These are my views, not anyone else's.)

The multiple choice section

1 *Be careful.* That's my main piece of advice to you – *be careful* in reading and answering the questions. For example, suppose you are asked:

> Which of the following is an **unstated** assumption that the writer makes in the passage?

When you are going through the possible answers supplied, remember that you are not *just* looking for an answer that identifies an assumption that the writer has made in making out his argument in the passage supplied. You are looking for an answer that identifies an assumption that the writer has made in making out his argument in the passage supplied that is also *not* stated in the passage supplied. So *don't* mark as correct an answer that identifies an assumption that the writer has expressly said that he is making in the passage supplied. That statement may represent an assumption that the writer made in making out his argument – but it's hardly unstated, is it?

2 *If you don't know the answer, you might as well guess.* In its present form, wrong answers in the multiple choice section of the LNAT are *not* given a negative mark. So if you do not know the answer to a given question, you might as well guess the answer. You won't be punished if your answer is wrong, and you might well be lucky and guess the right answer. The admissions tutors at the universities you are applying to will not see your answers to the multiple choice questions – all they will see is your total mark. So if your guess is wildly wrong, then again you won't be punished for that. No one will see your answers and think, 'Well – this candidate can't be very good if he or she thought that *that* was the right answer.'

Now, if you have come across a question in the LNAT that has completely stumped you, don't spend too long agonising over it. You can always go back to it if you finish the rest of the multiple choice section before the allotted 80 minutes is up. It's more important you move on to the other questions which you will probably have a better chance of knowing the answer to. So make your best guess as to what the answer is, and then swiftly move on. Once you have finished going through the whole of multiple choice section, *then* you can go back to the questions that you had real problems with and agonise over what the answers to those questions are.

3 *Getting through the test in time.* You will have to decide for yourself – by doing practice tests such as the one on the LNAT website or in the available books about the LNAT – what sort of approach to the multiple choice questions will best allow you to get through the multiple choice section of the LNAT in the time allowed.

Most people seem to adopt the following approach to answering multiple choice questions on a given passage in the LNAT. First of all they read the passage carefully; they then look at the questions; then they refer back to the passage to help them select the correct answers to those questions.

In doing the practice test on the LNAT website, I adopted a different approach. This was to look at the questions *first*, and then search the passage for the answers. This seems to me a great timesaver if you get a question like:

> What is the **main** point that the writer is making in the last paragraph?

To answer that question, you don't have to have read the whole of the passage supplied. You simply have to look at the last paragraph of the passage. Similarly, if you get a question like:

> Which of the following is **not** a reason why the writer refers to the 1990s as the 'golden age of television'?

Again, you don't have to have read the whole of the passage to answer that question – just look in the passage for the phrase 'the golden age of television' and then look around that phrase for the reasons why the writer thinks that the 1990s were the 'golden age of television'. And if you get a question asking:

> Which of the following is **not** a statement of opinion?
>
> or
>
> Which of the following **is** a statement of opinion?

– well, you don't need to have read the passage *at all* to answer that one.

I think my approach to doing the multiple choice section of the LNAT is a lot faster, and allows you to spend much more time on the really tricky questions. But you will have to find out for yourself whether my approach works for you – or whether you are more comfortable adopting the more conventional approach to going through the multiple choice section.

4 *The importance of practice.*   It is important – to give yourself the best possible chance of doing well in the multiple choice section of the LNAT – to do the practice tests on the LNAT website. (There are now three on the website.) This will get you used to the sort of questions that you might be asked in this section of the LNAT, and also the kind of tricks the question setters get up to in an attempt to find out how good your legal abilities really are.

The essay section

1 *Selecting your essay title.*   Be careful in choosing what essay to do in the essay section of the LNAT. Make sure that the essay title you pick allows you to write an *interesting* and *effective* essay that will *impress* an admissions tutor reading it. So pick an essay title that allows you to make some strong arguments – or, even better, an essay title that allows you to make an unexpected or surprising point. For example, in the year the LNAT was introduced, students were required to write an essay on *one* of the following five topics:

1 'Sporting achievement should not be limited by the prohibition on the use of certain performance-enhancing drugs.' Do you agree?

2 What is your response to the view that the purpose of education is to prepare young people for the world of work?

3 'Women now have the chance to achieve anything they want.' How do you respond to this statement?

4 'Modern society is too dependent on debt: we should all pay our way.' Do you agree?

5 Would you agree that travel and tourism exploit poorer nations and benefit only the richer ones?

(Nowadays, each student is given a choice of five essay questions that have been selected from a bank of possible essay questions. So different students will be given a different set of five essays to choose from.) Now –

which of these essays would a *good* student do? Well, a good student would rule out doing (4) straightaway. Why? Well, the statement is so silly that there's no possibility of agreeing with it. And any arguments that one might make against the statement are just so obvious (without incurring debts, people couldn't afford to buy homes and cars; companies could not survive through lean times; the government would collapse) that an essay arguing that the statement is wrong wouldn't make for particularly interesting reading.

A good student would also rule out doing (5). This is partly because, again, the basis of the essay question is a statement ('travel and tourism exploit poorer nations and benefit only the richer ones') that is so silly that one cannot do anything but disagree with it. So the scope for saying anything interesting in response to the essay title is virtually nil. In addition, to write an effective essay on this title would seem to require a good grasp of the economic data on tourism; and not many students will have that sort of information to hand.

For similar reasons, a good student would also rule out doing essay (3). The statement seems obviously wrong. A woman with a baby might want to be paid £50,000 a year for working one day a week in a law firm, thus allowing her to spend most of her time raising her baby. But it can hardly be supposed that any woman (or man) would be allowed to do that. However, an essay that made that point would not be particularly interesting. It might be possible to narrow the statement in some way so as to make it more plausible – one could interpret it as saying that 'Women now have the chance to do any kind of work they want.' But, again, it's hard to see how one could write an *interesting* essay on that topic. Either the available information indicates that women have that chance or it indicates that they do not – there does not seem to be much room for interesting debate or discussion, either way.

Our good student is running out of options! What about (2)? Well, there is no way any student applying to study at a university will want to be caught agreeing with the idea that education is simply about preparing young people to do a job. So a student who did essay (2) would *have* to argue that the purpose of education is more wide-ranging. Could a student write an interesting essay that took that kind of line? It depends on whether he or she could come up with an interesting and convincing line as to what the 'purpose' of education *is* if it's *not* to prepare young people for work. *Merely* saying that the purpose of education is to 'cultivate one's mind' or to 'expand one's horizons' or make one 'question everything' wouldn't be enough – saying *that* is just not very interesting.

One interesting line which would link in quite well with the statement in the essay title would be to argue that the purpose of education is not to prepare young people for *work* but to prepare them for *leisure*. You could argue that the purpose of education is to prepare young people for what they should be doing in their leisure time. And one could move from there to say that it's noticeable that as education has become more work-oriented (with Young Enterprise Schemes, work placements and so on), the way young people spend their leisure time has increasingly become a social problem (examples: binge drinking, bored youths hanging around estates, joyriding). You could then say that this makes it all the more necessary that we move back towards a notion of education as preparing young people for how they spend their leisure.

That would make for quite an interesting essay on (2) that would impress any admissions tutor who read it. And note that while an essay which took this kind of line might refer to some features of contemporary life to make its points, doing this essay would not require the sort of in-depth knowledge of the real world that one would have to have if one attempted essays (3) or (5).

Finally, what about (1)? Again, there seems to be some scope for writing an interesting and effective essay on this topic. It's not so obvious that using performance-enhancing drugs in sport should be banned that it's impossible to think of interesting arguments on either side of the issue. For example, one could observe – if one wanted to argue in favour of allowing the use of performance-enhancing drugs – that athletes already use dietary supplements to help them train. So why not allow them to use steroids to build up their stamina and help them train longer? Against this, one could argue that steroids are bad for you, and atheletes who do not want to endanger their health by using steroids should not be disadvantaged when competing against other athletes. There is scope here for getting an interesting debate going – which is simply not possible with essay (4). And there is no need to have access to very specialised knowledge to engage in that debate – something which, as we've seen, is not possible with essays (3) or (5). The debate is at the level of general principle, rather than hard fact.

So of these five essays, a *good* student would do essays (1) or (2). He or she would definitely not do essays (3), (4) or (5). So if you do the LNAT, be careful about your choice of essay – make sure you go through the same kind of process that I've gone through above. Discard the essay titles which, however do-able they might seem, offer little prospect of allowing you to write an interesting and effective essay.

2 *Essay structure.* Suppose you have been told to write an essay on 'Is *X* true?' You have probably been taught to write an essay on this topic using the following structure:

1 Introduction.
2 Arguments for thinking that *X* is true.
3 Arguments for thinking that *X* is not true.
4 Your opinion on whether *X* is true, given the balance of the arguments.
5 Conclusion.

Please don't adopt this kind of structure in writing your LNAT essay. (In fact, once you leave school, please don't ever write an essay along these lines ever again.) Nothing is more guaranteed to send an admissions tutor to sleep than an essay that goes, 'On the one hand, it could be argued that . . . On the other hand, it could be argued that . . . On balance, I think that . . . So we can conclude that . . .'. If you want to impress an admissions tutor who is reading your essay – and remember he or she will probably have a large pile of these essays to wade through so you will want to do something to catch his or her eye – you will have to adopt a quite different approach. I'd like to encourage you to adopt this structure in writing your LNAT essay:

1 Conclusion.
2 Arguments in favour of your conclusion.

>

> 3 Arguments against your conclusion, and an explanation as to why
> they do not work.
>
> 4 Restatement of your conclusion.

This is a much more direct way of writing your essay. There are three big advantages to writing your essay in this way. First, your essay will be very easy to follow and understand – by stating at the start where you stand, you make it obvious where you are 'coming from'. Secondly, your essay will be much more interesting than an essay written in the more careful, plodding style you have probably been brought up to use. Thirdly, your essay will be a lot less wordy – a big advantage when you only have 500–600 words to play with.

Of course, you can only employ this kind of essay structure if you know *before you begin* what your conclusion is going to be. So take some time before you start writing the essay to think it out and think about what sort of line you are going to take in the essay.

3 *Preparation.* It might be an idea to try a few practice essay questions to get used to this different style of writing essays that I'm encouraging you to adopt. But the other thing you *must* do by way of preparation for the essay section of the LNAT is to start reading – in full – a serious daily newspaper such as *The Times, The Daily Telegraph, The Independent* or *The Guardian.* Pay particular attention to the opinion/comment sections of the newspapers. It might be an idea to try to read the opinion/comment sections of both *The Daily Telegraph* and *The Guardian* each day, so that you are exposed to a variety of points of view. Also try, if you can, to read *The Spectator* or the *New Statesman* or *The Economist* every week.

Doing this will be of huge benefit to you in doing the essay section of the LNAT. First, reading serious newspapers and magazines will boost your knowledge of current affairs and therefore your ability to handle an essay question on current affairs. Secondly, doing this kind of reading will expose you to political ideas and discussions that you can then draw on in writing your essay. Thirdly, reading these kinds of newspapers and magazines will expose you to some good, serious debates on difficult issues, thus helping you see the sort of thing that you'll be expected to do in your essay.

So, that's all the advice I have to offer you on doing the LNAT. There is still a lot more to be said but you'll find everything else you need to know about doing the LNAT in the Shepherd and Hutton/Sampson books.

Hope this is helpful. Let me know how your applications go.

Best wishes,

Nick

Tips for Interview

- From: Nicholas J. McBride [dearnick@pearson.com]
- To: Brown, Jo
- Subject: Tips for Interview

Hey Jo,

Good luck for your admissions interview! I'm sure you'll do very well. It's inevitable that you're going to be nervous – but I hope you'll be able to give a good account of yourself. To help you with that, here are some tips:

● The interviewer is on your side

I guarantee that your interviewers will be eager to see you do well. Don't think for a second that they will be out to trip you up, or trap you into making a fool of yourself. All your interviewers will be desperate to find some really good students among all the candidates they are interviewing – so they will want to do as much as possible to help you do justice to yourself in the interview.

● Smile!

The interviewers would not only like to find some really good students among all the candidates they are interviewing – they would also like to find some really good students who they actually like the idea of spending the next three years with. So, don't be grouchy, or standoffish in the interview: be as positive, enthusiastic, and as cheerful as the circumstances allow you to be.

○ Be straightforward

Common sense is another thing your interviewers will be looking for in the people they interview. So if you are given a legal rule and asked to apply it to a given situation, be straightforward in applying the rule. Think about what the common sense meaning of the rule is, apply it to the situation and see what the outcome is. Don't try to prejudge what the outcome 'should' be, and don't try to detect any hidden traps, or meanings, or exceptions in the rule you've been asked to apply. If there are any, they will soon be pointed out to you – until that happens, just apply the plain, common sense meaning of the rule to determine how it applies in the situation you have been given.

○ Think!

The ability to think for yourself is another thing your interviewers will be looking out for. To test for this, your interviewers may well give you a situation, ask what you think the legal outcome should be in that situation, then give you a slightly altered situation, and ask you again what the legal outcome should be. If they do this, they are testing to see whether you can identify the distinctions between the two situations, and see whether you are capable of thinking for yourself whether those distinctions make a difference. For example, you might be asked to consider the following situation:

> 1 Two severely premature babies, Baby A and Baby B, are born at the same time. Neither of them can survive without being put in an incubator, but there is only one free incubator in the hospital. Who should be placed in the incubator?

Your answer will almost certainly be: whoever has the better chance of survival if they are placed in the incubator unit. Okay – consider now this next situation:

> 2 Two severely premature babies, Baby A and Baby B, are born within a few hours of each other. Neither of them can survive without
>
> >

being put in an incubator. Baby B is born first, and placed in the one remaining free incubator in the hospital. Baby A was born a few hours later, but there is no free incubator for him to be placed in. The chances of Baby B surviving in the incubator have been assessed at 25 per cent. It is clear that if Baby A were placed in Baby B's incubator, instead of Baby B, Baby A's chances of survival would be 75 per cent. Should the doctors take Baby B out of her incubator, and replace her with Baby A?

Your response to situation (1) might suggest that you would favour Baby B being taken out of the incubator, and being replaced by Baby A. But your interviewers have not asked you to consider situation (2) just so that you can repeat whoever has the higher chance of survival in the incubator should be placed in the incubator. They want to see if you can think for yourself: what are the distinctions between situations (1) and (2), and do those distinctions make a difference?

Well, let's consider the distinctions first. The key distinction is that in situation (2), Baby B is *already* in the incubator. So if you are going to put Baby A in the incubator, you have to do something *positive* to Baby B (take Baby B out of the incubator) that will have the effect of making Baby B worse off than she is at the moment. This is very different from situation (1), where if you put Baby A in the incubator, you are not doing anything positive to Baby B – you are merely *failing* to do something that would have the effect of saving Baby B's life. So: that's the distinction identified. The next issue is – does that distinction make a difference? Is doing something positive to Baby B, as a result of which act Baby B will die, worse than failing to do something for Baby B, as a result of which failure Baby B will die? Let's assume that you do think that it makes a difference. So you say that in situation (2), Baby B should not be taken out of the incubator. You might be asked to then consider this situation:

3 The same situation as situation (2), except Baby B was born five minutes before Baby A, and had only just been put in the incubator when Baby A was carried into the ward for severely premature babies. Should Baby B be taken out of the incubator, and replaced with Baby A?

In this situation, Baby B has only *just* been put in the incubator. Does this make a difference? Given that you thought Baby B should *not* be taken out of the incubator in (2), do you also think that Baby B should *not* be taken out of the incubator in (3)? Or does the fact that Baby B has not been in the incubator for very long make it more acceptable to take Baby B out of the incubator and replace her with Baby A?

● Argue!

Once you have taken a position, you will be expected to *argue* in favour of it. And by argue, I mean genuinely argue – present reasons for thinking that your position is correct. Don't just say 'Well, that's my opinion': that's not an argument, that's an assertion.

So – suppose you've said that Baby B should *not* be taken out of the incubator in (2), but that she *should* be in (3). You will be asked to account for this apparent inconsistency in your views. What you will need to do is show how you are not being inconsistent at all, but identify why there is a material difference between the two situations. One way might be to argue that in some sense, the incubator becomes part of Baby B the longer she stays in it – it becomes part of her life system, and it would be just as wrong to deprive her of that, as it would be for me to rip out your heart to give it to someone else who may, with your heart, enjoy a better chance of long-term survival than you do. So in (3), the incubator and Baby B are not yet – at the relevant level – 'attached' to each other, so it would not be wrong to take the incubator away from Baby B in the same way that it would be wrong to take the incubator away from Baby B in (2). Okay – this argument seems a bit mysterious and metaphysical, but at least it's an argument. And you are going to have to draw on some argument like that to establish that there is a significant difference between (2) and (3) – if you can't do that, you'll just be reduced to incoherent babbling.

Alternatively, let's suppose that you think that Baby B should *not* be taken out of the incubator in *either* situation (2) *or* situation (3). In that case an objection will be made to your view – and you will be expected to argue that that objection does not work. The objection would go like this: 'If you think that Baby B should not be taken out of the incubator in situation (3), then you are letting the morally arbitrary fact that Baby B was born a mere five minutes before Baby A determine who gets the incubator – surely this is unsatisfactory?' How do you overcome this objection? You have to establish that you are basing your position that Baby B should not be taken out of the incubator in situation (3) on something more than just the fact that Baby B was born first. Well, one way of establishing this would be to observe that in situation (3), the people running the ward for severely premature babies have taken on the job – in lawyers' language, 'assumed the responsibility' – of looking after Baby B, and have not (yet) taken on the job of looking after Baby A. So the people running the unit are 'attached' to Baby B in a way that they are not to Baby A. This is not a morally arbitrary fact. Attachments matter. Once an attachment has been formed, it counts for something, and this is so even if the attachment would never have been formed but for an initial, arbitrary, twist of fate. Again, the argument is a bit mysterious and metaphysical – but, again, at least it's an argument that helps you demolish the objection being made to your position.

● Don't stick to a hopeless position

But what if you are uninspired? What if you can't see an argument that will save your position? What if you've said that Baby B should not be taken out of the incubator in situation (2), but she should be in situation (3) – but you can't come up with a good argument to explain why there is a material difference between these two situations? If that's the case, then please, please don't 'stick to your guns'. Don't just blindly assert that there is a difference between (2) and (3), and that's your opinion and you are sticking to it. This will go down really badly – it will show a basic failure to think on your part. If you can't present a decent argument for thinking that there is a material difference between situations (2) and (3), you don't have a choice: you have to concede that there is no material difference between situations (2) and (3). And having made that concession, there are two ways you can go. You can stick with saying that in situation (2), Baby B should not be taken out of the incubator, and shift to saying that in situation (3), Baby B should also not be taken out of the incubator. Or you can shift your position on situation (2) and say that in that situation, Baby B should be taken out of the incubator, and say that given this, it's obvious that in situation (3) as well, Baby B should be taken out of the incubator. Don't think for a second that doing that will get you out of trouble – you will be expected to argue in favour of the new position that you have adopted. But it will at least show the interviewers that you are not a nutcase who sticks rigidly to a position even though you cannot come up with a single good reason for doing so.

● Don't avoid the issue

A lot of students – perhaps because they intelligently perceive the dangers of taking a position which they will then be asked to defend – try and avoid taking a position on an issue that they have been asked to address. They evade the issue, rather than tackling it head on. So, for example, let's go back to situation (2), where Baby B is in the incubator, and Baby A comes along, with a much better chance of survival if he is put in the incubator, in place of Baby B. The issue is whether Baby B should be taken out of the incubator and Baby A put in her place. Many students will avoid addressing that issue by saying something like, 'Well, I think in this situation the hospital authorities should try and find another incubator for Baby A to go in.' It's just a waste of time saying that – the interviewers will simply say, 'Let's assume that there isn't another incubator: what should happen then?', thus forcing the interviewee to address the issue. So don't avoid the issue. If you want to show the interviewers that you are aware there might be alternative solutions to the problem they are making you consider, then say something like, 'Assuming that there isn't another hospital nearby that would be able to care for Baby A, I think . . .'

● Don't assume that there is a clear right answer

I don't want to say that there is no right answer to the issue of what should be done in the incubator cases we have been considering – I believe in right answers, especially in the field of morality. However, I do want to say that there is no *clear* right answer to these issues. Whatever answer you come up with, objections and counter-arguments can be made to your position. So don't think that there is a clear right answer to the questions you are being asked to consider and that you are being expected to come up with that answer and that if someone comes up with an objection to something you've said, that shows you answered the question wrongly. That involves a complete misunderstanding of why your interviewers might ask you to consider a series of situations such as the incubator cases set out above. They are not so much interested in your answers, as they are in probing your answers to gauge how intelligent you are. Can you come up with an argument to support a position you are taking? Can you deal with an objection to that argument? Can you recognise when your position is hopeless, and shift your position accordingly? *These* are the questions that your interviewers will really be interested in getting some answers to – not what your views are on whether Baby B or Baby A should get the last incubator on the ward for severely premature babies.

Current affairs

Of course, you might not be asked at all about some hypothetical case and what should happen in that case. You might be asked about some recent incident or development that has made the news, and asked for your opinion about it. The interviewer's aim in asking you about this incident/development will be exactly the same – to probe your answers with a view to getting some idea as to how intelligent you are. But if you are asked about some recent incident/development in the news, you will be left hanging in the wind if you don't actually know much about it. So at least a couple of months before you attend your interview, make sure that you regularly read at least one of *The Spectator, The Economist* and *The New Statesman* each week, and that you read the news and opinion sections of a decent daily newspaper – that is *The Times, The Guardian, The Daily Telegraph, The Independent* or *The Financial Times* – each day. Doing this will not only keep you up to date with the news, it will also give you ideas for intelligent things to say in the interview if you are asked about something that has happened in the news.

Be prepared for the obvious questions

Your interview will probably open with a couple of questions about your personal statement on your UCAS form. These are meant to be 'soft' questions, designed to relax you and get you talking. But they can turn into a nightmare if you aren't prepared for them.

So if you have expressed an interest in reading fiction, be ready to say what you have read recently, and what you thought of it. If you say that you spent your summer holidays last year backpacking around Eastern Europe, be prepared to say something a little bit more enlightening about your experiences than just 'Yeah – it was great.' If you have said that you are deeply fascinated by the work of the International Criminal Court and you want study law because you would like to work there one day, be prepared – be very prepared – to talk about the International Criminal Court, what it does, why it's important, and what sort of cases it might handle in the future. That last example shows that you should be very careful in writing your personal statement not to make any claims that you cannot back up. So, for example, I have seen more than one personal statement in the past that has said something along the lines of, 'I spent a week working in my local solicitor's and my experience there has given me a great insight into the workings of our justice system.' Yeah, right. If you say something like that in your personal statement, you had better be ready to back it up with some examples of some 'insights' that you gained on your week's work experience – because you will definitely be asked for them.

There are other pretty obvious questions that you should have prepared to answer before your interview. Why do you want to study here? (Tricky one, that: it's pretty obvious what the answer is, but a bit sucky to come out with it. Just focus in on a few features of the place you are applying to and say that it was because of them that you were particularly attracted to the idea of studying there.) Why do you want to do law? How easy do you find it to balance your work with all your extra-curricular commitments? (Dangerous one, that: the interviewers don't want to admit someone who will be too busy with all sorts of extra-curricular activities to put in the effort required to do well in their legal studies.) Why do you want to take a gap year? (If you do.) Why are your AS marks in history not as good as your other AS marks? (That's a very important question as the interviewers do pay a lot of attention to things like GCSE marks and AS marks in gauging how well someone is likely to do as a law student. So if you have had a couple of disappointing marks at GCSE, or at AS-Level, then be prepared to explain them.)

Having said that you should prepare for these questions to come up, don't overprepare for them. Don't try and memorise an answer that you'd give for each of these questions – you'll just come across all unnatural in the interview. Just come up with a rough idea of what you would say, and then don't worry about it again.

◉ It's a conversation, not an interrogation

The best interviews are conversational in nature – there's a back and forth quality to them, where the interviewers say something, the interviewee says something that actually addresses what the interviewers have said, the interviewers then reply to the point that has been made to them, the interviewee responds, and so on. So try your best to go into the interview with the mentality that you are there to have a chat with the interviewers about some subjects that they are interested in talking about. Don't think that you are there to show off how clever you are, or to be pummelled into submission, or to be tested on how much you know about a particular subject. You are just there to have a chat for half an hour or so. So relax; listen to what's being said to you, and respond to it; and if you don't know what to say, be frank about that so the conversation can move on to some other topic that might be more productive.

◉ The interview isn't make or break

Finally, remember that the interview isn't the most crucial part of your application. Many interviewers are skeptical as to how valuable the interview actually is as a way of determining how well someone is going to do as a law student. I have certainly interviewed people who were completely disastrous in interview, but they were still admitted because the rest of their application – their reference and their exam results to date – was so outstanding, and they proved to be absolutely fine law students. So if you don't have such a good interview, it's not a disaster: there is lots of other information about you available to the interviewers that they can take into account in judging your application.

There are some other words of advice I'd like to give you, warning you against adopting certain disastrous ideas or habits of thought that seem to be particularly popular among people going to university, and which can result in your not doing so well in interview. But because the advice isn't just relevant to your upcoming interview, but will also be relevant for when you actually go to university, I'll deal with it separately in another letter. Read this one, think about it, and I'll be in touch again very soon.

Best wishes,

Nick

Some Traps to Avoid

○ From: Nicholas J. McBride [dearnick@pearson.com]
○ To: Brown, Jo
○ Subject: Some Traps to Avoid

Hi Jo,

As promised, here's a letter warning you about some bad mental habits that a lot of students your age fall into. I hope reading this letter will not only help you do well in interview, but also help you generally with your legal studies.

○ Relativism

Right at the start of his book *The Closing of the American Mind*, Allan Bloom – a very great American academic – observed, 'There is one thing a professor can be absolutely certain of: almost every student entering the university believes, or says he believes, that truth is relative.'

It's understandable why students should take this position. Students, as a whole, want to be nice, open-minded and tolerant people; and this is, of course, greatly to their credit. Now, suppose that I tell you that the world is flat. There are only two ways you can react. You can tell me that I am wrong, implying thereby that I am stupid and badly educated – which isn't very nice. Or you can say, 'Well, all truth is relative, so I'm not in a position to tell you that you're wrong. For you the world is flat; for me, it's roughly spherical – but there's nothing for us to disagree about. We're both right, from within our different perspectives.' This seems a much nicer, open-minded and tolerant response and is thus much more attractive to students.

However, it's extremely silly to think that 'all truth is relative'. The reason for this is very simple. We know for certain that the statement 'all truth is relative' *cannot* be absolutely true, because if this statement were absolutely true then not all truth would be relative. So only two possibilities remain. Either the statement 'all truth is relative' is absolutely false – in which case we shouldn't accept it. Or the statement 'all truth is relative' is only true for some people, and is false for some other people – in which case, why should *we* accept that it's true? Either way, it's senseless to think that 'all truth is relative'. As the philosopher Roger Scruton observes, 'A writer who says that there are no truths, or that all truth is "merely relative" is asking you not to believe him. So don't.'

'Well,' you may say, 'It may make no sense to think that "all truth is relative" when we are talking about questions of fact. But surely when we are talking about values or morality, everyone has different opinions, and it's simply not possible to say that one person's opinions are correct and another person's opinions are wrong. So in the area of values or morality, it *is* true to say that "all truth is relative".' If you think like this, you've already fallen into another trap that I want to urge you to avoid: the trap of **moral relativism**.

Let's try and get you out of the trap by considering a concrete example. In his great novel *The Brothers Karamazov*, Fyodor Dostoevsky set out a number of documented instances of cruelty to children that occurred a couple of centuries ago in Russia. This is the last one:

> There was a general at the beginning of the century, a general with high connections and a very wealthy landowner . . . He had hundreds of dogs in his kennels and nearly a hundred handlers . . . [O]ne day a house-serf, a little boy, only eight years old, threw a stone while he was playing and hurt the paw of the general's favourite hound. 'Why is my favourite dog limping?' It was reported to him that this boy had . . . hurt her paw. 'So it was you,' the general looked the boy up and down. 'Take him!' They took him, took him from his mother, and locked him up for the night. In the morning at dawn, the general rode out in

>

LETTER 8 SOME TRAPS TO AVOID

> full dress for the hunt . . . surrounded by . . . dogs, handlers, huntsmen, all on horseback. The house-serfs are gathered for their edification, the guilty boy's mother in front of them all. The boy is led out of the lockup . . . The general orders them to undress the boy; the child is stripped naked, he shivers, he's crazy with fear, he doesn't dare make a peep . . . 'Drive him!' the general commands. The huntsmen shout, 'Run, run!' The boy runs . . . '[Get] him!' screams the general and looses the whole pack of wolfhounds on him. He hunted him down before his mother's eyes, and the dogs tore the child to pieces . . .

A true story. So – what do you think? Was it morally wrong for the general to do what he did? I hope you will say, 'Yes it was – and anyone who thinks otherwise is wrong.' If you do, then you have to concede that moral relativism is incorrect: it is possible to say that someone's values or opinions on matters of morality are wrong.

Now – if you're anything like the students I see when I interview them for places at my college, you'll probably say, 'Well, it's my personal opinion that it was wrong for the general to do what he did, and if I could have stopped him I would have. At the same time, I recognise that other people might think it was okay for the general to do what he did – and if they do, I can't say they're incorrect. They're entitled to their opinion.' But if you say this, then you are contradicting yourself. If you genuinely think, 'It was wrong for the general to do what he did' then you *must* also think that the statement 'It was okay for the general to do what he did' is incorrect. But if you do think that that statement is incorrect, then you must think that you, me or anyone else would be making a mistake if we said that, 'It was okay for the general to do what he did'.

The truth is that moral relativism cannot be seriously defended. It's an affectation, adopted out of a laudable desire not to be offensive or cruel by telling other people that what they are doing is bad or morally wrong. Indeed, it's a self-refuting affectation because the people who adopt it would be the first to insist that it is morally wrong to be offensive or cruel to other people – and that anyone who thinks differently is simply wrong.

● Not taking human rights seriously

Imagine the following conversation between two people, A and B:

> A: Would it be wrong for me to torture you for fun?
>
> B: Of course it would.
>
> A: Why?
>
> B: Well, I have a human right not to be tortured.
>
> A: What if you were a terrorist and you had information about an impending terrorist attack that will kill thousands of people. Would it be wrong for me to torture you to get you to tell me the details of the attack?
>
> B: Er . . .

B is obviously not a moral relativist: he is happy to say that torture *is* wrong, and that he *does* have a human right not to be tortured. But B does not take the idea that there is a human right not to be tortured *seriously*. He hesitates on the issue of whether it would be wrong to torture a terrorist in order to prevent a terrorist attack. There are two possible sources of this hesitation; both of them are unjustified if we take seriously the idea that there is a human right not to be tortured.

Not wrong to torture the blameworthy?

B may be hesitating to say that it would be wrong to torture a terrorist in order to extract information about an impending attack because while he is completely confident that it would be wrong to torture someone who is completely blameless and innocent (such as a terrorist's 5-year-old daughter), he is less confident whether it would be wrong to torture someone who has been helping to plan the slaughter of thousands of people. But if there is a human right not to be tortured, then *everyone* has that right, the innocent and blameworthy alike. You cannot lose that right simply because you happen to be an evil person.

>

Society comes first?

The second possible source of B's hesitation may be a nagging thought that in the situation where we could prevent the deaths of thousands of people by torturing someone, surely the interests of those thousands of people must come before the interests of the person we are thinking of torturing. But again, if there is such a thing as a human right not to be tortured, this thought is unjustified. The whole point of human rights is that they place limits on what we can do to other people in the name of 'social welfare' or the 'public interest'. They assert the priority of the individual over society. (That is why Jeremy Bentham – who was the godfather of utilitarianism: the creed that tells us that sacrificing the interests of an individual is the right thing to do if the overall happiness of society will be increased as a result – was so hostile to the idea of human rights, declaring it to be 'nonsense on stilts'.) In the memorable phrase coined by the legal philosopher Ronald Dworkin, human rights are 'trumps' – if you have a human right not to be treated in a particular way, then that gives you the power to veto any proposal that you be treated in that way, no matter how overwhelming the public interest may be in the proposal being carried out.

It might be argued against this that many of the human rights recognised in the European Convention on Human Rights (ECHR) are qualified in nature. So, for example, the right to freedom of expression recognised in Article 10 of the (ECHR) may be limited or abridged so far as is 'necessary in a democratic society, in the interests of national security, territorial integrity or public safety, for the prevention of disorder or crime, for the protection of health or morals, for the protection of the reputation or rights of others, for preventing the disclosure of information received in confidence, or for maintaining the authority and impartiality of the judiciary.' Does this not show that what I've said in the previous paragraph is incorrect and that human rights can indeed be made to give way where the public interest demands it? The answer is 'no'.

To see why, we have to remind ourselves that human rights are enjoyed by everyone. Everyone has these rights because they are human beings, and as such are endowed with a certain dignity that

>

entitles them not to be treated as disposable commodities. If this is correct, the right to freedom of expression is not a genuine example of a *human* right. We don't have a right to freedom of expression because we are human beings. We have a right to freedom of expression because it is important for the health of our society that we be given a right to freedom of expression. History teaches us that democratic societies tend to flourish much more than undemocratic societies, and you cannot have a genuine democracy without giving people a right to freedom of expression. Given the *social* roots of the right to freedom of expression, it is hardly surprising that provision should be made for limiting this right where its exercise would work in an anti-social way. In contrast, the rights recognised by the ECHR that can be said to be genuine examples of *human* rights – the right not to be intentionally killed (Article 2), the right not to be subjected to 'torture or to inhuman or degrading treatment or punishment' (Article 3), the right not to 'be held in slavery or servitude' (Article 4), and the right to a fair trial (Article 6) – are completely unqualified, and cannot be set aside or limited when the public interest demands.

So, if there is such a thing as a human right not to be tortured, then B should not hesitate: he should say firmly that, yes, it would be wrong to torture a terrorist to extract information from him about a terrorist attack, even if thousands of people will die if the attack is carried out. But it may be that B could not bring himself to say this. If that is the case, B must concede that there is, in fact, no such thing as a human right not to be tortured. Does that then mean that it would be okay for A to torture B for fun? No: even if B does not have a human right not to be tortured, it would still be wrong for A to torture B for fun. This is because if we weigh the pain B will suffer if A tortures him against the pleasure A will get from torturing B, B's pain will outweigh A's pleasure and make it wrong for A to torture B. (Of course, such a balancing exercise produces a quite different conclusion in the scenario where B is a terrorist and we need to torture him to prevent an impending attack.)

B is typical of many students that I come across, particularly at interview stage. They are more than happy to talk the talk of human rights, but when it comes to walking the walk, they stumble and fall. They happily condemn what happened in Auschwitz on human rights grounds. But after only a few minutes' discussion, they are all too willing to concede that, in fact, it might be acceptable to torture people, or conduct medical experiments on unwilling patients, or destroy thousands of lives in a nuclear holocaust, if doing so would serve the 'greater good'. Don't fall into the same trap: if you are going to say that people have a human right not to be tortured, follow through and insist that it is *always* wrong to torture someone, no matter what the circumstances are and no matter what good might be done as a result.

● Finding human rights everywhere

The finality of human rights – the fact that the existence of a human right that x not be done allows the holder of that right to veto any proposal that x be done, no matter how advantageous doing x might be – means that there is a constant temptation to invoke human rights as a way of establishing that it would be wrong to go ahead with a particular course of action.

So, for example, if you are opposed to a local authority's plans to create a housing estate near your village, it is very tempting to try to win the argument that the housing estate should not be built by asserting that building the estate would violate your and the other villagers' human rights. If you can make this assertion stick, then you've won the day. If the local authority attempts to argue that it would be in the public interest to build the housing estate, you can argue back that that is irrelevant: your and the other villagers' human rights trump any considerations of the public interest.

Students like to invoke human rights for the same reason: it provides an easy way of closing down the discussion of an issue that might otherwise prove too thorny for them to handle. So, for example, in the case I discussed in the previous letter, where Baby B has been placed in a hospital's last remaining free incubator, and Baby A is then wheeled into the ward for severely premature babies, and the issue is whether Baby A should be placed in Baby B's incubator, in place of Baby B, many students might feel tempted to short-circuit the discussion of what should be done by simply asserting that Baby B has a 'human right' to stay in the incubator.

Try to resist this temptation if it comes calling. Recognise what a difficult thing it is to establish that someone has a human right not to be treated in a particular way. Remember that human rights are based on the idea that all human beings are special, and as such deserve not to be treated like trash. This places a serious limit on when we can reasonably say that a proposed course of action will violate someone else's human rights. Choosing to replace Baby B in the incubator with Baby A because Baby B is black and Baby A is white would certainly violate Baby B's human rights because making such a choice involves a refusal to recognise that Baby B is just as special as Baby A. But it's hard to see how it could be argued that Baby B's human rights would be violated if we chose to replace Baby B in the incubator with Baby A simply because Baby A has a better chance of survival. Making that kind of choice does not involve any disregard, or contempt, for Baby B. (Though it may still be wrong to take Baby B out of the incubator, even if Baby A has a better chance of survival, for the reasons I discussed in my previous letter.)

Another way of making the same point about how difficult it is to establish that someone has a human right not to be treated in a certain way is – remember how *final* human rights are. That is, remember that if someone has a human right not to be treated in a particular way, then it would *always* be wrong to treat them in that way, no matter how beneficial the consequences of treating them in that way might be. This also places a serious limit on when we can reasonably say that a proposed course of action will violate someone's human rights. How many things that one person can do to another would you be willing to say are always absolutely wrong, no matter how beneficial the consequences of doing that sort of thing might be? I can only come up with eight:

1 executing someone else – that is, intentionally killing someone else after you have decided in a calm and collected state that that is what you are going to do;

2 torturing someone else;

3 having sex with someone without their consent;

4 intentionally sterilising someone without their consent;

>

5 experimenting on someone without their consent;

6 depriving someone of their liberty for an indefinite period;

7 intentionally destroying or getting in the way of someone's friendship with another;

8 treating someone with a contempt that is not based on an honest assessment of that person's character.

If I'm right, and there are no more than eight things that you can do to someone else that are always wrong, no matter what the circumstances, then there are only eight genuine human rights. And, of course, there are even fewer if, for example, it would in fact be justifiable in certain circumstances to torture someone, or execute someone.

○ Assumptions about certainty in the law

Another common trap that I would counsel you against falling into is the belief that the law on every issue is always certain. This is simply not true: it's often very difficult to say what the law says on a particular issue. The sources of uncertainty in the law are threefold.

Gaps

The law is full of **gaps**. That is, there are lots of areas and issues where we don't know what the law says, because Parliament hasn't legislated to cover that area or issue and the courts haven't yet been asked to decide what the law says on that area or issue. For example, suppose that I write a play that receives a great deal of acclaim. I subsequently allow the play to be performed at a theatre for six months, on the basis that I'm to receive 10 per cent of the box office. Suppose the play closes after two nights because the acting and the production received universally bad reviews in the newspapers. Could I sue the actors and the producer of the play for the money I would have earned had their acting and staging of the play been halfway competent? Nobody really knows: there's no statute governing the issue, and the

>

issue has never come up to be decided by the courts. The law on this issue is therefore uncertain.

Vagueness

Legal rules are often **vague**, making it very hard to know how they apply in concrete situations. So, for example, the Unfair Terms in Consumer Contracts Regulations 1999 provide that a term in a contract between a consumer and a business will be invalid if 'contrary to the requirement of good faith, it causes a significant imbalance in the parties' rights and obligations arising under the contract, to the detriment of the consumer'. This is so incredibly vague it will often be very hard to tell whether a given term in a contract between a business and a consumer will be valid or invalid. For example, suppose that I hire a car from you, and the car hire contract provides that if the car suffers any damage for any reason while it is in my possession, then I am obliged to compensate the car hire company for the damage done. It's uncertain whether this term is valid or not under the 1999 Regulations.

Contradiction

On occasion the law is **contradictory**. One legal rule will point in one direction while another legal rule will point in another direction, and it's hard to know which legal rule one should follow. For example, let's suppose there are two children called Adrian and Brooke, and let's suppose that Adrian is under 18 and Brooke is under 13. Now, sections 9 and 13(1) of the Sexual Offences Act 2003 combined provide that Adrian will commit the offence of 'sexual activity with a child' if he intentionally touches Brooke and his touching is 'sexual'. Because Adrian is under 18, section 13(2) provides that in this situation the maximum punishment Adrian can receive is imprisonment for 5 years. However, section 7 of the Sexual Offences Act 2003 provides that if Adrian intentionally touches Brooke and his touching is 'sexual' then he will also commit the offence of 'sexual assault of a child under 13' – and the maximum punishment for committing that offence is imprisonment for 14 years. But this seems to contradict the effect of section 13(2). What is the point of Parliament having provided in

>

section 13(2) that if Adrian intentionally touches Brooke in a 'sexual' way, the maximum punishment he can receive is 5 years' imprisonment if prosecutors can evade the effect of this provision by charging Adrian with an offence under section 7? This contradiction – or tension – within the Sexual Offences Act 2003 makes it very uncertain what the legal position will be if Adrian intentionally touches Brooke in a sexual way.

Thinking that the law is always certain can be damaging in interview if you dogmatically insist that a particular legal provision means *x*, and fail to acknowledge that it is actually difficult to tell what it means. It can also be damaging to you as a law student in answering problem questions. If you assume that the law on every issue is perfectly certain, your answer to a problem question will almost certainly be overly simplistic and fail to attend to all the issues raised by that question.

So try in your studies to embrace the idea that the law *is* uncertain on various issues and questions. Indeed, it would be a very good idea to carry around an 'Uncertainty Book' in which you can write down any issues or questions on which the law is uncertain and suggestions as to how that uncertainty might be resolved. This will prove invaluable for your exams, as examiners often set questions around areas of the law where the law is uncertain in order: (1) to test your ability to recognise that the law in those areas is uncertain; and (2) to see whether you can intelligently discuss how the courts might resolve that uncertainty if they are called upon to do so.

But don't go throwing the baby out with the bathwater. While you should embrace the idea that the law isn't always certain; but you should reject the idea that the law is always uncertain. This idea – which is most closely associated with an American school of thought called the **Critical Legal Studies Movement** – is demonstrably untrue.

If I, being of sound mind, take a rifle, climb to the top of a tower in the middle of a square, and shoot dead someone walking around in the square below, I *will* have committed murder. If I contract to paint your house on Sunday, and I spend that Sunday watching football instead, you *will* be entitled to sue me for damages. If I am an examiner and I charge a student £1,000 to get an advance look at the paper that I have set, the exam board for which I'm working *will* be entitled to sue me for that £1,000 and anything that I've acquired with it. If a local authority has been allocated money by Parliament to improve transport facilities in its area, and it decides to use that money to buy cars for members of the party that controls the local authority, disaffected council tax payers *will* be entitled to bring an action for judicial review and have the local authority's decision set aside. There is as little doubt that these things will happen as there is doubt that apples that fall off trees will always fall towards the ground.

The idea that the law is always uncertain is, admittedly, very liberating for lawyers – it gives them a lot more freedom to fool around with legal rules and doctrines to achieve whatever results they want to achieve. But that feeling of liberation doesn't make the idea any more true. If I think I can fly, I may feel more liberated – but I still won't be able to fly. The truth is that if the law were always uncertain, then there'd be no point in our having a legal system at all. After all, what is the point of our having laws if they don't provide us with any effective guidance as to what we can and cannot do; if they don't provide us with any reliable information as to what actions we can bring against other people and in what circumstances; if they don't place any real limits on what the State may do to us? What are our laws for if not that? Fortunately, the law for the most part is certain and you should resist the temptation to think that the law is always uncertain, however dizzyingly exciting such a thought may seem.

Okay, that's enough advice from me for now. Again, good luck with your interview. Let me know how it goes.

All best wishes,

Nick

Advance Reading

○ From: Nicholas J. McBride [dearnick@pearson.com]
○ To: Brown, Jo
○ Subject: Advance Reading

Hi Jo,

That's excellent news about your offer – I'm sure you'll have no trouble getting the A-Level grades you need to meet it. Do I have any advice as to some books it might be useful for you to read between now and October when (all being well) you'll start studying law? Of course I do!

Whoever's going to be teaching you in October will probably send you a list of books to read before you go to university. My advice on that would be to have a look at the books, but don't carry on reading them if they're boring you. If you're reading a book (any book) and you're bored by it, then there's absolutely no point in carrying on with it. The information in the book will simply not go into your head. And if you are set a book on a particular subject that you'll be studying next year like tort law or criminal law, my advice would be – don't try to read the whole book. Again, it's just too much information for you to absorb. Read two or three of the opening chapters, and try and get to know them really well so that you've completely absorbed the information in those opening chapters by the time you get to university. Then you'll be in a good position to make a great start to your studies when you get to university. As to what other books you should read, my advice would be threefold.

First, read a lot of books before you go to university. You'll be reading a lot of material when you get to university, so if you start reading a lot of books now, studying at university won't come as such a culture shock.

Secondly, try and read books that you won't have much time to read when you're at university. So try not to spend too much time reading books that are about subjects that you'll be studying at university. You'll be able to read those books when you get to university. Instead, you should try and read some good books that will give you tips on how you should approach your studies when you get to university, and absorb the lessons that they have to teach you so that you'll be ready to apply them from day one of your studies. Remember that you'll have so much to read once you get to university, you won't necessarily have time to read any books that give you tips on how you should approach your studies. So it's important to take advantage of the free time you have *now* to read such books.

Thirdly, do you remember what I said in my second letter to you about how important it is that you cultivate an interest in political and economic ideas if you are going to do well as a law student? I meet and teach so many students who are utterly bland and colourless in their views – and they are always rewarded with bland and colourless marks in their end of year exams. So take the opportunity between now and October to expand your mind a bit and spice up your views by reading interesting and challenging books of *ideas*, particularly on political and economic issues.

In light of all that, here are some recommendations as to what you might read between now and October that almost certainly won't make any official 'summer reading list' that your future teachers will send you.

Books about philosophy

Julian Baggini, *The Pig That Wants To Be Eaten* (Ganta, 2008)

Peter Cave, *Can A Robot Be Human* (Oneworld Publications, 2007)

>

Peter Cave, *What's Wrong With Eating People* (Oneworld Publications, 2008)

James Garvey, *The Twenty Greatest Philosophy Books* (Continuum International Publishing Group Ltd, 2006)

Books about politics

James Bartholomew, *The Welfare State We're In* (Methuen, 2006)

Michel Feher (ed.), *Nongovernmental politics* (by far the biggest and most expensive book on this list, but extremely stimulating and informative) (Zone Books, 2007)

C.S. Lewis, *The Abolition of Man* (1943)

Books about economics

Tim Harford, *The Undercover Economist* (Oxford University Press, 2005)

Henry Hazlitt, *Economics in One Lesson* (1946)

David Smith, *Free Lunch: Easily Digestible Economics* (Profile Books, 2008)

Books about law

Philip K. Howard, *The Death of Common Sense* (Random House, 1994)

Philip K. Howard, *The Lost Art of Drawing the Line* (Random House, 2001)

Novels of ideas

Quick reads

Douglas Coupland, *Girlfriend in a Coma* (Harper Collins, 1998)

Russell Hoban, *Riddley Walker* (Jonathan Cape, 1980)

Donna Tartt, *The Secret History*

>

Longer and more testing

Fyodor Dostoevsky, *The Brothers Karamazov* (1881)

Hermann Hesse, *The Glass Bead Game* (1943)

C.S. Lewis, *The Space Trilogy* (*Out of the Silent Planet* (1938), *Perelandra* (1943), *That Hideous Strength* (1945))

Ayn Rand, *Atlas Shrugged* (skim over the long speeches) (1957)

None of these books are at all boring to read, and all of them amount to 'brain food': reading them will help you look at the world differently, and make you think more, and more creatively, than you do at the moment. I strongly recommend that you try to read quite a few of these books before you go to university. All of them are available on Amazon (both new and secondhand), and most of them can also be found on the second-hand book website, www.abebooks.com.

Happy reading!

Nick

A Mini-Dictionary of English Law

10

From: Nicholas J. McBride [dearnick@pearson.com]
To: Brown, Jo
Subject: A Mini-Dictionary of English Law

Hey Jo,

I've written something for you! It's a mini-dictionary of English law. It's designed to get you acquainted with a lot of the terms and concepts you'll come across this year. My hope is that reading this through will help minimise the disorientation that you might experience in beginning to read about law, and help get you talking and thinking like a lawyer as quickly as possible. I've highlighted the most important terms and concepts that you will need to know about for this coming year. (Incidentally, whenever you come across the abbreviation 'q.v.' – which is short for 'quod vide', which means 'which see' – that means that there is an entry in this dictionary for the term immediately preceding the abbreviation 'q.v.'.)

Act of Parliament. See 'Legislation', below.

Common law. The term 'common law' is used to refer to a few different things.

First of all, the term 'common law' is often used, loosely, to describe 'judge-made law'. This is law that does not derive from a statute, but from the decisions of the judges as to what the law says in concrete

>

cases. Technically, such decisions only amount to *evidence* of what the law says – with the judge in his or her decision expressing his or her *opinion* as to what the law says (which opinion is then binding on the parties to the case, and creates a mini-law for their case). However, if it is clear that a particular opinion that the law says *x* would be accepted as correct by all the judges, then for the time being we can confidently say that the law *does* say *x*. And if the proposition *x* cannot be found in a statute then we say that it is a piece of judge-made law, and part of the 'common law'. Such propositions include: 'A promise will only be legally binding if something of value in the eye of the law is given in return for it, or if it is made in a deed'; 'Manufacturers of consumer products owe those who will ultimately use those products a legal duty to take care to see that those products are reasonably safe to use'; 'A decision of a public authority can be set aside as invalid and of no effect if no reasonable public authority would ever make such a decision'. There is no statute that says any of these things; but these propositions are still part of our law because they would be accepted as correct by the judges.

Secondly, the term 'common law' is sometimes used, more strictly, to describe areas of 'judge-made law' that derive ultimately from the decisions of judges in concrete cases heard by the courts of Common Law, in the days when the English legal system had separate courts of Common Law and courts of Equity. The Common Law courts would have general jurisdiction to hear all cases raising a legal issue. In contrast, the courts of Equity would only hear a case if – in the view of the Equity judges – there was a danger that applying the rules of the Common Law to the case would result in a serious injustice being done. So the courts of Equity acted as a corrective to the Common Law courts – either granting a remedy to a deserving claimant who would not be entitled to a remedy from the Common Law courts, or by ordering (on pain of going to prison for contempt of court if the order were disregarded) a claimant who would be entitled to a remedy from the Common Law courts not to pursue that remedy if it would be 'unconscionable' to do so. In the nineteenth century, the distinction between courts of Common Law and courts of Equity was

\>

abolished and from then on the rules of Common Law and Equity were supposed to be applied by a unified set of courts. But if a given bit of law has its origin in the decisions of the old courts of Common Law, lawyers will still mark that fact by referring to a 'common law interest' or 'common law action' or 'wrong at common law'; and if it has its origin in the decision of the old courts of Equity, lawyers will again mark that fact that by talking about an 'equitable interest' or an 'action in equity' or an 'equitable wrong'.

Thirdly, the term 'common law' is sometimes used as a catch-all term to describe those countries who have legal systems that are ultimately based on English law. So the United States, Canada, Australia, and New Zealand are the major common law countries outside England and Wales. In contrast, so called 'civilian' jurisdictions are those countries whose legal systems are ultimately based on 'civil law' (q.v.) – that is, the law of the old Roman Empire. Most countries in Europe count as 'civilian jurisdictions'. There is an entire subject – comparative law – that is devoted to comparing the common law approaches to various legal issues, with the civilian approaches to those legal issues. Many universities offer their students the chance to interrupt their studies for a year to go to a civilian jurisdiction – usually France – to get acquainted with its distinctive system of law.

Civil law. The term 'civil law' has a couple of different meanings.

First of all, the term 'civil law' is used by English lawyers to describe that part of English law that determines what rights (in the first sense of the word 'right' (q.v.)) private individuals enjoy against each other. Of the subjects you might study at university, tort law, contract law, land law, trusts law, family law, and labour law all belong to the field of 'civil law'. 'Civil law', in this sense, is opposed to 'public law' which is the area of law which specifically governs relationships between public bodies and private individuals, and 'criminal law' which governs when the government may punish someone for behaving in an anti-social fashion.

Secondly, 'civil law' is often used (along with 'Roman law') to refer to the law of the old Roman Empire, on which the legal systems of many countries on the European mainland are based. These countries are often known as 'civilian' or 'civil law' jurisdictions as a result. Because of the importance of civil law (in this secondary sense) for the development of legal systems on the European mainland, many universities offer courses in 'civil law' (or 'Roman law').

Claimant. Someone who commences litigation against someone else. Before 2000, someone who commenced litigation against someone else would be known as a 'plaintiff'. The person against whom litigation is brought has always been known as a 'defendant'.

Contract. Many people would say that a contract is a promise that is legally binding. However, there are many occasions when a promise will be legally binding on an individual without there being any kind of contract involved. It would be better to say that *contract law* provides people with a facility for making undertakings to each other that will be legally binding, and that a *contract* is what two people enter into when they take advantage of that facility.

Courts. Opposite is a very simplified diagram setting out the names and relationships between the main types of courts that decide cases in England and Wales. The courts are arranged in a hierarchy, so that if you are unhappy with the result of your case, it may be possible to appeal to a higher court either to have the result in your case reversed in your favour, or to have the higher court order that your case be reheard by a lower court. The highest court in the land is the Supreme Court of the United Kingdom. (The highest court in the land was formerly known as the Appellate Committee of the House of Lords, but it was thought desirable on separation of powers (q.v.) grounds that there should not be any kind of link between the highest court in the land and the House of Lords, and that members of the highest court in the land should not have the power to sit in the House of Lords and contribute to its discussions of legislation. So the Constitutional Reform Act 2005 abolished the Appellate Committee of the House of Lords and put in its place the Supreme Court of the United Kingdom, which is due to start hearing cases in late 2009.)

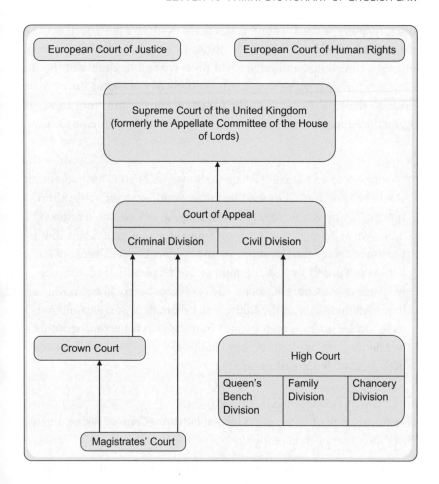

Criminal cases are heard in either the Crown Court or Magistrates' Court, with appeals from those courts ultimately going to the Court of Appeal Criminal Division, and from there (if the Supreme Court gives leave to appeal) to the Supreme Court.

Most of the non-criminal cases you will read as a student will have originated in the High Court. The Queen's Bench Division of the High Court typically hears cases involving disputes over land (q.v.) and claims for damages (q.v.). A subdivision of the Queen's Bench Division is the Administrative Court, which considers applications for judicial review (q.v.). The Family Division, as the name suggests, deals with all matrimonial disputes, and child custody cases. The Chancery Division deals with a wide range of cases, typically centred around issues that would have been dealt with by the old courts of Equity (q.v.). So issues relating to equitable claims or interests, companies, and intellectual property will be dealt with by the Chancery Division. Appeals against decisions of the High Court can be made to the Civil Division of the Court of Appeal, and from there (if, again, the Supreme Court gives leave to appeal) to the Supreme Court.

(A quick note on names: if Adam Smith were a High Court judge, he would be known as 'The Hon. Mr Justice Smith' or 'Smith J.' for short. If Adam Smith were a judge in the Court of Appeal, he would normally be known as 'Lord Justice Smith', or 'Smith LJ'. However, if Adam Smith were in charge of the Court of Appeal Criminal Division, he would be known as 'Lord Chief Justice Smith', or 'Lord Smith CJ'; and if he were in charge of the Court of Appeal Civil Division, he would be known as 'Lord Smith, Master of the Rolls', or 'Lord Smith MR'. If Adam Smith were a judge in the Supreme Court of the United Kingdom, he would be known as 'Lord Smith' or 'Lord Smith of _____' (insert placename dear to Adam Smith's heart here).)

Standing over all of these courts are the *European Court of Justice*, and the *European Court of Human Rights*.

The *European Court of Justice* is the ultimate authority on all issues relating to European Union (q.v.) law and the UK courts must follow its decisions in deciding any legal cases that raise issues of European Union law. Any UK court is free to refer a case raising a tricky issue of European Union law to the European Court of Justice, which will give its opinion and then refer the case back to the UK court from where it came.

The *European Court of Human Rights* is the ultimate authority on how the European Convention on Human Rights (q.v.) should be interpreted. Under the Human Rights Act 1998 (q.v.), the UK courts are required to take into account the decisions of the European Court of Human Rights in determining whether someone's rights under the Convention have been violated. But they are, in theory, free to disregard those decisions where they think the European Court of Human Rights has got it wrong.

Crime. A crime is an act or omission which is punishable under the law in some way – either through imprisonment, or a fine, or an order to perform community service, or through some other sanction. It is often the case that the act or omission does not in itself amount to a crime; instead the act or omission will only amount to a crime if it is accompanied by a so-called 'guilty mind' or *mens rea*. For example, it is not a crime to take a bar of chocolate off a supermarket shelf and put it in your pocket; but it is if you do so dishonestly, and with the intent to keep the bar of chocolate for yourself or somebody else.

There are thousands of crimes recognised under English law. The crimes that make up the core of the criminal law are acts which involve someone's deliberately or recklessly violating someone else's rights (in the first sense of the word 'right' (q.v.)). Crimes of this type include murder, rape, assault, battery, theft, criminal damage to property, and fraud. Around this core are thousands of crimes that do not necessarily involve the violation of anyone else's rights, but involve some form of anti-social conduct that Parliament has thought it necessary to discourage by making it criminal. Such crimes include speeding, possessing dangerous drugs, false advertising, selling goods by weight without providing a price by metric unit, travelling on a train without a valid ticket, and possessing a firearm without a licence.

Damages. Damages are a monetary remedy (q.v.) that may be sued for in a case where someone has violated someone else's rights (in the first sense of the word 'right' (q.v.)). There are a few different types of damages.

The principal form of damages is *compensatory damages*. These are designed – as the name suggests – to compensate a claimant (q.v.) for some or all of the losses that he or she has suffered as a result of someone's rights being violated. They aim to put the claimant in the monetary equivalent of the position that he or she would have been in had the rights violation not occurred; of course, they often fall short of achieving that aim.

English courts sometimes – though rarely – award *exemplary damages* against a defendant. These are designed to punish a defendant who has deliberately and outrageously violated a claimant's rights. Exemplary damages perform the same function as the criminal law, though without the controls that exist as to when someone will be subjected to criminal punishment. For example, someone can only be held guilty of committing a serious crime (q.v.) if their guilt is established 'beyond a reasonable doubt'. In contrast, someone can be held liable to pay exemplary damages if it merely seems 'more likely than not' that he or she deliberately and outrageously violated a claimant's rights.

Delegated legislation. Delegated legislation is legislation that is created by someone – almost always a government minister – who has been given the power to make law by an Act of Parliament. The power to make delegated legislation is usually exercised by issuing what is called a *statutory instrument.*

(Delegated legislation that is of some constitutional significance is usually created by the Queen's issuing an *Order in Council.* (Of course, the Queen will do as her government advises.) The Terrorism (United Nations Measures) Order 2006 was created in this way. This gave the Treasury the power to freeze someone's bank accounts if there were 'reasonable grounds' for believing that he or she was involved in terrorist activities. This provision was later (and rightly) condemned by the courts for violating people's rights under the Human Rights Act 2008 (q.v.).)

There were 3,399 statutory instruments issued in 2008, in contrast to 31 Acts of Parliament. The creation of law through statutory instruments undermines the existence of the rule of law (q.v.) in the UK: the fact that so many statutory instruments are issued each year makes it impossible to keep track of what the law actually says.

See also 'Henry VIII clause', below.

Duty (legal). Someone will have a legal duty to act in a particular way if they are required under the law to act in that way.

If A has a legal duty to do *x*, we can say that that duty is a *private law* duty if it was imposed on A for the benefit of a particular individual, B. In such a case, B is usually said to have a 'right' (q.v.) that A do *x*, and if A does not do *x*, B will normally be entitled to sue A for damages (q.v.).

A's legal duty to do *x* can be said to be a *public law* duty if A is a public body, and that duty was imposed on A to help ensure that A acts in the public interest. A breach of a public law duty is normally remedied through an application for judicial review (q.v.), though it may also amount to a crime (q.v.) for which A can be prosecuted.

Equity. See 'Common law', above.

European Union. The European Union ('EU' for short) is an organisation of 27 European states, including the United Kingdom, bound together by a series of treaties (such as the Treaty of Rome 1957, the Maastricht Treaty 1992, and the Lisbon Treaty 2007), which commit the member states of the EU to maintain a single market within the borders of the EU (within which borders there is to be free movement of peoples, goods, services and capital) and to pursue common policies on a range of other areas, such as agriculture and fishing.

To achieve these objectives there exist a range of different European institutions. The EU is run on a day-to-day basis by the *European Commission*, which comes up with suggestions for legislation that might be created by the EU's legislature. The EU's legislature is made up of the *European Parliament* (which is, in turn, made up of elected representatives from all regions of the EU) and the *Council of Ministers* (which is made up of ministers from each of the member states of the EU, with the ministers making up the Council at any one time varying according to what the Council is discussing at that time).

The United Kingdom has been a member of the EU (at the time, the 'European Economic Community') since 1973.

Under the European Communities Act 1972, provisions in any treaty entered into by the member states of the EU automatically become part of English law (and override any inconsistent parts of English law) once the treaty is approved by the UK Parliament.

Any *regulations* created by the EU's legislature will automatically become part of English law (and automatically override any inconsistent elements in English law, irrespective of whether those elements pre-date or post-date the regulation in question), again as a result of the European Communities Act 1972.

The EU's legislature is also empowered to issue *directives* to the member states of the EU, requiring the member states to change their national laws so that the law on a particular point or issue is the same across the EU. For example, Council Directive 85/374/EEC directed each member state of the (then) European Economic Community to change its law so that the manufacturer of a dangerously defective product that did harm to someone's person or property would be held strictly liable for that harm (that is, without the need to prove that the manufacturer was at fault for the existence of that defect). That directive was implemented in the UK by passing the Consumer Protection Act 1987. (Directives are more usually implemented through the issuing of a statutory instrument, which is a form of delegated legislation (q.v.).)

If a member state of the EU fails to implement a directive correctly, it is required under EU law to compensate anyone who suffers financial loss as a result of that failure. Who says so? The *European Court of Justice* ('ECJ' for short) which so ruled in the case of *Francovich* v *Italy*. The ECJ, which is based in Luxembourg, is the ultimate authority on all issues of EU law. It interprets the treaties of the EU and the legislation issued by the European legislature, and decides such issues as whether a member state has failed to implement a directive correctly, or whether a particular aspect of the domestic law of a member state is inconsistent with a EU regulation or treaty provision. In theory, a member state of the EU is free to disregard an order issued against it by the ECJ (just as a member state of the EU is free to disregard a directive that has been issued by the European legislature) – but doing so would put it in breach of its obligations as a member of the EU, and put its continued membership of the EU in question.

European Convention on Human Rights. The European Convention on Human Rights ('ECHR' for short) was created by the 47 member states of the *Council of Europe* in 1950. Signatories to the Convention (which include the United Kingdom, as well as non-EU countries such as Russia, Switzerland and Norway) agreed to observe certain fundamental rights and freedoms, including the right to life (Article 2), the right not to be tortured or subjected to 'inhuman and degrading treatment' (Article 3), the right to liberty and security of person (Article 5), the right to a fair trial (Article 6), the right to respect for one's 'private and family life' (Article 8), and the right to freedom of expression (Article 10). Since its inception, the Convention has been supplemented by a number of Protocols. Signatories to Article 1 of the First Protocol undertake to respect people's rights to peaceful enjoyment of their possessions.

The *European Court of Human Rights* ('ECtHR' for short) was set up in Strasbourg, France, to monitor whether signatories to the Convention were in breach of their obligations under the Convention and to provide a satisfactory remedy in cases where someone had suffered loss as a result of a signatory's failure to abide by its obligations under the Convention. For example, a prisoner in the UK who was denied access to a solicitor could complain to the ECtHR that the UK government was violating his right to a fair trial, and if the Court found that the complaint was made out, it would order the UK to compensate the prisoner for the violation of his rights and to cease violating his rights. If the UK did not comply with this order, it would be in breach of its obligations under the ECHR, which would be embarrassing both at a political and public relations level. So in practice the UK does comply with orders of the ECtHR.

The need for UK citizens to take cases to the ECtHR has been lessened by the enactment of the Human Rights Act 1998 which imposes on public authorities a legal duty (q.v.) not to violate people's rights under the ECHR. A claimant (q.v.) who alleges that he has suffered loss as a result

>

of a public authority breaching this duty may now take his case to be heard by an English court, which will grant a satisfactory remedy if – taking into account the ECtHR's interpretation of the ECHR – it is persuaded that the claimant's rights under the ECHR have been violated. The UK Parliament (q.v.) is exempt from this duty – if it were not, the traditional rule of Parliamentary sovereignty (q.v.) over the courts would have been abolished – but in cases where it is alleged that Parliament has passed legislation (q.v.) that violates people's rights under the ECHR, the courts have the power to issue a *declaration of incompatibility*, saying that the legislation is in violation of the ECHR. In such a case, political and public relations considerations could be expected to force Parliament to repeal the relevant legislation.

It is a common mistake of students (and journalists) to think that the ECHR has something to do with the European Union (q.v.). This is quite wrong: the ECHR has nothing to do with the EU. In fact, as the EU (as distinct from the member states of the European Union) is not a signatory to the ECHR (and has no power to become such, as the European Union is not – yet – a state), the institutions of the EU are not bound by the ECHR, and are therefore not required to respect, for example, the freedom of speech of whistleblowers exposing corruption within the EU. To eliminate this loophole, it was proposed to create a *Charter of Fundamental Rights* that would be binding under EU law both on the institutions of the EU, and the member states of the EU. The Charter has now been drawn up and has been agreed by the members states of the EU, but at the time I am writing this letter, it has yet to come into legal force.

Henry VIII clause. A 'Henry VIII clause' is a provision in an Act of Parliament (q.v.) that empowers a government minister to change the terms of an Act of Parliament or a statutory instrument (q.v.). (Such a provision is called a 'Henry VIII clause' because the Statute of Proclamations 1539 gives us a very early example of such a provision. That Act provided that Henry VIII's 'proclamations' had the full force of law 'as though they were made by act of parliament'.)

Examples of very wide Henry VIII clauses are provided by section 1 of the Legislative and Regulatory Reform Act 2006 ('A Minister of the Crown may by order make any provision which he considers would . . . remov[e] or reduc[e] any burden, or the overall burdens, resulting directly or indirectly for any person from any legislation') and sections 19–24 of the Civil Contingencies Act 2004, which provide that 'Her Majesty by Order in Council' (i.e. the government) may create 'emergency regulations' that have the effect of 'disapply[ing] or modify[ing] an enactment or a provision made by or under an enactment' if it is urgently 'necessary to make provision for the purpose of preventing, controlling or mitigating an aspect or effect of [an] emergency.' (An 'emergency' is defined as, among other things, 'an event or situation which threatens serious damage to human welfare in the United Kingdom or in a Part or region.')

Human Rights Act 1998. See 'European Convention on Human Rights', above.

Judicial review. A claimant (q.v.) who brings an application for judicial review is asking a court to determine whether or not a public body exceeded its powers (in Latin, acted '*ultra vires*') in making a particular decision or in acting in a particular way or in failing to act in a particular way.

If the court finds that the public body is exceeding, or has exceeded, its powers in acting in a particular way, there are a variety of remedies (q.v.) that the court could award. In the case where a public body has made a decision that is *ultra vires* (for example, deciding to grant planning permission to a company to construct a supermarket), the court could issue an order of *certiorari*, quashing the decision. In the case where a public body has exceeded its powers by failing to act in a particular way (for example, by refusing to consider someone's objections to the construction of a new supermarket in a particular location), the court could issue an order of *mandamus*, ordering the public body to act in that way. In the case where a public body is continuously exceeding its powers by acting in a particular way (for example, by making a

>

yearly grant to a company in return for its running a supermarket in a particular location), the court could issue an order of *prohibition*, ordering the public body to cease acting in excess of its powers.

There are a number of different reasons why a court might find that a public body has acted, or is acting, in excess of its powers. The public body may have misinterpreted the powers granted it by a particular piece of legislation (thereby making an *error of law*), or made an *error of fact* which made it think it was empowered to act in a particular way, when in fact it was not. The public body may have used the powers granted it by a particular piece of legislation for an *improper purpose* or may have exercised those powers in a way that *no reasonable person would have exercised them*. The public body may have exercised its powers without granting someone affected by them a *fair hearing* before deciding what to do, or the person making the decision as to how the public body should exercise its powers may have had a *financial interest* in the public body's exercising its powers in the way it did. Finally, the public body may have acted in a way that violated someone's rights under the European Convention on Human Rights (q.v.), something which it is barred from doing under the Human Rights Act 1998 (q.v.).

Virtually all public bodies are susceptible to having their decisions and actions challenged through an application for judicial review. The major exception to this rule is that no one can make an application for judicial review to ask the courts to quash an Act of Parliament on the ground, for example, that no reasonable person would have created such an Act, or that it violates someone's rights under the European Convention on Human Rights. (Though in the latter case, it is open to the courts to make a *declaration of incompatibility* between the Act and the Convention.) This is because of the doctrine of Parliamentary sovereignty (q.v.). No such bar to judicial review applies in the case of delegated legislation (q.v.). For example, if a Minister creates a statutory instrument (q.v.) under legislation empowering her to do so, a claimant could make an application to the courts asking for the statutory instrument to be quashed on the ground that the Minister exceeded her powers in creating that instrument, for one of the reasons set out above.

Jurisprudence. In ancient times, the term 'philosophy' was used to describe the study of the entire field of human knowledge. (The word 'philosophy' is derived from the Greek *philos* (meaning 'love') and *sophia* (meaning 'knowledge').) But then different branches of knowledge acquired their own titles – mathematics, physics, biology, chemistry . . . – and were hived off from 'philosophy', which as a term simply came to describe 'whatever we study when we don't study mathematics or physics or biology or chemistry or . . .'. The same thing has happened to the term 'jurisprudence', which as a term used to describe the entire field of legal studies (so that an undergraduate who obtains a law degree from Oxford is still said to obtain a BA in 'Jurisprudence'). But as different branches of the study of law have acquired their own titles – contract law, tort law, criminal law, public law . . . – those branches have become distinct from 'jurisprudence', which as a term has simply come to describe 'whatever we study when we study law but don't study contract law, tort law, criminal law, public law . . .'. As such, 'jurisprudence' as a subject is now concerned with theoretical issues affecting the other branches of legal study such as: What is law? How do we tell what the law says on a particular issue? Can the law on a particular issue ever be certain? Is it ever justifiable to punish someone for acting in a particular way? What is the basis of the remedies that courts award when someone's rights (q.v.) have been violated?

Legislation. Legislation is law that has been deliberately created by a law-making body. There are two forms of legislation in English law. First: primary legislation, which is made up of laws contained in Acts of Parliament passed by Parliament (q.v.). Second: delegated legislation (q.v.), which is made up of laws created by someone (usually a government minister) empowered to make law by an Act of Parliament.

Some say that judges act in a legislative capacity when they decide cases where the law is uncertain: that they make new law in deciding the case. The better view would seem to be that judges hardly ever act as legislators. In other words, a judge hardly ever decides a case with the conscious intention, 'I will now lay down what the law will say on this particular issue from now on'. Instead, he will express his *opinion* on what the law says on that issue, and then wait to see if his fellow judges will accept his opinion. If they do, then his opinion will represent the law (for the time being). If they do not, then his opinion won't be worth the paper it was written on. But, unlike a true legislator, no judge acting alone has the power to affect what the law says.

Omission. English law draws a big distinction between acts and omissions. Roughly speaking, acts make people worse off; omissions merely fail to make people better off. If I run you over in my car, that is an act. If I fail to shout out a warning when I see that you are in danger of being run over by someone else, that is an omission.

Under English law, you have lots of rights (in the first sense of the word 'right' (q.v.)) that other people not make you worse off; but rights that other people make you better off are much rarer. You have a right against everyone that they take care not to do something that foreseeably would cause you physical injury. But if you are in danger of suffering some kind of physical injury, you will only normally have a right against someone that they take care to save you from that danger if you are in a *special relationship* with them. A complete stranger will not normally be under any kind of duty (q.v.) to save you from that danger. As a result he will not normally commit any kind of tort (q.v.) or crime (q.v.) if he leaves you to your fate.

Parliament. Under the UK constitution, the Parliament of the United Kingdom has the power to make law for the UK. Under the doctrine of Parliamentary sovereignty (q.v.), there are no restraints on how this power may be exercised.

The Parliament of the United Kingdom is made up of three parts:

1 The *House of Commons*. This is currently made up of 646 Members of Parliament ('MP' for short), each of whom represents a constituency within the UK and was elected to Parliament by that constituency. Almost all MPs belong to a party. The party that has an absolute majority of MPs makes up *the government*, with the leader of that party acting as *Prime Minister*.

2 The *House of Lords*. This is currently made up of 740 members, almost all of whom were appointed to serve in the House of Lords

by the Sovereign, acting on the advice of the Prime Minister, who in turn allows the other parties in the House of Commons to nominate people to represent their interests in the House of Lords.

3 The *Sovereign*. The Sovereign is the UK's Head of State and is currently Queen Elizabeth II.

Parliament makes law by considering proposals to change the law, known as Bills. Bills are almost always introduced into Parliament by the government, though MPs are also given some Parliamentary time to offer their own Bills for approval by Parliament.

Normally, for a Bill to become an Act of Parliament, it has to be approved by all three parts of the Parliament of the United Kingdom. The Parliament Acts of 1911 and 1949 placed a limit on the power of the House of Lords to stop a Bill becoming an Act of Parliament by refusing to approve it. A Bill dealing with taxation, and a Bill that has been approved by the House of Commons in two separate sessions, can become an Act of Parliament without the approval of the House of Lords. The approval of the Sovereign – known as the Royal Assent – is *always* required for a Bill to become an Act of Parliament. In practice, the Sovereign never refuses to give the Royal Assent to a Bill that is presented to him or her for approval. However, the fact that the Royal Assent is required to turn a Bill into law is thought by some to be a residual bulwark against a government using its majority in the House of Commons to instal itself permanently in power as a dictatorship.

Parliamentary sovereignty. The 'doctrine of Parliamentary sovereignty' has two sides to it: the first deals with the relationship between Parliament and the courts; the second deals with the relationship between the current Parliament, and future Parliaments.

The doctrine of Parliamentary sovereignty says, first of all, that the courts will be required to give effect to each provision in a Act of Parliament until that provision is repealed by a subsequent Act of

>

Parliament; and this is so no matter how objectionable that provision may be. In other words, the courts are subordinate to Parliament.

The doctrine of Parliamentary sovereignty says, secondly, that any Act of Parliament can be repealed by Parliament, and that an Act of Parliament that has been repealed will no longer have any legal effect. In other words, Parliament cannot bind its successors. It follows from this that Parliament cannot place any hurdles in the way of a future Parliament repealing a given Act of Parliament, that would make that Act harder to repeal than it was to pass. In other words, Parliament cannot entrench legislation, protecting it against successor Parliaments that might want to repeal it.

The doctrine of Parliamentary sovereignty is fundamentally democratic in nature: it proclaims the supremacy of the elected legislature over unelected judges, and the current legislature, which represents the current views of the people, over previous legislatures. Given this, it might be wondered whether there should be an exception to the doctrine of Parliamentary sovereignty where a Parliament attempts to undermine democracy by, for example, passing laws against public demonstrations, or by passing laws that make it easier to engage in corrupt electoral practices. But no exception is made to the doctrine of Parliamentary sovereignty in such cases. However, there *are* two major exceptions to the doctrine of Parliamentary sovereignty.

First, a provision in an Act of Parliament will not be given effect to by the courts if it is inconsistent with European Union (q.v.) law (as incorporated into English law by the European Communities Act 1972) unless Parliament has made it absolutely clear that it is to be given effect to even if it is so inconsistent.

Secondly, Parliament is free – within as yet unspecified limits – to pass legislation that will have the effect of changing the definition of what counts as an Act of Parliament. It remains uncertain whether this power can be used to entrench either other legislation ('An Act purporting to repeal the Human Rights Act 1998 will not count as a valid Act of Parliament') or the very legislation that has the effect of

>

changing the definition of what counts as an Act of Parliament ('An Act that purports to repeal this legislation but does not command the support of 75 per cent of the House of Commons will not count as a valid Act of Parliament').

Precedent. A precedent is a legal case that has been decided by some court in the past.

A *binding precedent* is a legal case that was decided by a court on the basis of some rule or principle which other courts must give effect to under the *rules of precedent* if they have to decide a case where that rule or principle applies. Under the rules of precedent:

1 Decisions of the Supreme Court of the United Kingdom (and the Appellate Committee of the House of Lords) are binding on all UK courts (q.v.) other than the Supreme Court of the United Kingdom unless and until they are *overruled* (declared no longer to be correct) by the Supreme Court (or have already been overruled by the Appellate Committee of the House of Lords).

2 Decisions of the Court of Appeal are binding on future Court of Appeals, and all courts lower than the Court of Appeal, unless and until they are overruled by the Supreme Court (or have already been overruled by the Appellate Committee of the House of Lords).

A *persuasive precedent* is a case that was decided by a court on the basis of some rule or principle which another court is not bound to give effect to under the rules of precendent, but the legal wisdom and authority of the judges who decided that case is such that it is likely that other courts will accept that rule or principle as being correct.

The rules of precedent are rendered less important than you might think because of the fact that it is almost always a matter of debate what rule or principle underlay a decision of a court in a particular case. So, for example, if the Supreme Court decides in *Doe* v *Brown* that Doe must pay Brown damages (q.v.), the Court of Appeal will be bound by that decision. At the same time, it will usually be a matter of debate what rule or principle underlay the decision of the Supreme Court in *Doe* v *Brown*. If this is so, it will be up to the Court of Appeal to decide for itself what rule or principle underlay the Supreme Court's decision in *Doe* v *Brown* and therefore what rule or principle it is going to be bound by under the rules of precedent.

Property. Lawyers use the term 'property' to refer to three different things, and are not always careful enough about distinguishing between them:

1 They use the term 'property' to refer, first of all, to the things that can amount to property. These things are separated into two categories. First, *tangible property*. This category is made up of things that can amount to property that you can touch such as land, and cars, and computers, and CDs. Secondly, *intangible property*. This category is made up of things that can amount to property that you cannot touch. Intangible property always takes the form of a right (in the second and third senses of the word 'right' (q.v.)) of some kind. For example: copyrights (which give someone the right not to have their work copied by someone else), patents (which give someone the exclusive right to exploit a particular invention), rights to draw money from a bank account, and rights to sue someone for money.

2 Lawyers also use the term 'property' to refer, secondly, to the *interests* that one can have in a thing that amounts to property. The greatest interest one can have in such a thing is *legal ownership*. But English law recognises many other interests that one can have in a thing, such as *equitable ownership* (otherwise known as a *beneficial interest*), a *lease*, and a *charge*. These interests can be traded, and can be held simultaneously in the same thing by different people. So a piece of land could be legally owned by A, but at the same time B has a beneficial interest in it (in which case A is said to hold the property *on trust* for B), and the land is leased out to C for a year, and D Bank has a charge over the land to secure the money D Bank lent A to acquire the land.

>

3   Lawyers also use the term 'property' to refer, thirdly, to the *rights* (in the first sense of the word 'right' (q.v.)) that someone who has an interest in property will have that others not interfere with that interest. So someone who *legally owns* a thing will have rights against virtually everyone else that they not interfere with his ability to enjoy and exploit that thing. If B has a *beneficial interest* in a thing that is legally owned by A, B will have a right against A that A exploit that thing for B's benefit. If C *leases* a thing that is legally owned by A, C will have a right against virtually everyone else (including A) that they not interfere with her ability to enjoy and exploit that thing for the duration of the lease. If D Bank has a *charge* over a thing legally owned by A, it will have a right against A that A sell that thing and use the money realised by the sale to pay off a debt that A owes D Bank. (D Bank will not, of course, seek to enforce this right unless it becomes worried about A's ability to pay off his debt to D Bank without selling the thing that D Bank has a charge over.)

Remedy. 'Remedy' is a catch all term for the range of orders, awards and sanctions that a claimant (q.v.) who brings a case to court may be seeking.

In a case where a claimant complains that a defendant has violated his rights (in the first sense of the word 'right' (q.v.)), the normal remedy that he will be seeking is damages (q.v.). But in a case where a defendant is continuously violating the claimant's rights, the claimant may also seek an *injunction* – an order of the court that the defendant stop violating the claimant's rights. (Disregarding such an order after it has been issued will amount to a *contempt of court*, which is a crime (q.v.) punishable by imprisonment.)

A claimant may bring a case seeking a *declaration* that he has an interest in a particular piece of property (q.v.) that is being held or exploited by the defendant, and that as a result he has certain rights against the defendant (in the first sense of the word 'right' (q.v.)).

A claimant may also bring an application for *judicial review* (q.v.) against a public body, seeking a range of remedies designed to ensure that that public body does not exceed its powers.

Right (legal). Confusingly, lawyers use the term 'legal right' to describe three different things:

1 The situation where the law imposes on B a duty to do *x*, and that duty is imposed on B purely for A's benefit. In such a situation lawyers say that A has a legal right that B do *x*. For example: 'A has a legal right that B not harass him', or 'A has a legal right that B take care not to injure him'.

2 The situation where the law gives A the power to perform a particular legal act, such as suing someone, or entering into a contract with someone else, or making someone your agent. In such a situation, lawyers say that A has a legal right to perform the act in question. For example: 'A has a legal right to sue B for damages', or 'A has a legal right to terminate his contract with B'.

3 The situation where the law protects to a limited degree some freedom or interest of A's against being interfered with by other people. In such a situation, lawyers say that A has a legal right to enjoy that freedom or interest. For example: 'A has a legal right to freedom of speech', or 'A has a legal right to enjoy his property', or 'A has a legal right to bodily integrity'.

The fact that the word 'right' is used in these different ways creates room for confusion – either on the part of the person using the word, or the people he or she is speaking to. For example, suppose that Freddie is making a controversial speech at Nantwich University, and some student protestors are trying to shout him down. Freddie may try and silence the protestors by claiming (either to them or the police) that he has a 'right to freedom of speech', and that they should respect that. But in saying this, he is trying to pull a fast one. He does indeed have a 'right to freedom of speech' because the law – to a limited extent – protects his freedom of speech from being interfered with by the government. But that has nothing to do with the protestors. Unless the law gives Freddie a right (in sense (1), above) that the protestors not shout him down (which it does not, unless their conduct amounts to unreasonable harassment), the protestors are free, and should feel themselves free, to make as much noise as they want.

Rule of law. Academics use the term 'rule of law' in a number of different ways.

First, some use the term 'rule of law' to describe the conditions that have to be satisfied if a legal system is to work effectively as a legal system, that is, as a system for guiding people's behaviour by laying down rules for them to follow. Such people say that the rule of law demands that a legal system's laws be certain, consistent, prospective, easy to understand, easy to remember, easy to find out. It also demands that people generally must be inclined to obey the law, and there must exist effective remedies and sanctions that are applied to those who are not willing to obey the law.

Secondly, some think of the 'rule of law' as the antithesis of the 'rule of men' – as in the phrase, 'we live under the rule of law, not men'. According to this view, we can only say that we live in a country governed by the rule of law if: (i) our country's legal system places strict limits on when the State may use coercive force against someone; (ii) those limits are normally observed; and (iii) when those limits are violated, there exist effective remedies and sanctions that are applied against the State.

Thirdly, others think that if the ideal of living under the 'rule of law, not men' is to be achieved, the power to make law must be constrained, so that those who make the law are themselves subject to a higher law in the way they exercise their power. On this view, we can only say that we live in a country governed by the rule of law if – in addition to (i), (ii) and (iii), above – (iv) there exist mechanisms in our country that work effectively to ensure that the power to make law is not exercised arbitrarily or irrationally or immorally.

Separation of powers. The French philosopher, Montesquieu (1689–1755), praised the British constitution for splitting the government into three different branches: the legislature (which makes the law), the executive (which enforces the law, and employs the power of the State within the limits placed on it by the law), and the judiciary (which interprets the law, and resolves legal disputes). This arrangement, he claimed, prevented governmental power being concentrated in the hands of any one person, or one group of people, and therefore helped to ensure that governmental power was not abused.

It seems hard to deny that Montesquieu's analysis of the British constitution no longer holds true (if it ever did). There is no longer an effective separation of powers within the UK of the type Montesquieu advocated. The fact that the leading figures in the government are drawn from the majority party in the House of Commons (and the fact that the House of Lords cannot block legislation that the majority party in the House of Commons is determined to introduce) means there is no longer any solid dividing line in the UK constitution between the legislature and the executive. The line is dissolved even further by the existence of delegated legislation (q.v.), which is legislation created by government ministers, and Henry VIII clauses (q.v.), which allow government ministers to rewrite Acts of Parliament after they have been passed. Turning to Montesquieu's third branch of the government, while the judiciary is theoretically independent of the executive under the UK constitution, the law reports contain very few cases where the courts have decided a case in a way that is seriously embarrassing for the government; there are, in contrast, plenty of cases where the courts have re-interpreted and twisted the law to avoid deciding cases in a way that would embarrass the government. In practice, the courts are careful not to exercise their powers in a way that might provoke a seriously adverse reaction from the all-powerful executive.

Statutory instrument. See 'Delegated legislation', above.

Tort. A tort involves the violation of a legal right (in the first sense of the word 'right' (q.v.) that does not arise from a contract (q.v.) and which may be remedied through the award of damages (q.v.).

There are a large number of different torts recognised under English law, corresponding to the large number of legal rights that English law endows people with even before they have entered into a contract

>

with someone else. The range of torts recognised under English law includs: *trespass to the person* (touching someone else without justification – *battery*, threatening someone else without justification – *assault*, and locking someone else up without justification – *false imprisonment*); *trespass to land* (going onto someone else's land without justification); *negligence* (failing to take care not to injure someone or protect their interests when they had a right that you take such care); and *defamation* (damaging someone's reputation without justification).

So – that's my mini-dictionary of law! I'd recommend that you read this through a few times before you start studying law – once you are completely familiar with it, you should be able to hit the ground running when your studies begin. Having said that, it would be a good idea for you to buy a dictionary of law, as you will be coming across a lot of other strange words and concepts in the course of your studies that you will need to come to grips with. Jonathan Law and Elizabeth Martin's *Oxford Dictionary of Law* (7th edn) looks really good. If you have a lot of money, it might also be worth investing in *The New Oxford Companion to Law*, edited by Peter Cane and Joanne Conaghan (both titles published by Oxford University Press).

Best wishes,

Nick

Some Last Advice Before You Start

From: Nicholas J. McBride [dearnick@pearson.com]
To: Brown, Jo
Subject: Some Last Advice Before You Start

Hey Jo,

Thanks for your letter asking me if I have any last minute tips for you before you go to university. Here they are:

● Listen

This is the most important tip I can give you – not least because if you don't take this piece of advice on board, everything else I have to say to you will be a waste of time. Listen to any advice that you are given. You are starting an entirely new subject and you will need a lot of guidance to make a success of your studies. Now, I'm not saying that all the guidance you will get will be helpful, but almost all of it will be – so keep your ears open and pay attention to everything your teachers have to tell you. In order to do this, you will need to do a couple of other things:

Be humble

Try to realise that you have a lot to learn, and act accordingly. If your teacher tells you something about the law or gives you a bit of advice about your work, try to stop yourself thinking straightaway, 'That's ridiculous!' or 'That can't be true!' or 'She's talking rubbish!' or 'Well,

>

disagree' or 'Nobody's ever told me that before – he can't know what he's talking about'. These sorts of instant reactions are the brain's way of shutting up shop – of refusing to listen to what it is being told. Instead, try to keep an open mind. Try to recognise that you don't know everything and that what your teacher has told you probably has a lot of merit.

Don't distract yourself

Make it easy for yourself to listen to what you are being told. If you are being taught in a small group, you won't be able to pay attention to anything your teacher is saying if you haven't done any of the work that you've been told to do for that session, with the result that you are sitting there worrying about whether the teacher is going to call on you to say something and show you up in front of everyone else. Instead of being focused on what your teacher has to say, your mind will be on the clock – you'll be thinking 'Only 20 more minutes to go until I'm off the hook' or 'We've *still* got 45 minutes to go??? – It feels like I've been here an hour already!' So make sure that when you have a small group teaching session that you are extremely well prepared for it, so that you can walk into the session with confidence, eager to listen to whatever your teacher has to tell you.

If you are in a lecture, you won't be able to hear anything the lecturer is saying if you are thinking about what you are going to be doing tonight, or about what you did last night, or worrying about a small group session you've got this afternoon that you haven't done any work for, or checking out which students in the lecture hall are particularly good looking, or reading notes passed to you by other students. Try to avoid doing all of these things in lectures. Keep your mind (and your eyes) focused on the front of the hall.

⦿ Be self-critical

Do you remember what I said in my second letter to you about studying law being very much like taking a ride in a helicopter and looking down at the ground below? If you 'fly high' the ground looks smooth and uniform;

it's only when you 'fly low' that you get to see the detailed features of the ground and see where it's broken up and where it changes colour.

This feature of studying law means that law is a great subject for giving students a false sense of security. They can be lulled into thinking that the law's no problem, that they understand it, and that they're going to be fine in the exams – when none of those things are true. What they've been doing is 'flying high' all the time in their studies – only learning the law in a very superficial way, and not coming to grips with its difficulties and complexities. And it's only when they do their exams and see their results that they realise that they never really 'got' law at all.

Don't be like them. Ask yourself constantly: Am I going into this subject deeply enough? What don't I know – what do I still have to learn? Do the books I'm using look like the sort of books that top students would use? If not, what sort of books do top students use and how can I get hold of them? Is this book that I'm using inviting me to 'fly high' over the law by constantly skating over difficult issues? (Danger phrases to look out for are: 'Broadly speaking . . .'; 'It's safe to assume . . .'; 'Generally, . . .'; 'Usually, . . .'.)

○ Be positive

You will find studying law a very tough experience at times. You will be studying a whole new subject from scratch, one that is unlike any other subject you have studied before. You will be acquiring a whole new set of skills and taking what skills you have for making notes and writing essays to a whole new level. Doing this will be hard – but it is do-able. The important thing is not to get discouraged, but to keep on going.

The first time you read a case, you are likely to find it a bewildering experience. But if you stick with it and keep reading cases, the feelings of disorientation will disappear and you will start to understand how judges reach their decisions – and how you have to reason and argue when you are discussing points of law. The same is true of reading text-books and articles and going to lectures and doing written work – you will feel an initial sense of discouragement because what you are doing is unfamiliar to you. You need to put that sense of discouragement aside and stick with your studies; eventually, everything will come good in the end.

● Speak up

If there's some point you don't understand about the law, don't be afraid to ask your teachers about it when you get the chance. Don't think, 'I don't want to embarrass myself in front of everyone else by making myself look stupid.' Chances are everyone else is having a problem with that point as well and they'll be grateful to you for speaking up and giving your teachers the chance to address it in front of everyone.

Similarly, if you are having a problem with your studies, don't be afraid to go to whoever is in charge of your studies to tell them about it and ask for their help. The problem you're having is probably one they have come across before and they'll be able to draw on their experience to give you some good advice. Don't be afraid to ask for and get as much help as you need. You have the right to freedom of speech. Exercise it.

● Be nice

Because of the work I do, from time to time I get contacted by sixth-form students like you asking me questions about studying law at university. I always try to do my best to answer their questions – but am always amazed at how often it happens that after I've replied to a particular student, that they don't get back in touch with me to thank me for giving up some of my time to deal with whatever issue they were asking me about. And even among the students I know here, or students who have left university and are now making their way in the world, 'thank you' seem to be the hardest words of all.

Don't be like that. Be nice – thank everyone for helping you out, whether or not it's part of their job to do so, and they will be more willing to help you out in future. In small-group teaching sessions be friendly, full of questions and radiate eagerness to learn. Your teacher will respond to this and will end up doing far more for you than he or she would if you were hostile and uncommunicative. Look out for your fellow students. If someone is going through a hard time, don't just ignore that – reach out to them, and help them out. Your kindness will be repaid in ways you can't imagine. Don't be secretive and competitive in your studying – let other students share in the fruits of your labours, and your example will encourage them to do the same for you, and for others. Always ask yourself – would I like it, if someone were to do that to me? If the answer is 'no', then don't do it.

● Try to fall in love with the law

This may sound like a strange piece of advice. But again it's common sense. If you are going to be successful in your studies, you are going to have to spend most of the next three years studying law. Now – imagine that the law is a person. If you were going to be spending most of the next three years living with a particular person, would you choose to live with someone you loved or someone you hated? Obviously, you'd choose to live with someone you loved. And the reason why is obvious too – if you had to spend most of the next three years living with a particular person, those three years would be far more pleasant if you loved that person than if you hated them.

In the same way, your next three years will be far pleasanter if you some-how manage to fall in love with the law. And how do you manage to do that? Well, again, how do you fall in love with someone? The answer's obvious – you spend a lot of time with them, getting to know a lot about them. In the same way, if you are going to fall in love with the law, you need to spend a lot of time with it, studying it and reading about it. With luck, in time you should find yourself falling in love with the law and get-ting excited about the idea of finding out new things about it. So, really commit yourself to your studies, and give law a chance to cast its spell on you. If it does, then your next three years will be a lot easier than if you start your studies half-heartedly, don't really give the law a chance, and as a result end up dreading every hour that you have to spend study-ing law.

● Make the most of your time

There's going to be a lot to read and do if you are going to do well as a law student. So make the most of your time. Each day, work out some goals that you want to achieve that day. And then try your best to stick to your plan. If you succeed, then you'll get a great feeling of satisfaction – that you've done a good day's work. If you don't then review your day – was your plan a bit too ambitious, or were you a bit too weak-willed to resist the lure of a 'quick coffee'? If the former, then adjust your plan for tomorrow. If the latter, then resolve to do better tomorrow.

● Start thinking about the exams from day one

Another difference between doing A-Levels and studying law at university is that as a law student you have to start preparing for your exams almost as soon as you start studying. You can't afford to leave everything until six weeks before the exams – there is just too much information that you will need to assimilate and too much preparation that you will need to do for that to be a feasible option.

So start thinking about the exams as soon as you start studying. When you are reading a textbook, ask yourself: What points or issues are likely to come up in an exam? and pay special attention to those. When you are reading an article, try and condense its basic argument down to a few lines that can be reproduced in an essay in the exam. When you are writing an essay or answering a legal problem, don't write any more than you could write in an exam. When one of your teachers sets you some reading to do on a particular topic, before you even start going through the reading list, have a look at the past exam papers and see what sort of questions are set on that topic and direct your reading towards putting yourself in a position to answer those kinds of questions.

● Take time off from your studies

My final bit of advice is – don't spend all your time studying law. You don't want to get burned-out from studying law every hour of the day. Try to ensure that you do something nice at the end of every day to reward yourself for the effort you've put in studying law during the course of the day, and make sure that one day a week you spend half of the day having a good time doing something other than law.

So – good luck with your studies! Let me know how you are getting on.

Best wishes,

Nick

PART 3

Studying Law

The General Approach

- From: Nicholas J. McBride [dearnick@pearson.com]
- To: Brown, Jo
- Subject: The General Approach

Dear Jo,

Sorry you were disappointed with my last letter because it didn't actually contain any advice on how should go about studying law. I suppose I shied away from talking about that because it's such a big subject, with so many different angles to it. What I'll do is try and break it down for you by writing you a series of letters over the next couple of weeks. This letter will give you some general words of advice on how to approach your studies. I'll then give you some advice in subsequent letters about using textbooks, and reading cases and statutes, reading articles, using the Internet, and getting the most out of the lectures and small group teaching sessions that are lined up for you.

So these are my general tips for how you should go about studying law.

Don't be passive

This is my number one, most important, tip. If you don't remember anything else that I tell you in this letter, remember this. Anyone who studies law properly has to learn how to absorb and retain a huge amount of information. You cannot do that by simply lying back and letting information wash over you: you will absorb very little of that information and retain even less in your long-term memory. You can test this for yourself. Ask yourself – Can I remember what Nick told me in the first ever letter he wrote to me? I would be willing to bet a lot of money that you can't remember a lot of what I said. The reason for this is that *all* you did was *read* my letter. You let the information in the letter wash over you, and as a result almost all of it simply washed off you; and what information didn't wash off you evaporated away soon afterwards. By *merely* reading my letter you didn't make your brain do the work that it needed to do in order to **absorb and retain** the information that my letter was offering you. So: don't be passive in approaching your studies. Don't study law by *simply* reading about the law. Do more than that.

◉ Always ask questions

So what more should you do? Well, this is my next tip: the most effective way of absorbing information is by **asking questions and having them answered**. For example, suppose we are both standing in front of a tree. I know everything there is to know about the tree, and you don't know anything about the tree. Now, there are two basic ways you could attempt to find out as much as possible about the tree. You could passively listen to me giving you a one hour lecture about the tree. That's a pretty awful way of achieving your objective. Your attention will soon start to wander, and after about half an hour you will find it impossible to focus on anything that I have to say. Another way of finding out as much as possible about the tree is to ask me questions about it: What sort of tree is this? How old is it? How did it come to be here? What are the characteristics of this kind of tree? Is there any history attached to this tree? What sort of birds and animals use this tree? How long is it likely to live? Has anyone ever photographed or painted this tree? How many trees like this are in the UK? And so on, and so on. This is a much better way of finding out as much as possible about the tree because it is so much more active than the first method, which just involved you listening to me go on about the tree. Under this method, *you* are in charge, not me. *You* get to dictate what I talk about, and the pace with which I give you information about the tree. If I say something that is unclear, *you* have the power to make me express myself more clearly by asking me to try to answer your question again. Because you are more involved in the process of learning as much as possible about the tree, you are more engaged in the process and will therefore pay more attention to what I have to say. As a result, you will learn far more about the tree using this method of finding out as much as possible about the tree than you would if you just listened to me give you a lecture.

Of course, universities have not yet caught on to this basic fact about education. Their basic method for delivering information about a subject to their students is through lectures. Imagine how exciting it would be to attend a university where lectures were abolished and replaced by question and answer (Q&A) sessions, where the 'lecturer' simply stood in front of the students and answered their questions about a particular subject. How much more students would learn in that university, than they do at the moment! You may think that I'm a dreamer, and that what I'm suggesting simply wouldn't work because the students wouldn't know what to ask. But that just shows the sort of damage that 14 years of schooling in the UK can do to you. Little children have absolutely no problem with asking all sorts of questions about things they know nothing about. It's because they know nothing that they ask the questions! Now: suppose you turned up to a Q&A session on jurisprudence – a subject you know nothing about. Are you sure you can't think of a single question that you could ask about this subject? How about the most basic one: What is this subject about? Once you know the answer to that, you will know enough to ask a host of other questions about jurisprudence, and the answers to those questions will unlock yet more questions that need to be answered, and so on, and so on. Before you even knew it, you would know – by asking all these questions and having them answered – far more about jurisprudence than a student who went to a conventional series of lectures on jurisprudence could ever hope to absorb.

Well, just because universities are still locked into nineteenth century notions of how best to communicate information to their students, that's no reason why you should be. *Learn by asking questions and finding out what the answers to those questions are.* If you are studying a particular subject, approach it with the following questions in mind:

- What is this subject about?
- Why is it important to know about it?

And then go from there. If you are studying a particular area of law, ask yourself:

- Why does this area of law exist?
- Who is affected by this area of law?
- How are they affected?
- Who benefits from this area of law?
- How do they benefit?
- Where does this area of law come from – the legislature? the judges? or a mixture of both?
- What effect has that had on this area of law?
- Are there any basic principles or ideas that underlie this area of law?
- Could this area of the law be profitably reformed?

And then go from there. If you are studying a particular legal rule, ask the same questions that you would if you were studying a particular area of law, but also:

- Is this rule actually part of English law?
- How does this rule apply in practice?
- Are there any exceptions to it?
- Is it inconsistent with any other rules?

And go from there.

If you get into the habit of approaching your studies with a set of key questions in mind that you want answers to, then you'll find that the process of studying law will be a lot more interesting and stimulating than it would be if you approached your studies by simply 'hitting the books' from 9 to 5 every day.

● Use it or lose it

So, that's the basic method for absorbing information in the course of your legal studies. But how do you make sure that you retain the information you absorb? Again the key is not to be passive. Most law students try to drum the names and facts of cases, and the essentials of the various legal rules they have to know about, into their long-term memory through constantly going over their notes, reading them again and again, or by making notes about their notes. This works to some extent – but at the price of boredom, and frustration, and anxiety (has the information really gone into my long-term memory? how can I tell?). A much more effective method of getting information into your long-term memory is to use it constantly. The more you use the information, the more it becomes ingrained into your brain. By using the information, you transfer it back and forth between different parts of your brain, and it seems that every time you do this, a bit of the information rubs off on your brain and is transferred into its long-term memory, never to be lost again.

So use the information that you have gathered from your studies *constantly*:

1 write lots and lots of essays (even if no one gets to see most of them);

2 answer loads of problem questions (ditto);

3 compose textbook-style summaries of various areas of the law;

4 participate in as many moots as your time allows (a moot is a mock court hearing where two 'barristers' on each side will debate two issues of law, with a judge deciding both the issues of law and who performed best in arguing those issues; your university law society will almost inevitably organise mooting competitions);

5 talk about the law as much as possible with your fellow law students (and don't be put off doing this by the thought that 'it's uncool');

6 if your university law society runs a magazine, get involved with it.

● Go beyond the reading list

If you are going to do well in your legal studies, it is essential that you start reading books and articles (and possibly cases as well) that are not on the reading lists that your teachers will supply to you. There are two reasons for this.

1 *The target audience.*   You've got to remember that any reading lists that you're given are pitched at students of average ability. Obviously, your teachers aren't going to set reading lists that are really easy to get through; but neither are they going to set reading lists which only really brilliant students can handle. Instead, they set reading lists which are somewhere in middle – taxing, but not too taxing. So students who want to do really well in their exams – and show themselves to be of above-average ability – should constantly be looking to move beyond their reading lists, and read things which aren't on the reading lists.

How do you find out what else you should read? Well, there are a variety of ways of doing this. You could ask your teachers if they could recommend any extra reading. You could look in the footnotes of the textbooks and articles that you've already been referred to and see whether they refer to any other books or articles that might be worth looking up. You could do searches on the Internet for resources that even your teachers might not know about – particularly American articles. (Because the American legal system is derived from the English legal system, you can frequently find American articles on topics that are also highly relevant to English law – though remember that American law is different from English law in many respects, and you've got be on the lookout for those differences.) Or you could just walk along the shelves of your law library, opening relevant-sounding journals and collections of papers, and seeing what's in them.

2 *The need to develop interesting ideas.*   To write good essays about the law, you have to develop some interesting ideas about the law. That's why I've emphasised a few times now the importance of your developing a knowledge of political and economic ideas, which can give you a starting point for thinking about the law, and thinking about whether it needs to be reformed. It's not likely that your reading lists will provide you with sufficient material to write interestingly about the law: almost by definition, an essay that is based on an article or book that is well-known enough to get onto a reading list will not say anything interesting. It will just be repeating ideas that are already very familiar to the sort of person who will be reading the essay.

So, if you are studying a subject where exam questions about that subject tend to ask you to write an essay rather than answer a problem question, put yourself in a position to write interesting essays about that subject by looking out for books that contain some sparky, provocative, interesting ideas about topics or issues relating to the subject you are studying. These books have to be short because you won't have that much time to spend reading them (plus long books tend not be sparky, provocative, or interesting). But don't think that these books have to be about the law – they can just contain some interesting ideas relating to your subject that you can then adapt to discussing the law relating to that subject. And definitely don't think that these books have to be by academics – it's often journalists, or people with hands-on experience in the world relating to the subject you are studying, who are most adept at coming up with the sort of sparky, provocative, interesting commentary that you are looking for.

To give you a better idea of what I'm talking about – and to save you a bit of time – I had a look in one of my local bookshops for short, interesting books relating to subjects that tend to be essay-heavy when it comes to the exams. I didn't just look in the 'Law' section of the bookshop; I also looked in the 'Politics', 'Economics', and 'Sociology' sections. Having found some interesting books, I looked them up on Amazon and chased up other books that people who bought those books had also bought. After all of that, I came up with the following list of books that I think that any student would find very helpful at generating some interesting ideas for essays on the following subjects:

Constitutional law

Peter Oborne, *The Triumph of the Political Class* (Pocket Books, 2008)

Dominic Raab, *The Assault on Liberty* (Fourth Estate Ltd, 2009)

Family law

Martin Guggenheim, *What's Wrong with Children's Rights* (Harvard University Press, 2007)

Mark Harris, *Family Court Hell*

>

Criminology

William Ian Miller, *An Eye for an Eye* (Cambridge University Press, 2007)

Peter Hitchens, *The Abolition of Liberty* (Atlantic Books, 2004)

International law

Mark R. Amstutz, *The Rules of the Game* (Paradigm, 2008)

Roy Gutman, David Rieff and Anthony Dworkin (eds), *Crimes of War 2.0* (W.W. Norton & Co., 2007)

Robert Cooper, *The Breaking of Nations* (Atlantic Books, 2007)

European Union law

Larry Siedentop, *Democracy in Europe* (Penguin, 2001)

Alberto Alesina and Francesco Giavazzi, *The Future of Europe* (MIT Press, 2006)

Anand Menon, *Europe: The State of the Union* (Atlantic Books, 2008)

I am sure if you follow the same methods, you will be able to build on this list considerably.

○ Your notes

I'll say a lot more about how to make notes in the letters to come, but, just to anticipate a bit: your notes should be organised around questions. Whether you make notes on a textbook, an article, a case or a statute, your notes should always be organised around a set of key questions. I'll tell you in future letters what key questions you should be asking when making notes on a particular piece of legal material. (You can guess what some of them will be from what I've already said.) But here I just want to talk about *how* your notes should be presented.

Many students take notes in a very boring, straight down the page, style. For example, I enclose a photocopy of the Preface to my textbook, *Tort*

Law (co-authored with Roderick Bagshaw).[1] Many (good) students' notes on this Preface (assuming that they read it at all, which they should!) will look something like the following.

Two rival camps:

Modern view – tort law about determining when A liable to compensate B for loss that A has caused B to suffer. (Popular in 1960s and 70s.)

Traditional view – tort law about determining whether A has committed wrong to B/violated B's rights and if so, what remedies will be available to B against A. (Revived in 80s and 90s.)

Disagreement matters because:

(i) Tort law much wider on modern view (applies in every case where A has caused B loss) than on narrow view (only applies where wrongdoing/rights violation).

(ii) Affects scope of tort textbooks.

(iii) Cases decided in way that supports traditional view (courts ask before allowing claim in tort whether claimant's victim of wrong or had rights violated) so people who believe modern view more likely to support conspiracy theories about way tort cases decided (courts not being honest about reasons for decision and deciding cases on secret, policy, grounds).

(iv) On modern view, lot more factors should be taken into account in judging tort cases than on traditional view.

McBride and Bagshaw argue traditional view is correct: way cases are decided and outcome of cases support traditional view (no remedy to third party in fraud case – easy to explain on traditional view (no right violated); hard to explain either on modern view (fraudster = bad, why not hold him liable?))

>

---

[1] A copy of this Preface can be found in the Appendix of this book (see page 349).

McBride and Bagshaw criticise people who adopt traditional view but also say that public policy is *never* relevant to tort cases:

(i) Need to take into account public policy to see whether someone has right (can't have right not to be offended because against public policy).

(ii) Public policy relevant to determining remedies available where tort committed.

That's actually not a bad set of notes – they manage to reduce almost eight pages of text down to not more than one A4 sheet of paper. And they're clear, well-structured, and easy to read. But with the same A4 sheet of paper, I think we can come up with something that is a bit more interesting and exciting to look at, and therefore much more memorable.

Landscape, not portrait

Think 'landscape', not 'portrait' – there's no reason why your notes should be written on an A4 page starting at the top and working their way to the bottom. Think about turning the A4 page on its side, and starting your notes in the centre of the page, with them working their way out to the edges of the page. (To do this, it helps if the A4 page is blank, rather than lined – so when you buy an A4 pad of paper, you should seriously think about buying a pad of blank paper, rather than lined.)

Organise your notes around key questions

This will help you remember your notes – a piece of information that is hooked up to a question is easier to remember than a piece of information that is floating in mid-air, not related to anything else. (Memory experts remember the order of a pack of cards by 'placing' the cards in their mind along a route which contains 52 memorable locations – when they have to recall the order of the cards, they just walk along the route in their mind, seeing the cards that they placed along the route as they go by. But to remember what each

>

card was, it has to be associated with a location along the route: it can't just be thrown on the ground.)

Get artistic

Use drawings and symbols in your notes to summarise key ideas. If you are making notes on a Preface called 'The Tort Wars', it's a good idea to build at least the centre of your notes around an image of a battle – that helps dramatise the idea that you are trying to summarise in your notes, and also makes that idea much more memorable.

Taking all these points into account, try to come with an 'alternative' set of notes on the Preface to my tort textbook. Compare them with my version, at the end of this letter. Can you see how much more fun and interesting our 'alternative' set of notes is, compared with the set of notes above? As I said, this makes them a lot more memorable when you look at them. But because the process of coming up with these notes is so much more creative than writing a set of straight down the page notes, you'll probably never have to look at these notes again to remember what they say. The creative activity involved in putting these notes together is so intense that the information on the page will have been fused into your long-term memory simply by putting it down on the page.

● Your files

For virtually every subject you study (that is, any subject which isn't completely theoretical), you should have two files – a **'cases and statutes' file** (or 'case file' for short), and a **'secondary materials' file**. As the name indicates, the 'cases and statutes' file is where you file your notes on cases and statutes. The 'secondary materials' file is where you file your notes on textbooks and articles. Any essays or problem questions you do can be stuck away in a section at the back of the 'secondary materials' file. If you work predominantly on a computer (which I don't advise, as it is extremely difficult to make fun and interesting notes on a computer unless it is hooked up to a really high quality graphics tablet that you can draw on), then the same point applies – for almost every subject you study, you should create a 'cases and statutes' file and a 'secondary materials' file, for you to post your notes into as you create them on your computer. And *make sure* you back up your work *every day*, saving the files onto memory sticks, just in case your computer crashes and you lose all the data on it.

Study groups

I used to be in favour of the idea of forming study groups with other students, to share the burden of getting through a long reading list, or to share out the task of reading extra articles and books to add interest to one's essays. However, on reflection, I don't think that was one of my more inspired ideas. In principle, it's a good idea, but in practice, the reality always falls some way short of the ideal. People's abilities always vary, and that creates a big problem with making the study group work the way it should. Those of greater ability obviously don't get much illumination from those of lesser ability; but the same is also true vice versa – people of greater ability often find it hard to communicate effectively with people of lesser ability, because they assume everyone is as good as they are, and understands as much as they do. So, on reflection, I think it's better just to get on with your work as best you can – drawing on the advice above and the advice I will give you – and not get involved with anything as formal as a study group for the purposes of learning the law.

Having said all that, study groups do have a role to play. It would be good practice for writing essays in the exam (and also for your teachers) if you could get together with other students to go through essay titles to come up with interesting 'lines' in response to those essay titles. Often two (or three, or four) heads are better than one, and someone else will be able to come up with an interesting 'angle' on an essay question that you haven't thought of, and simply wouldn't be able to think of. Defending your ideas for how an essay should be approached is also a good way of clarifying your ideas and getting a firm grip on what you actually want to say, and how you want to say it. And looking at essay titles together will firmly encourage you not to be lazy, and just go for the first idea you think of how to do a particular essay – if you have to tell other people how you would approach an essay, you are going to want to come up with a really good idea for how to do the essay, rather than something which is obviously pants. (I'm convinced this is the reason why in Oxford small group teaching sessions, students are made to read out their essays in front of the other students in the session – I don't know of anything which could encourage you more to ensure your essay was absolutely top quality.) Study groups can also be very useful for improving your answers to problem questions. If you could get together with some fellow law students and each write an answer to the same problem question, comparing your answers would help each of you see any issues you had missed, and help each of you get pointers from the others as to how best to address those issues.

Right, that's enough advice from me for the time being – I'll write to you shortly to talk about how to get the most out of your textbooks. But in the meantime, if you want any more general advice on how to approach your studies, I would recommend you have a look at one or more of the following: Mark Black, *The Insider's Guide to Getting a First* (White Ladder Press, 2005); Thomas Dixon, *How to Get a First* (Routledge, 2004); and Adam Robinson, *What Smart Students Know* (Three Rivers Press, 1993).

Best wishes,

Nick

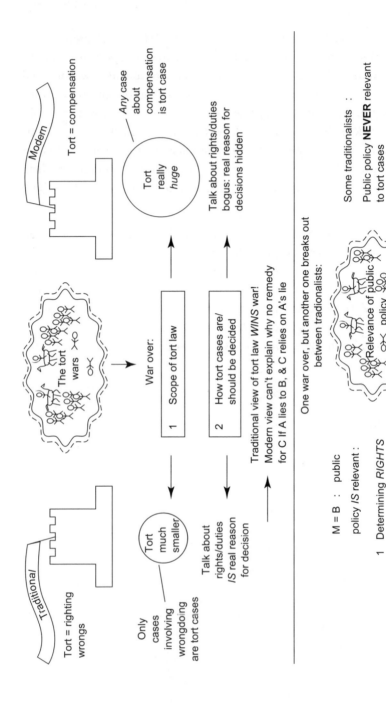

Traditional

Tort = righting wrongs

Only cases involving wrongdoing are tort cases

Tort much smaller

Talk about rights/duties *IS* real reason for decision

The tort wars

War over:

1 | Scope of tort law

2 | How tort cases are/ should be decided

Traditional view of tort law *WINS* war!
Modern view can't explain why no remedy for C if A lies to B, & C relies on A's lie

Modern

Tort = compensation

Any case about compensation is tort case

Tort really *huge*

Talk about rights/duties bogus: real reason for decisions hidden

One war over, but another one breaks out between tradionalists:

Relevance of public policy

M = B : public policy *IS* relevant :

1 Determining *RIGHTS*

2 Determining *REMEDIES*

Some traditionalists :
Public policy **NEVER** relevant to tort cases

Using a Textbook

- From: Nicholas J. McBride [dearnick@pearson.com]
- To: Brown, Jo
- Subject: Using a Textbook

Hey Jo,

Okay – as promised, here's some advice on what you should do in going through a textbook.

The basic approach

So let's assume you've been given a reading list. Normally, the reading list will start with a reference to a chapter from a textbook. This is intended to give you an overview of the subject that is the focus of the reading list. So – how should you go about reading the chapter? Well, the answer is: go through it three times. For me to explain what you should do on going through the chapter the third time round, I'll have to write you another letter, on how you should read a law case. But this letter will explain what you should do the first two times you go through a chapter in a law textbook.

The *first time* you read the chapter, as you are reading it, write down the key questions that are either addressed in that chapter, or that come into your head as you are reading the chapter. (For the time being, until this process of asking questions becomes second nature to you, it might be an idea, before starting your reading, to refer back to the list of key questions set out under the heading 'Always ask questions', so that you do your reading with a set of questions already in mind that you can write down immediately.) The second time you read the chapter, make notes on the chapter arranged around those questions.

For example, suppose that you are studying constitutional law, and you have been told to read a chapter from a constitutional law textbook on the 'rule of law'. When you read the chapter first time round, you might jot down the following questions – either because the chapter addresses those questions, or because they float into your head in the course of your reading.

What is the rule of law?

Why is it important?

What do people think is required by the rule of law?

Why do people disagree about this?

Are there any 'core' elements of the rule of law that everyone can agree are part of the rule of law?

What elements of the UK constitution can be said to be consistent with/inconsistent with the rule of law?

Having made a note those questions, try to see which of them are the most fundamental, or 'key' to understanding the rule of law. (Here, I would say 'What is the rule of law?', 'Why is it important?' and 'What elements of the UK constitution can be said to be consistent with/inconsistent with the rule of law?' are the key questions; the other questions are just aspects of these key questions, and can easily be answered if you can answer these key questions.) Now that you've identified the key questions to your subject, go through the textbook a *second time*, and make notes on what it has to say about those subjects. When you make your notes, remember my advice at the end of the last letter – try and make your notes fun and interesting to write and read. Aim to devote one sheet of A4 (but no more than one sheet) to each key question. And think about turning the A4 sheet on its side, putting the key question at the centre of the page and then working out from there, using images and symbols to illustrate the points being made in your notes.

Once you have finished your notes on the textbook chapter, file them away safely in your secondary materials file – but don't then forget about them! Have a look at other constitutional law textbooks to see whether they have anything more to say on these key questions – if they do, incorporate what they have to say into your existing notes. And whenever you come across an article, or an idea in a lecture, that is of some relevance to these key questions, dig out your notes again and incorporate that idea into them. In this way, your notes on the chapter from your textbook that you were told to read will transform in time into a window on a large number of different people's answers to the key questions you have identified.

The same approach should be adopted in reading a textbook chapter not on some legal concept, but on a particular area of law, or a particular legal rule, or set of rules. Let's suppose, for example, that you have been assigned a chapter from a tort law textbook on liability for omissions (failures to save other people from harm). As you read the textbook for the first time, you will probably jot down the following questions:

> What is an omission?
>
> What is the general rule governing liability for omissions?
>
> What are the exceptions to this rule?
>
> What values underlie this area of the law?
>
> Should this area of the law be reformed?

These questions all look 'key', so in going back through the textbook, you should note what it has to say in response to all of these questions, devoting one A4 sheet to each one. And then, once you have finished with the textbook, put your notes safely away in your secondary materials file, and then explore what other writers have to say about these issues – if they have anything more to add, dig the notes out and expand them.

That's basically it. But before I finish this letter, a few more words of advice.

● Don't rely too much on your textbooks

One of the most important differences between doing A-Levels and doing a law degree is the attitude you should have towards your textbooks. At A-Level, you could count on your textbooks to be correct and to tell you everything you needed to know to get a good grade in your exams. Neither of these things are likely to be true of the textbooks you will be looking at when doing a law degree.

First of all, legal textbooks *frequently* get the law wrong or make statements or assumptions about the law that are debatable. So if a textbook says 'The law says *x*' you shouldn't necessarily think that the law does actually say *x*. (A particular danger sign that a textbook is telling you something that is either debatable or simply wrong is when it makes a statement about the law without backing it up by reference to any cases or statutes.)

Secondly, most textbooks do *not* tell you everything you need to know about the law to get a good mark in the exams. For reasons of space, most textbooks do not spend much time discussing how the law should be developed or reformed – and what discussion there is, is likely to be quite superficial. For in-depth discussions of how the law should be reformed or developed, you need to look at monographs (short books on a single issue) or articles. In addition, most textbooks 'play safe' and spend almost all of their time simply reporting what the decided cases say; they spend very little time going beyond the cases and discussing what the legal position is in various hypothetical, problematic situations. But these are precisely the sort of situations you are likely to be confronted with in your exams.

So you should treat textbooks as *fallible introductions* to the various subjects you are studying. They get you started and give you some idea of terrain over which you are going to be moving – but it's dangerous to over-rely on them.

● Use more than one textbook

It's even more dangerous just to rely on one textbook. As I've already said, after you've gone though one textbook, have a look at what the other textbooks have to say about the subject you are studying. No one textbook can be the font of all wisdom on a particular subject. (Though some textbooks come closer than others . . .) If you take virtually any legal textbook, there are going to be some chapters where the writers did a really good job and some chapters were the writers weren't quite on their game. So consulting a variety of textbooks is essential to ensure that you get the best possible education available about the particular subject that you are reading about.

○ Remember that textbooks get out of date

This point may be a bit too obvious to be worth making – but it sometimes catches inexperienced students out. There are some areas of law that change quite a lot over short periods of time – tort law and criminal law are examples – with the result that textbooks in those areas get out of date quite quickly. If you are studying one of these areas, be careful about using a textbook which is more than three or four years old – many of its statements about what the law says could be out of date. (Though if you are, as I advise, consulting a variety of textbooks, you'll soon detect any out of date statements.)

○ Look at the footnotes

Don't ignore the footnotes in a textbook. They can often be the source of:

- very useful observations about the law which didn't fit easily into the flow of the main text and were therefore relegated to the footnotes;
- suggestions as to articles and other books that it might be helpful to read, and, if you are really lucky, summaries of what those articles and books say, thus saving the trouble of looking at them yourself;
- criticisms of other writers' views which will come in handy when trying to make up your mind whose views you agree or disagree with.

● Boredom

If you're getting bored reading a textbook what should you do? (Note that this is highly unlikely to happen if you adopt the above approach to going through the textbook.) The answer is: stop reading. If you're bored, you won't be taking anything in, and there's no point in carrying on reading when you're not taking in anything of what you're reading. Deal with the source of the boredom before you carry on reading. It may be that you've been working too long and your brain has decided it's had enough. In which case, take a break. Or it may be that the textbook is at fault: the writer hasn't made enough effort to make the bit of the textbook you are reading interesting enough. In which case, search out another textbook that covers the same area but is more interesting. Or it may be that there's something on your mind that stops you focusing on what the textbook has to say. In which case, deal with the thing that's on your mind and then come back to the textbook. (Easier said than done in many cases, I know.)

I said at the start of this letter that when you are told to read a chapter from a particular legal textbook, you should go through it three times – but that I couldn't tell you what you do on the third run through the chapter until I'd written to you about how to read a legal case. So that's what I'll write to you about next. Until then, I don't have anything more to say about textbooks, and will sign myself off with.

Best wishes,

Nick

Reading a Case

○ From: Nicholas J. McBride [dearnick@pearson.com]
○ To: Brown, Jo
○ Subject: Reading a Case

Hi Jo,

Up until the twentieth century, most English law was caselaw – law that emerged from the concrete decisions of the courts. Out of thousands and thousands of cases, each presenting a set of facts and a question: 'What does the law say in this situation?', there emerged a body of rules and principles that was known as 'the common law'. The tidal wave of legislation in the twentieth century has reduced the importance of the common law, but large swathes of our law are still very much based on caselaw.

Administrative law – the law governing when a public body will be found to have exceeded its powers – is almost entirely made up of caselaw (though now supplemented by the Human Rights Act 1998). Tort law is mainly caselaw, with a few statutes at the fringes, intervening to adjust tort law where the legislature judges that it has gone wrong. Statute law has a more prominent role in contract law – but the basic rules on what is a contract, how a contract is formed, how one determines what the parties to a contract are required to do, and what remedies will be available when someone fails to do what they are required to do under their contract with someone else, are still almost entirely supplied by caselaw. Criminal law and land law are increasingly statute-based, but the statutes that loom large over these areas of law are so vague or so confused that it won't be long before both subjects are re-covered with a thick moss of caselaw – as has happened to family law already.

So if you are studying law, you have to get used to reading cases. In this letter, I will give you some tips on how you should approach the job of reading cases, taking notes on cases, and remembering them once you've read them. But first of all, a basic question:

● Why should I read cases?

Many law students complete their law degrees without reading any cases whatsoever – they simply find out what the cases on a particular area of law say by consulting textbooks and potted summaries of the law. So why should you read cases? I suppose there are five reasons why it's important that you should read cases:

1 *Legal reasoning.* Reading cases gives you an education into how lawyers think and reason. Read *any* case. Look at the facts of the case. Look at how the judge lays out the legal questions raised by those facts. Look at how he goes through the previously decided cases and statutes that are relevant to those legal questions. Look at how he discovers from those cases and statutes a legal rule or principle that can be used to resolve those questions. Look at how he checks that rule or principle to ensure that it is sound – that a special exception to it shouldn't be created in this case to ensure that it doesn't work an injustice. Look at how the judge, reassured, applies the rule or principle and moves towards a conclusion.

You will have to do exactly *the same thing whenever you are asked to give an opinion as to what the law says in a particular situation.* So reading cases helps educate you how to be a lawyer. What would we think of a trainee surgeon who, on being invited to watch a particularly tricky operation so that he can learn from the experience, replies, 'Sorry, no – I never watch other people operating'? Well, a student who doesn't read cases is no different.

2 *Golden nuggets.* Cases are treasure houses of important insights into the law. They contain hosts of observations (known as '**dicta**') from judges about:

- how the law should be reformed;
- why the law should not be reformed in a certain way;
- how the law might develop in the future;
- what the law might say in certain hypothetical situations that might become the focus of a case (or a problem question in an exam) in the future;
- what principles underlie the law;
- why the law has developed in the way it has;
- why the decision in a particular case that was decided in the past was fundamentally flawed with the result that the case should be ignored;
- why a particular case that was decided in the past is extremely important.

and so on, and so on. If you don't read cases you are turning your back on all these insights and your notes will be much the poorer for it.

3 *Evaluating the law.* Reading cases encourages you to think about the law. If you read a line of cases, you start to think – how do these cases fit together? Does one principle underlie all of them or more than one? What principle or principles are at play here? By thinking in these terms, you enhance your understanding of the law and your interest in it.

Again – whenever, in the course of reading a case, you come across a judge criticising or defending the law, you should adopt exactly the same procedure as I suggested you adopt when you come across an academic criticising or defending the law in a textbook or in an article. You shouldn't just make a note of the judge's criticism or defence and then move on – you should pause to think about whether you agree with the judge. And in the process of thinking about whether you agree with the judge, your own views about the law will develop.

If you don't read cases, then you will miss out on lots of opportunities to deepen your understanding of the law and thereby increase your interest in it.

4 *Seeing both sides of the story.* Reading cases helps you to see that in many situations, the legal outcome of a case was not fixed in stone before the case was ever heard. Both sides to a case may have good arguments on their side. It's simply not possible in many cases to predict what the judge will say.

Reading cases makes you realise this – and that, in turn, will make you into a better student when answering problem questions. Instead of rushing into an answer that says, 'D is definitely guilty of . . .' or 'D will undoubtedly be held liable to . . .', you'll be encouraged to think: 'Hang on, can *nothing* be said here in D's favour to get him off the hook?' After all, in real life lawyers don't normally say, 'It's a fair cop, my client's guilty – you'd better get straight onto sentencing him'; and they don't normally say either, 'Yes – there's no doubt my client's liable. Why don't you just get on and determine how much he should pay by way of damages?' Right at the moment you look to see what can be said in D's favour, you may see an argument for D that you would never have seen had you not been encouraged, through the process of reading cases, to realise that in many situations the law is not completely clear-cut.

5 *Interest.* Reading cases makes studying law more interesting than it otherwise would be. You get to see how the law has in the past impacted on real people's lives, real people's problems. The law comes to life in and through cases. Why wouldn't you want to read cases? Cases are the soul of the law – without them, the law can become very dull and turgid.

6 *Legal skills.* You are going to have to read cases at some point in your life – so why not start now and become an expert at reading them?

If you are going to be a practising lawyer, you are simply going to have to be able to read cases – to be able to make arguments in court, to give clients legal advice, and generally to keep up to date with recent developments in the law. Given this, you should really try to acquire the skill of reading cases while you are at university and have a fair amount of time to acquire that skill – the alternative is to try to acquire the skill in just a few days when you start practising as a lawyer.

And even if you are not going to be a practising lawyer, to prepare for your exams, you are going to have to be well-acquainted with all the recent cases that came out round about the time the exams were set and will undoubtedly have provided the examiners with much inspiration when setting questions for the exams. How are you going to get acquainted with those cases except by reading them? You certainly won't find those cases in your textbook or casebook, both of which were probably published two or three years ago.

● How to read a case

How, then, should you approach the task of reading a case? Well, in my last two letters, I've laid down the basic approach. Your reading of a case should be question-driven. These are the key questions you should be asking yourself, and seeking answers to, as you are going through a case:

- What were the facts of this case?
- What was the result?
- Why was the case decided the way it was?
- Does the case contain any interesting *dicta*?
- Was the case decided correctly?

Let's look at each of these questions in more detail.

1 *Facts.* You shouldn't try to get the facts of the case from the judgments in that case – the facts, as set out in the judgments, will be far too long-winded. Instead, look at the brief summary of the case which you will always find at the start of the case. This brief summary is called the 'headnote'. The **headnote** will usually summarise the facts adequately enough for your purpose. But *don't* just copy the facts as set out in the headnote. Try to reduce the summary of the facts still further (this will usually be possible), and use your own words. Forcing yourself to do this will help ensure that you fully understand the facts.

Having said that, some modern cases are so complicated that the headnote and even a look at the judgments won't leave you any wiser as to what actually happened in the case. In this situation, you should try to see if anyone has written a **casenote** on the case you are reading. A casenote consists in a summary of, and comments on, a case. The *Law Quarterly Review* and the *Cambridge Law Journal* are a good source of casenotes. You can also find casenotes (in smaller quantities) in the *Modern Law Review*. The *Criminal Law Review* always has very good casenotes on all the important criminal law cases; as does *The Conveyancer and Property Lawyer* on land law cases. A search on Westlaw UK (insert the name of the case into the search box and instruct it to search 'Legal Journals' only) will tell you where casenotes on a particular case have been published. If you find a casenote on the case you are reading that will probably provide you with a good, clear summary of the facts of the case that you can use as a basis for your own summary of the facts.

One aspect of the facts of a case that is usually worth noting – and for which you will probably have to dip into the judgments in the case to find out – is the *names* of the parties involved in the case. Knowing the names of the parties makes it easier to distinguish the different characters involved in the case, and helps make the case itself a bit more memorable than would be the case if your notes simply referred to 'C' (for claimant) and 'D1' (for first defendant) and 'D2' (for second defendant). But however you choose to refer to the parties to the case in your notes, *definitely, definitely, definitely* do *not* – I repeat, *do not* – refer to the parties as the 'appellant' and 'respondent'. The **appellant** in a particular case is the party appealing against the judgment of the court below that found against him/her/it. The **respondent** is the person who won in the court below and is now responding to the appeal, arguing that the court that is now hearing the case should uphold the judgment of the court below. For your purposes, it does not matter who was the appellant and who was the respondent in a particular case, and you definitely will never be able to remember this information in the long-term. So don't pay any attention to who was the appellant and who was the respondent – instead just make a note of the proper names of the parties involved.

2 *Result.* By 'the result', I just mean: 'What was the outcome of the case?' If in a particular case a claimant was suing a defendant, who won? And if it was the claimant, what did the claimant get? If a defendant was being

prosecuted for committing a crime, was he found guilty or innocent? The headnote will tell you the answer to these questions, so that's all you need to look at to find out the result of the case.

3 *Reasoning.* This is the most important part of any case – the reasons why the judges decided a particular case the way they did. The headnote of the case will give you a very rough idea about this, but it will only be a *very* rough idea – to fully understand the judges' reasons why they decided a case the way they did you *have* to read their judgments. But not all of their judgments.

First, for the purpose of understanding the reasons why a case was decided the way it was – and for this purpose *only* – you can ignore any dissenting judgments. To explain: most cases in the Court of Appeal are decided by a three-judge panel, and almost all cases in the Supreme Court are decided by a five-judge panel. It frequently happens that the judges on the panel deciding a case will disagree on how the case should be decided. In such a case, the majority wins: the case is decided the way the 'majority judges' thought it should be decided, and the judgments of the minority judges are called 'dissenting judgments'. In trying to find out why a case was decided the way it was, you should focus on the judgments delivered by the majority judges.

Secondly, in reading through a judgment, you don't have to read every word, or even every page, of the judgment. You can skip the judge's summary of the facts of the case – you will have already got those from the headnote, or a casenote. You can also skip any quotes from other cases that the judge has inserted into his judgment – you are not interested in those: you are only interested in what that judge has to say. (You can easily spot when a judge is quoting from another case because the text of the judgment will be indented at that point – so if you see an entire page where the text is indented, just flick past it.) Just following those two rules will cut down by about 90 per cent the amount you have to read when looking at a judgment. And don't feel at all bad about skipping over passages where a judge is talking about the facts of a case or quoting from other people's decisions. Doing this is essential if you are going to learn how to get through cases quickly.

In reading through a judgment and trying to find out why the judge decided the case the way he/she did, it's worth bearing in mind that there are basically *four* different reasons why a judge might decide a case in a particular way – so in going through the judgment, your basic task is to identify which of these four basic reasons formed the basis of the judge's decision. (Though note that a judge's decision can be based on more than one of these four basic reasons.) To demonstrate this point, let's consider the following (imaginary) case.

Rick asks Talia to have sex with him. Talia is attracted to Rick but turns him down, saying that she is in a steady relationship with Jeremy, and she doesn't want to wreck that. Rick lies to Talia and tells her that he heard that Jeremy is having an affair with Talia's best friend. Talia is devastated and sleeps with Rick. When the truth comes out, Talia feels utterly betrayed by Rick and goes to the police. The police charge Rick with rape, which can be defined as 'having sex with a woman without her consent when you know, or have reasonable grounds to believe, that she is not consenting.'

Let's assume that five judges – Tom, Dick, Harry, Larry and Moe – have to decide the case.

Tom says:

Rick is not guilty of rape. Talia clearly consented to have sex with Rick. She was not unconscious while Rick was having sex with her; nor was she forced to have sex with Rick. She knew what she was doing, and who she was doing it with. It matters not that she was tricked into giving her consent. She still gave her consent.

The basic reason underlying Tom's judgment is his **interpretation of the rule** governing when someone will be guilty of rape. So we can say that Tom's judgment is **rule-based** in nature (such judgments are sometimes called '**formalistic**').

Dick says:

Rick is guilty of rape here. While I acknowledge Tom's point that Talia knew what she was doing and who she was doing it with when she had sex with Rick, there are lots of cases decided by our courts which seem to be based on, and give effect to, the idea that some-one cannot be said to have truly consented to act in a particular way if they have been tricked into acting that way. This is why, for exam-ple, if B induces A to enter into a contract with him by lying to A, A will be allowed to get out of the contract: B's lie means that A did not truly consent to enter into the contract with B. The same if B induces A to give him some money by lying to her: A will be entitled to her money back, because she did not truly consent to give it to B. So here: Rick's lie means that Talia did not truly consent to have sex with Rick, and because Rick knew that Talia was sleeping with him because of his lie, he knew she was not truly consenting to have sex with him. So he is guilty of rape.

The basic reason why Dick decided Rick's case the way he did is that he has gleaned from the available legal materials a **legal principle** – that someone cannot be said to have consented to do something if they were tricked into doing that thing – and that principle, when applied to Rick's case, suggests that he is guilty of rape. We can say then that Dick's judg-ment is **principle-based** in nature.

Larry says:

Rick is not guilty of rape here. If we found him guilty of rape here, as Dick proposes that we should, we would unacceptably extend the scope of the law on rape. Any lie that induced a woman to have sex with a man would turn the man into a rapist. Our jails would be filled with people who were guilty of no more than being economical with the truth in order to smooth things over with their loved ones before being intimate with them. The stigma attached to a rape conviction would be diluted, and some seriously dangerous individuals would be able to take advantage of that to reassure other people, including

>

vulnerable women, that their convictions for rape were 'nothing serious'. There is a difference between force and fraud, and we will rue
the day that in an attempt to do a more perfect justice, we extend the
law on rape to cases such as Rick's.

Larry's judgment focuses on the **consequences** of finding Rick guilty of
rape here. He rules that Rick should be acquitted because of the harm that
would be done to the public interest if Rick were found guilty. So we can
say that Larry's judgment is **policy-based** in nature.

Harry says:

Rick is not guilty of rape here. Our courts have never before found
someone guilty of rape in a case like this – where the alleged victim
of the rape knew what she was doing in having sex, and where vio-
lence was not used to force the alleged victim into having sex. Given
this, it would be unfair to find Rick guilty of rape. It is unjust to subject
someone to criminal punishment for acting in a particular way when
they could have had no idea at the time they acted that the courts
might view their conduct as criminal. So Rick must be acquitted. But
the fact that some of my fellow judges take a different view will now
put people on warning that if they follow Rick's example, they may
well be found guilty of rape. As a result, if a case were to arise in
future that presented us with facts similar to those in the case at hand,
I would have no hesitation in finding the defendant in that future case
guilty of rape. But given the state of the authorities at the time Rick
acted, I see no alternative but to vote in favour of his acquittal.

The basic reason underlying Harry's decision that Rick should be acquitted is one of **fairness** or **justice**: he thinks it would be wrong to find that
Rick was guilty of rape. We can say that Harry's decision is **justice-based**.

Moe says:

Of the other four judges deciding this case, I understand that three
are in favour of acquittal, and only one is in favour of finding Rick guilty.

>

It therefore matters little what I say. However, I would like to express my agreement with Dick's judgment. I regret that we have been unable to convince our fellow judges to reach what is plainly the right conclusion on this occasion, but I take comfort from the fact that, as Harry's judgment makes clear, if a similar case were to come before us at some point in the future, we might well see justice done on that occasion.

It is unclear what the basis of Moe's judgment is: it's relatively **opaque**. Moe's judgment could be principle-based, just like Dick's judgment, with which Moe says he agrees. The judgment could also (or alternatively) be rule-based: after all, Moe does say that finding Rick guilty of rape is 'plainly the right conclusion', which may indicate that he thinks that the definition of rape, properly interpreted, clearly applies in this case. But you could also argue that Moe's judgment is (in whole or in part) justice-based: you could argue that he thinks that Rick should be found guilty of rape because he deserves to be labelled as a rapist. And though Moe does not mention the public interest in his judgment, it may be that considerations of policy played some part in his deciding the case the way he did: he may have thought that finding people like Rick not guilty of rape would have undesirable consequences that should be avoided (such as bringing the legal system into disrepute, or sending out a message to men that it is legitimate to trick women into having sex with you). So it's hard to know what the basis of Moe's judgment is – all you can really do is note that he was in favour of finding Rick guilty.

Now that you understand a bit more about the possible reasons that might underlie a judge's decision in a particular case, I want to make two more points about judicial reasons.

Public expectations

First, people generally expect judges to decide cases in the way that Tom and Harry did in deciding whether Rick was guilty of rape. The public expect judges to decide cases by applying legal rules and

>

principles to those cases, where those rules and principles have either been laid down by Parliament or are implicit in the cases that have already been decided by the courts. The public is suspicious of judges who decide cases according to what they think the public interest, or fairness and justice, requires.

The public is right to think this way. Anyone who goes to court is entitled to expect that the outcome of his/her case will *not* depend on who the judge deciding the case happens to be. But if the judge decides the case according to *his or her* perceptions of what is in the public interest, or according to *his or her* perceptions of what fairness and justice requires in this case, then the losing party is entitled to feel aggrieved. He or she may well think that if his/her case had been heard by a different judge, with different views as to what is in the public interest or as to what fairness and justice requires, then the outcome of his/her case may well have been different. It is different if the judge decides the case by applying established rules and principles to that case. The losing party can console him/herself by thinking that whichever judge his/her case was heard by, he or she would still have lost. It was the law – the legal rules and principles that applied in this case – that was against him/her, not the judge.

The judges are well aware of the need to reassure the people who appear before them that what they will get from the courts is impersonal justice – that is, what the law demands – and not personal justice – that is, what the judge happens to think is the 'right' result on the day. So, for example, when a judge decides a case on an issue where the law is uncertain, when the judge delivers his/her judgment, the judgment will not admit that what the judge is really doing is making new law according to his view of what the law should say on the issue at hand. Instead, the judge will purport to *find out* what the law says on that issue, as if he is an explorer digging for treasure that has been buried for ages, but can be found if you just look hard enough. The reason for this is that if the judge admitted that the law applying to a particular case is very uncertain, and the only way he/she can decide the case is to give effect to what he/she thinks the law *should* say in this case, then the losing party would be aggrieved, and think: 'Well, what if a different judge had

>

decided my case? Maybe they would have had a different view as to what the law should say.' It's better to pretend that the law on any issue is always 'out there', just waiting to be discovered. (This is known as the '**declaratory theory of law**'.) Then the losing party can console themselves that their loss was nothing personal: it was just the law that was against them.

So oftentimes a decision in a particular case will *look* as though it was rule-based or principle-based, whereas *really* it was actually policy-based or justice-based. The judge has taken a view as to how the case should be decided according to what the public interest, or justice and fairness, requires, and then dressed his/her judgment up as based on a legal rule or principle so as to reassure the losing party that the law gave the judge no choice but to decide the case the way it was decided. So whenever you come across a judgment that is rule-based or principle-based, always think to yourself: Is that *really* why the judge decided the case? Or has he/she engaged in some *creative* interpretation of a legal rule, or the decided cases, in order to reach the result that he/she thinks that the public interest, or justice and fairness, requires? But please don't – as so many academics do – go overboard with this approach. There are lots of times where a judgment in a case is genuinely rule-based or principle-based, and the judge is not pursuing any hidden agenda. Don't go finding conspiracies and secret plots where there are none to be found.

Covering up

The second point I want to make is that a judge will sometimes use completely opaque language to justify his/her decision. For example, he/she might say, 'The defendant is liable here because he acted *unconscionably*' or 'The defendant is not liable because it would not be *fair, just and reasonable* to find her liable' or 'It would be *inequitable* to deny the claimant an interest in the defendant's land in this case'. Terms like 'unconscionable', 'fair, just and reasonable', 'inequitable' have very little meaning – of and in themselves, they amount to nothing more than legalese for 'bad' or 'good' – and as a result they cannot possibly explain why the judge decided the case

>

the way he/she did. There must be something more: some reason underlying this language that explains the judge's decision. It may be impossible to find the reason – it may be lost forever beneath the opacity of the judge's language. But you should search for it. You shouldn't think that you understand the reason why a judge decided a case the way he/she did if you wouldn't be able to explain the reason for the decision to a five-year-old child. If you cannot reduce the judge's reasoning down to the level that a five-year-old would understand, you are just fooling yourself that you understand why the case was decided the way it was.

4 *Dicta.* By '*dicta*' (which is Latin for 'words') I mean observations made by the judges in deciding a case that weren't strictly speaking essential parts of their reasoning towards the conclusion that they reached in that case, but are still worth knowing about because:

- they indicate some limits on the rule or principle on which the judges are basing their decision in this case;
- they indicate how another case with slightly different facts from the one at hand might have been decided;
- they contain some useful/interesting criticisms/justifications of the law as it stands at the moment.

So, for example, in Harry's judgment, above, his observations as to how he would decided a similar case to Rick's in the future amount to *dicta* – they aren't part of the reason why he decided that Rick should be acquitted (he decided that Rick should be acquitted because Rick could not have been reasonably expected to know at the time he acted that he might be convicted of rape for acting in that way) but they are worth knowing about because they indicate that were a case similar to Rick's to come before the courts again, the outcome might be very different. (In fact, in such a case, the prosecution would be able to argue that there was a 3:2 majority in Rick's case in favour of a 'guilty' verdict being returned in the case at hand.)

Any of the judgments in a particular case may contain interesting *dicta* about the law – so in looking for such useful *dicta*, do not confine yourself to the majority judgments.

5 *Correctness.* The final question you should be seeking to address in reading a case is: Was this case correctly decided? A case can only be said to have been correctly decided if the judges in that case reached the right result, *and for the right reasons.* The fact that the judges reached the right result in a particular case will matter very little if they reached that result for the wrong reasons. This is because the reasons why the judges reached a decision in a particular case can have a big effect on how future cases are decided. If the judges reached that decision on the basis that a particular rule or principle is part of English law, then future judges may well accept that that particular rule or principle *is* part of English law, and base their own decisions on that rule or principle. This is fine if the rule or principle in question makes sense, but disastrous if the rule or principle in question is irrational.

For example, in a case called *Mogul Steamship Co* v *McGregor*, decided in 1891, the defendants tried to corner the market in shipping tea from China to England. The claimant also wanted to ship tea from China to England but found it impossible to get any business because, in an attempt to drive the claimant out of business, the defendants undercut his prices. So he sued the defendants, claiming that they should pay him compensation because they had combined together to make him worse off. The House of Lords dismissed the claimant's claim. This was the right result. But the House of Lords got the reason for the decision wrong. Instead of saying – as they did six years later in the case of *Allen* v *Flood*, where an individual was sued for intentionally making the claimant worse off – that the claimant couldn't sue because you only have a right that someone not intentionally make you worse off if they use unlawful means to do so, the House of Lords in *Mogul* said that the claimant couldn't sue the defendants because the defendants weren't acting *maliciously* in trying to make the claimant worse off: they were only trying to drive the claimant out of business in order to protect and promote their businesses. So, 10 years after the *Mogul* decision, and four years after the decision in *Allen* v *Flood*, the House of Lords was faced with a case called *Quinn* v *Leathem* where some trade unionists had combined together to drive the claimant out of business because they were furious with him that he had refused to employ trade union workers in his business, and wanted to teach him a lesson that you don't mess with the brothers. Because this was – like *Mogul* and unlike *Allen* v *Flood* – a case of people combining together to make someone worse off, the House of Lords applied what had been said in the earlier *Mogul* case and found that as the trade unionists here had acted out of malice in trying to drive the claimant out of business, they were liable for doing so. And this was so even though the means they used to drive the claimant out of business – persuading the claimant's customers not to trade with him – were perfectly lawful.

So ever since these cases were decided, the courts have drawn an irrational distinction between cases where an individual intentionally drives someone out of business, and cases where two or more people combine together and intentionally drive someone out of business. In the first case, the claimant can only sue if the defendant used unlawful means to drive him out of business. In the second case, if the claimant can establish that the defendants acted maliciously in driving him out of business, the claimant can sue even if the means that the defendants used to drive him out of business were perfectly lawful. And this is all because the House of Lords in one case that was decided over 100 years ago reached the right result, but for the wrong reasons.

In thinking about whether a case was correctly decided, try and resist the understandable temptation to think that judges are pretty clever people who can be relied upon to reach the right decision, and for the right reasons. There's no reason to think this. Think about the typical career path of an English judge. University education, go to the Bar, spend about 20 years arguing cases, specialising in a particular area of the law (such as commercial law, or public law), and then accept an offer to become a judge. There is no reason to think that someone with that kind of background will be particularly wise. Indeed, there's no reason to think that he/she will have much of a clue when it comes to deciding cases outside the area of law that he/she specialised in as a barrister. So resist the temptation to be deferential and start thinking instead –

- Are there any flaws in the judges' reasons for their decision, or arguments they simply failed to consider?
- Is their decision, and their reasons for that decision, consistent with other judgments I've read?
- Does the decision in the case, or the judges' reasons for that decision, start us down the slippery slope to some disastrous destination?
- Do the judges' reasons for their decision make the law unacceptably uncertain?

To help you answer these questions, it's always useful – if you have the time – to read some casenotes on the case you are reading. Look back at the mini-section on '*Facts*' in this section of my letter for my advice on finding casenotes on a particular case. And also pay attention to any comments or criticisms that your textbook might have to make of a particular case. So if you remember your textbook saying a lot about a particular case, go back and remind yourself of what the textbook had to say about that case.

○ Taking notes on a case

So, to recap, the five questions you should be asking yourself while going through a case are:

- What were the facts of this case?
- What was the result?
- Why was the case decided the way it was?
- Does the case contain any interesting *dicta*?
- Was the case decided correctly?

And as you are going through a case, you should be making notes on the case organised around these questions.

Make sure that you devote a separate sheet of A4 to *each* case you make notes on. Do *not* make notes on more than one case on the same sheet of

A4 paper. Keeping to the one case per A4 piece of paper rule will make it much easier for you to organise your notes in your case file. You may choose to organise your notes on cases **alphabetically** – this will make your notes on an individual case very easy to find in a hurry. Or you may choose to organise your notes **thematically** – placing together notes on cases that are linked in some way as dealing with a common issue, or a common idea. Whatever system of organisation you choose to employ, having more than one case noted on a single sheet of A4 paper is sure to mess it up. So keep your notes on individual cases separate. Even if this means only having two lines on a particular case on one A4 page, it's still worth it in the long run. (Incidentally, if you choose to organise your notes on cases thematically, and you have a case that deals with more than one issue, just photocopy your notes on that case so that you can put them in two different places in your case file.)

When you are making notes on a case, all my tips for making notes on your textbook apply. Make your notes fun and interesting to look at. Try and get all the information you need on one side of A4. Think about turning the A4 page on its side, and starting your notes from the centre of the page (with the facts of the case at the centre, and your notes on the result, the reasoning, and so on, leading off from the facts at the centre), with the name of the case (and its citation) forming a title at the top of the page. Use diagrams and pictures to illustrate and illuminate any points you want to make in your notes.

◉ Supplementing your notes

Once you have made notes on all the cases on your reading list, you can supplement your notes in three ways:

Textbooks

Go back through the relevant chapters of your textbook (this should be the *third time* you will go through those chapters), looking out for any summaries of important-looking cases that you weren't referred to on your reading list. Whenever you come across such a case, get a fresh sheet of A4 paper and use what the textbook says as the basis for making some notes on that case.

Articles

Do exactly the same with any article you read. After you've been through it once, and extracted from it what its main point is, go through it again looking for summaries of significant cases that aren't on your reading list, and comments on cases that are on your reading list. If you come across anything useful, make a note of it in the appropriate place in your casefile.

Lectures

And the same applies again when one of your lecturers starts talking about a case that isn't currently in your casefile. Make a note of what the lecturer has to say, and then when you have a bit more time, get a fresh sheet of A4 and use your lecture notes as the basis for making some notes on that case. And obviously, if your lecturer has talked about a case that is currently noted in your case file, at some point fish out your notes on that case from your casefile and make a note of any interesting points that your lecturer made about that case.

Remembering cases

Students often find it a challenge to remember cases. Cases are a lot like small, shiny beads. If I told you to hold out your hand and I poured 50 such beads into it, it's doubtful whether you'd be able to keep hold of more than 10 of them. All the rest would simply bounce out of your hand and fall onto the floor. But if I ran a string through 50 beads and tied the two ends of the string together, you'd have no problem keeping hold of all of the beads in one hand. In fact, all you'd have to do is hold *one* of the beads, and all the rest would be under your control.

Cases are the same. If you try to remember them individually, the likelihood is that you'll only remember one-fifth of them. But string them together and you won't forget a single case. So how do you string cases together? Well, what you've got to do is come up with a *story* that helps explain why the cases were decided the way they were. Say you've got 15 cases to remember and those cases were decided over 40 years. There are a number of different stories that you could tell to try and link these cases together.

1 *Politics.* Try to see if the decisions in those cases were affected by political ideas and views that held sway at the time those cases were decided. If they were, then you've got a story onto which you can thread your 15 cases. You can say 'In the 1950s and 1960s, the political consensus was that the interests of society were very much more important than the interests of the individual and you can see the judges giving effect to that consensus in cases *A*, *B* and *C*. But that consensus started to break down in the 1970s, and by the 1980s, there was a new emphasis on protecting the interests of the individual and letting society 'look after itself' – and the decisions in cases *X*, *Y* and *Z* illustrate that new consensus at work.' To help you look at cases this way, get familiar with the various different political theories that judges might give effect to in deciding cases:

- *Libertarianism*: The only thing the State should do is to protect us from being harmed by other people.
- *Utilitarianism*: The State should take steps to maximise the net welfare or happiness that exists in society as a whole. So, on this view, the State should do *x* if its doing so would increase the overall level of happiness in society, even if doing *x* will decrease certain people's happiness.
- *Liberalism* (*right wing*): The State should generally act to maximise everyone's freedom to live their lives as they want.
- *Liberalism* (*left wing*): The State should generally act to minimise inequalities of income and opportunity in society.
- *Perfectionism*: The State should encourage people to live morally worthwhile lives.
- *Communitarianism*: The State should protect, elaborate, and give effect to the shared understandings, practices and traditions that are essential features of our community.

2 *Principle/policy.* Alternatively, you could try to come up with a principle or policy that underlies almost all of the 15 cases. If you can, then

again you've got a story that can link all of your cases – even the ones that don't give effect to the principle or policy in question. You could say, 'Almost all of these cases give effect to the following principle/policy . . . For example, in case *A* . . . Similarly, in case *B* . . . This is also true of case *C* . . . However, in cases *X*, *Y* and *Z* the courts chose not to give effect to this principle/policy. For example, had the courts given effect to this principle/policy in case *X*, we would have expected them to find in favour of . . . But they didn't . . . Similarly, in case *Y* . . .'

A more radical version of the same story would identify a fundamental conflict in the law – with roughly half of your 15 cases giving effect to one principle or policy and the other half giving effect to a completely different and opposed principle or policy. A 'battle of the cases' story line can prove very effective at helping you to remember a large number of cases because battles are always interesting and therefore memorable. But don't invent battles where none exist – the story that you come up with to link your cases must actually *work*. Otherwise the story will have no plausibility and will be extremely hard to remember – just as it's hard to remember the details of a crazy dream where all sorts of people were acting in odd ways.

3 *Line of descent.*   A third possible story line is to link your 15 cases to one 'master' case, which all your 15 cases have 'descended' from. For example, a very effective story line that would link your 15 cases together might go, 'In *Roe* v *Doe*, the House of Lords decided that . . . Applying this decision has created huge problems for the courts ever since. In case *A*, the courts applied *Roe* v *Doe* to find . . . But in the very similar case *B*, the courts came to a very different conclusion, holding that . . .' and so on.

4 *Form/substance.*   A fourth possible story line that could help you link your 15 cases may be provided by the *way* the cases were decided. In some of the cases did the judges adopt a very **formalistic** approach and decide the case by simply applying the law as it was established at the time? In the other cases, did the judges adopt a much more **substantive** approach and simply decide the case on its merits, not paying much regard to what the established law said? If so, then you again have a story that you can use to provide a link between your 15 cases. You can say, 'Well, in cases *A*, *B* and *C*

the judges adopted a very formalistic approach to deciding the cases, but in time they gradually loosened up and became much more willing to depart from the established law if the merits of case demanded it – cases *X*, *Y* and *Z* are examples of that.'

So, if you want to remember lots of cases, remember them in *groups*, where each group of cases is linked by a story that helps explain why they were decided the way they were. (This is why it's *so* important to ask the third of the seven questions that you should ask yourself whenever you are reading a case – Where does this case fit in?) Remembering cases in this way will not only work wonders for your ability to recall cases in the end of year exams – but it will also, of course, help deepen your understanding of, and interest in, the law. Which is all to the good.

And of course, don't miss out on any opportunity to *use* cases. Talk about them with your fellow lawyers. Form study groups where you can have regular discussions about them. Participate in moots where you will be called upon to use cases. Write as many essays and problem answers as you can – even if no one else ever sees them. Take advantage of *any* chance you get to talk about or write about cases you have studied. The more you use cases, the more deeply they will penetrate into your memory.

● Casebooks

There are now casebooks available covering every area of English law. These reproduce excerpts from important cases in a particular area of law, usually alongside short summaries of other relevant cases, as well as some commentary on the cases and the way they were decided.

Students often find using casebooks a useful substitute to reading cases in the law reports. (And, indeed, many students never even read cases in the law reports, but simply rely on casebooks to improve their knowledge of the case law affecting a particular area of law.) It's easy to see why. Instead of searching through a report of a case to find passages that are relevant to the topic or issue you are looking into, a casebook does the hard work for you, finds the relevant passages for you and presents them to you on a plate.

Despite their usefulness, it's dangerous to rely on casebooks too much:

1 *Material left on the cutting room floor.*   There is a limit to how much material from a case can be set out in a casebook. A typical case will be about 25 pages long in a law report. Of course, the editors of a casebook won't reproduce the whole case because doing so won't leave them room to cover that many cases in their casebook. So, they'll be looking to get their coverage of the case down to about 5 pages. To reduce 25 pages to 5 pages, you have to cut a lot of material, and some of the material that's left on the floor can be very useful. So, if you rely exclusively on a casebook to read a particular case, you can often miss out on some very useful *dicta* and ideas in the judgments in that case.

2 *Boredom.*   If you spend all your time reading the same book, boredom can quickly set in. To keep it stimulated and active, the mind needs variety. So, if you buy a 1,000-page casebook (which is the sort of size a casebook needs to be to have any hope of being comprehensive enough to be useful), it is doubtful how much information you will retain from going through that book after reading a few pages in each session you use it.

3 *The importance of reading cases for yourself.*   It can be good for you to have to search through case reports yourself to find the passages that are relevant to the topic or issue that you are studying. It helps develop your skills at reading cases and finding your way around them – and it also means you get a bit more satisfaction out of reading cases.

However, I must emphasise that I don't want to put you off looking at casebooks entirely. As I said, they can be very useful at helping you see why exactly a case is significant. In addition, some of them provide the reader with a lot of stimulating and interesting commentary on the law. (I am thinking in particular here of Tony Weir's classic *A Casebook on Tort*, 10th edn (Sweet & Maxwell, 2004), which is well worth reading for the comments alone.) Further, in certain subjects such as international law (where the official case reports are ridiculously long), casebooks are indispensable. Finally, if you don't have access to a decent law library with a full set of law reports, they are a lifesaver. (Though remember, a lot of cases can now be accessed over the Internet – something I'll talk about in another letter.)

◉ Two final points

Don't get discouraged

Reading cases is a bit like riding a bike. When you start reading cases, you don't get very far and the whole process is quite painful. But if you stick at it, and follow the advice in this letter, I promise things will get better and you will find that reading cases gets easier and easier – and pretty soon you'll be flying through them. But you'll never get to that stage of development unless you are willing to grit your teeth and go through the pains involved in reading cases for the first time.

Ratio decidendi

If you've read any introductory books on studying law, you may have been expecting me to give you some advice in this letter on how you discover the **ratio decidendi** of a case. (Just in case you haven't read any introductory books on studying law, the *ratio decidendi* – or *ratio* for short – of a case is the rule of law that underlay the decision in that case.)

In practical terms, the only time you'll ever have to worry about finding the *ratio* of a case is *after* you've left university and you've started practising law. If you are arguing a case in court, you may well be called upon to discuss what the *ratio* of a case was. For example, suppose there is a *dictum* in a previously decided case that is unhelpful to your argument. If you can establish that the *dictum* was *obiter* – that is, not essential to the outcome of the case (in other words, not part of the *ratio* of the case) – then you can invite the court deciding your case to disregard that *dictum*. Alternatively, suppose there is a *dictum* in a previously decided case that is very helpful to your argument. In that situation, you will want to establish that that *dictum was* part of the *ratio* of the case – with the result that the court before which you are arguing your case may be bound to apply it.

>

But as a law *student*, you'll never have to spend time determining what the *ratio* of a case was. You obviously need to know what the judges' reasons were for deciding a case in a particular way, but you don't need to know how to take the further step of determining from those reasons what we can say was *the* reason for the decision. So I'm not going to waste your time (and mine) discussing such things as how you determine what the *ratio* of a case was when three judges all decided the case in the same way but they all gave different reasons for their decision. Instead, I'll finish now and write to you in a few days about how you should approach the job of reading a statute.

Best wishes,

Nick

Looking at Statutes

○ From: Nicholas J. McBride [dearnick@pearson.com]
○ To: Brown, Jo
○ Subject: Looking at Statutes

Hey Jo,

Students find reading statutes extremely boring. Unlike cases, statutes tend to be very dry and technical. As a result, it is hard to work up any enthusiasm for reading a statute, and it's even harder to remember a statute once you've read it. I'm not going to pretend that I have any magic method for taking the pain out of reading statutes, but following the approach below will inject a little bit of interest into the job of reading a statute, and make the job of remembering what that statute says a little bit easier.

● The basic approach

Suppose you have been told to read a statute, or some sections from a statute. (You may not be familiar with the term 'section', so I'll briefly explain. Every Act of Parliament is made up of sections, or 's.' for short. A section in an Act of Parliament is usually divided up into subsections, where each subsection is denoted by a number in brackets. So if you want to refer to subsection 1 of section 1 of the Guard Dogs Act 1975, you would simply write 's.1(1) of the Guard Dogs Act 1975'.) Of course, you shouldn't just read the statute – you should also make some notes about the statute in your case file. (Remember, 'case file' is short for 'cases and statutes file'.)

Now, in making notes on the statute, you *shouldn't* try to *summarise* what the statute says. There's a very good saying that 'You can't paraphrase a statute'. In other words, if you attempt to summarise what a statute says, your summary will always omit some crucial details. And if you attempt to avoid missing out any crucial details in making your summary, you will usually simply end up copying out the statute. And copying out the statute is the *last* thing you want to do. Copying out a statute is such a passive activity that you will simply get bored, your brain will shut up shop and you won't take anything in of what the statute says.

So – how should you make notes on a statute? Well, you'll probably not be surprised to hear me say that your notes on a statute should be question-driven. Suppose that you have been told to read sections 1–10 of the Theft Act 1968. Take a separate A4 sheet for each section. Write the name and title of the section in the middle of the sheet. (The title of the section is literally that – the short title that appears above the section.) Around the name write five questions:

- Why was this section enacted?
- How does this section apply in concrete situations?
- Why does this section go as far as it does?
- Why doesn't this section go further than it does?
- Is this section in need of reform?

Then, on the same A4 sheet of paper, make notes on the answers to these questions by consulting the statute, textbooks, articles, and your brain. Let's now look at these five questions in more detail, by seeing how they would apply to certain sections of the Theft Act 1968.

1 *Why was this section enacted?* Section 1(1) of the Theft Act 1968 (title: 'Basic definition of theft') provides that:

A person is guilty of theft if he dishonestly appropriates property belonging to another with the intention of permanently depriving the other of it; and 'theft' and 'steal' shall be construed accordingly.

If you are told to read s.1(1) of the Theft Act 1968, the first thing you should do is ask yourself: Why has this section been enacted? Why does the law criminalise the dishonest appropriation of property belonging to another when that property was appropriated with the intention of permanently depriving that other of it? Why doesn't the law simply allow the owner to sue for his property back – why does the criminal law have to get involved here at all? Use your textbook, your brain, any relevant articles you have read, and any relevant *dicta* in any relevant cases you have read to come up with some answers to these questions, and make notes of the answers in the appropriate place in your case file.

No doubt the answers to these questions are pretty obvious. However, the important thing is that by asking these questions, you are *thinking* about s.1(1) of the Theft Act 1968 instead of just passively reading it. And your thinking about s.1(1) is doing three things:

- it is helping to make s.1(1) more interesting and therefore more enjoyable to read;
- it is deepening your understanding of s.1(1), thus putting you in a great position to answer questions about it later;
- it is helping to cement the place of s.1(1) in your memory, which again is helping to put you in a great position to answer questions about it later.

2 *How does this section apply in concrete situations?* Section 2 of the Theft Act 1968 (title: 'Dishonestly') provides that:

(1) A person's appropriation of property belonging to another is not to be regarded as dishonest –

(a) if he appropriates property in the belief that he has in law the right to deprive the other of it, on behalf of himself or of a third person; or

(b) if he appropriates the property in the belief that he would have the other's consent if the other knew of the appropriation and the circumstances of it; or

>

> (c) (except where the property came to him as trustee or personal representative) if he appropriates the property in the belief that the person to whom the property belongs cannot be discovered by taking reasonable steps.
>
> (2) A person's appropriation of property belonging to another may be dishonest notwithstanding that he is willing to pay for the property.

Let's assume you've considered why this section has been enacted. Now you've got to ask yourself – How does this section apply in concrete situations? To answer this question, you should come up with a number of different hypothetical scenarios, and see how the section applies in each of them. You should consider *at least* as many scenarios as there are rules laid down in the section. So for a section like this, which lays down four rules, you should probably make notes on how the section will apply in *at least* four different hypothetical scenarios. But to really come to grips with this section, you should probably consider how it applies in eight different hypothetical situations.

Try to think up the scenarios yourself and make them as memorable as possible by using the names of people you know about, preferably doing things that they would never do in real life. (These kinds of scenarios will stay longer in your memory than scenarios that might have been supplied to you by a textbook.) Here are some examples of scenarios you might come up with:

> 1 Peter realises that a DVD in a shop has been wrongly priced as being for sale for £1.59, rather than £15.99 (which is what other identical DVDs are being sold for in the shop). He takes the DVD up to the counter and pays £1.59 for it.
>
> 2 Hannah finds a wallet that has been dropped in the street by Siobhan. There is a £20 note in it. She hands the wallet in at a nearby police station but keeps the £20 note as a 'finder's fee'.
>
> >

3 Megan, a student living in college, makes a cake for everyone on her staircase using ingredients that she has found in the fridge that everyone on the staircase uses to keep their food in. None of the ingredients belong to her, but she figures that as everyone on the staircase is going to get to eat some of the cake, the rightful owner of the ingredients won't mind her using them.

4 Hugh owes Beka £5 but is refusing to pay up. Beka takes one of Hugh's DVDs out of his room when he isn't looking and auctions it on eBay. Someone pays her £10 for the DVD. Beka keeps £5 and slips the remaining £5 into Hugh's wallet when he isn't looking.

5 Maryam has read a textbook on 'Natural Law' which says that 'no law is valid if it is contrary to the will of God'. Believing that God desires all living creatures to be free, she releases Clare's parrot into the wild.

Having come up with some such scenarios, work out when s.2 will apply to acquit someone of being dishonest in these scenarios – and when it won't. (To do this, make use of your textbooks, any relevant articles, your brain and – importantly – any cases that have helped clarify how s.2 of the Theft Act 1968 is to be applied.) In your notes, make a note of these scenarios, how s.2 will apply in those scenarios, and the reason it applies or does not apply in each of those scenarios.

It may be pretty obvious how s.2 will apply in the above scenarios. But the point of going through these scenarios isn't to anticipate potential problem questions that you might be asked in the exam, which questions will probably pose more tricky issues than the scenarios set out above. The point of going through these scenarios is to get a solid grasp of how s.2 of the Theft Act 1968 applies in concrete situations. This will help you to remember how s.2 works. This, in turn, will help you apply s.2 with confidence when you are faced with trickier problem questions about s.2 in the end of year exam.

3 *Why does this section go as far as it does?* Section 3(1) of the Theft Act 1968 (title: 'Appropriates') provides that:

> Any assumption by a person of the rights of an owner amounts to an appropriation, and this includes, where he has come by the property (innocently or not) without stealing it, any later assumption of a right to it by keeping or dealing with it as owner.

Let's assume you've considered why this section has been enacted, and have got a good grasp of how it applies in concrete situations. The third question you have to ask yourself is – Why does this section go as far as it does?

You will have discovered in considering the second question – how does this section apply? – that the case law seems to suggest that merely touching an item of property will amount to an 'appropriation' of an object. Why should merely touching an item of property potentially amount to a criminal act? Or was s.3(1) never intended to have that effect – have the courts misinterpreted it?

Again, make notes on the answers to these questions using your textbooks, any relevant articles, any relevant *dicta* in any relevant cases, and your brain. Asking and answering these questions will:

- help you to remember what s.3(1) says;
- deepen your understanding of, and interest in, s.3(1);
- put you in a good position to answer our fifth question about s.3(1) (Is this section in need of reform?);
- put you in a great position to answer any essay questions that might be set on s.3(1) in the end of year exam.

4 *Why doesn't this section go further than it does?* Section 4 of the Theft Act 1968 (title 'Property') provides that:

> (1) 'Property' includes money and all other property, real or personal, including things in action and other intangible property.
>
> >

(2)   A person cannot steal land . . .

(3)   A person who picks mushrooms growing wild on any land, or who picks flowers, fruit or foliage from a plant growing wild on any land, does not (although not in possession of the land) steal what he picks, unless he does it for reward or for sale or for other commercial purposes.

For purposes of this subsection 'mushroom' includes any fungus, and 'plant' includes any shrub or tree.

(4)   Wild creatures, tamed or untamed, shall be regarded as property; but a person cannot steal a wild creature not tamed nor ordinarily kept in captivity, or the [carcass] of any such creature, unless either it has been reduced into possession by or on behalf of another person and possession of it has not since been lost or abandoned, or another person is in the course of reducing it into possession.

Let's assume you've taken notes on the first three questions relating to this section. So you can now move on to consider our fourth question: Why doesn't this section go further than it does? This raises a host of sub-questions.

Dead bodies don't normally count as 'property' – so why doesn't the law of theft cover someone's taking away a dead body? Is it because there are already other areas of law that criminalise this sort of conduct? Information doesn't normally count as 'property' – so why doesn't the law of theft cover the situation where someone sneaks an advance peak at an exam paper, or gives out advance copies of an exam paper to his friends? Why can't someone steal land? (Note, however, that you can in certain situations – s.4(2) is quite long and to save space I have cut it down.) What would stealing land involve? Is this sort of conduct covered by some other area of the law? Why are you potentially guilty of theft if you pick wild mushrooms on someone else's land for reward but not if you pick them to deprive the owner of the land of the opportunity to pick them himself? Is doing something for reward worse than doing something out of malice?

The point of asking and trying to answer these questions should be obvious by now. Doing this will:

- help cement the details of s.4 into your memory;
- deepen your understanding of – and therefore interest in – s.4;
- put you in a good position to answer our fifth question about s.4 (Is this section in need of reform?);
- put you in a great position to answer any essay question that you might be set on s.4.

5 *Is this section in need of reform?* Section 5(1) of the Theft Act 1968 (title: 'Belonging to another') provides that:

Property shall be regarded as belonging to any person having possession or control of it, or having in it any proprietary right or interest (not being an equitable interest arising only from an agreement to transfer or grant an interest)

Let's assume that you've run through the first four of our questions relating to this section. Having done so, you'll have realised that s.5(1) means that someone can be convicted of theft for stealing his own property. This happened in one case where a man left his car with a garage to be repaired, and after it had been repaired, he drove the car away without paying for the repairs. Because the garage had possession and control of the car at the time the car-owner drove the car away, the courts held that the car 'belonged' to the garage under s.5(1) at the time it was driven away, with the result that the car's owner could be convicted of stealing it.

The fifth question you should ask yourself about this section and make notes on is: Is this section in need of reform? Is it right that someone can be convicted of stealing his own property? Should the law of theft go beyond protecting the ownership of property and help protect people's possession of property? Asking these questions and trying to answer them (again, with the help of your textbooks, any relevant articles, any relevant *dicta* in any relevant cases, and any thoughts you yourself might have) will help deepen your understanding of – and therefore interest in – the law of theft as a whole and its functions and put you in a great position to answer essay questions either specifically on s.5 of the Theft Act 1968, or on the law of theft as a whole.

● Three more points

So – that's the basic approach you should adopt in reading statutes (or statutory instruments, for that matter). I don't have any further tips for you on how you should approach the job of reading a statute. However, there are three more points that I want to make.

Statute books and the exams

Almost all universities now allow their law students to take statute books into their exams so that they can consult them in the course of answering problem questions or writing essays. Given this, you may wonder if there is any point doing work which is geared to helping you to remember what particular statutes say. I think there is.

The more time you spend in the exam looking through a statute book trying to find out what a particular statute says and trying to figure out how it applies, the less writing time you will have in the exam. You want to maximise the amount of writing time you have in your exams – so it is very important that by the time you do your exams, you have a good knowledge of all the statutes that you will need to know about for the exams.

Only look at statutes that you are going to be examined on

While I normally encourage you to do more reading than you are actually asked to do by your teachers, this doesn't apply to statutes. There is no real point in knowing about a statute that isn't going to figure in the exam – so unless you have been told about or asked to read a particular statute, the chances are that it's not worth knowing about and you shouldn't bother looking it up.

>

Statutory interpretation

Again, if you've read any introductory books on studying law, you may have been expecting me to say something in this section on various techniques that can be used to interpret statutes, such as the 'literal rule' (where words in a statute are interpreted according to their plain meaning) or the 'mischief rule' (where words in a statute are interpreted in light of the problem or evil that the statute was trying to address) or the 'golden rule' (where the courts try to avoid interpreting words in a statute in a fatuous or stupid way). Again, I'm not going to waste your time by talking about such things. If a particular word in a statute is ambiguous or needs to be interpreted, your textbooks will give you sufficient guidance as to how that word has and should be interpreted. You won't need to worry about what rule you should apply to interpret that word. This is something you may need to worry about if you are a practising lawyer advising people on how a new statute applies – but for the time being, you have better things to worry about.

I will be in touch again soon about how to read, and make notes on, an article.

Best wishes,

Nick

Reading an Article

● From: Nicholas J. McBride [dearnick@pearson.com]
● To: Brown, Jo
● Subject: Reading an Article

Hey Jo,

It's important that you read lots of articles written by legal academics. Other than writing legal essays yourself, there is no better way of improving your legal essay writing skills than to read legal articles. They provide you with models of how to argue properly when you are writing an essay, and are a fertile source of ideas and arguments that you can draw on or react against in writing your essays. So – here are my tips on getting the most out of reading articles.

● The basic approach

Okay – so you are going to read a particular article. What should be your basic approach? Go through the article *twice*.

The first time, you are trying to get an idea of what the article is basically saying – what the overall point of the article is, and what arguments are being made (or dismissed) in order to make that point out. The second time, you should look through the article to see if it has anything interesting to say about any particular cases, which observations you can then make a note of in your case file, under the name of the case in question.

Your aim in going through the article for the first time should be to enhance your *understanding* of the law, thereby helping you to critically evaluate the law and write good, solid essays about it. Your aim in going through the article for the second time should be to enhance your *knowledge* of the law, thereby helping you to appreciate the full range of legal issues raised by a specific legal problem.

◉ The first run-through

When I say 'run-through' I *mean* it. *Hustle* through the article. Don't make notes as you go through it – that will just slow you up and make you feel miserable. Read the article *at speed*, asking the following key questions *all the time*:

> 1 What is this article basically saying?
>
> 2 What arguments are being made in favour of the article's basic point?
>
> 3 What are the arguments against the article's basic point, and how does the author dismiss them?
>
> 4 What do I think of the author's arguments?

Those are the *only* things you want to know on the first run-through.

Once you've read the entire article through, getting an idea of what the article has to say (if it has anything to say) on these issues, then take a fresh A4 piece of paper and make some notes about the article *from memory*, organised around these key questions, referring back to a specific part of the article only if necessary to refresh your memory. Once your note is complete, file the piece of A4 paper away in your secondary materials file.

> ### What is the article basically saying?
>
> In making a note on question (1), try and reduce the basic message of the article down to five or six lines at most. If you can't do that, then it's doubtful whether the article is going to be that much help: either it is very unclear in what it wants to say, or you are very unclear about what it wants to say, and either way the article's not going to be of much help to you. If you have a nagging feeling that you have
>
> >

completely missed the point of what the article has to say, Google search it to see what other people have to say about it, or ask your fellow students what they throught of it, or ask your teachers what they think its basic message is.

What are the arguments being made/being dismissed?

In making notes on questions (2) and (3), use *numbers* to identify the different arguments that the author makes in favour of his/her basic point, and the reasons why an author thinks that an argument that might be made against his/her basic point should be rejected. If the author is making four arguments for what he/she wants to say, then your notes should reflect that and number those arguments one to four. Numbering the arguments helps you get clearer about what the author is actually saying – instead of a mish-mash of jumbled assertions, you have four crisp (and make sure that when you make a note of the author's arguments, you express them as crisply as possible) arguments on which the worth of the article will depend.

What do I think?

In making notes on question (4) (and in reading the entire article) . . .

○ . . . Be aggressive

In the excellent film *Searching for Bobby Fischer* (highly, highly recommended), Laurence Fishburne's street speedchess player intimidates his opponent with some trashtalk:

> What's that . . . Is that the best you got? Is that the best you got? Uh-huh . . . you ain't got nothin' . . . No . . . that ain't it . . . Hmmm . . . that ain't it either . . . You're going to have to do much better than that, boss . . . Much better than that . . . C'mon, show me something . . . show me something, grandmaster . . .

That is *exactly* the sort of mentality I want you to adopt on going through an article for the first time. You should be hustling through the article, challenging it to 'show me something' – to tell you something interesting about the law. If the article doesn't *seem* to have anything worthwhile to say (which may well be the case), don't be afraid to conclude that it doesn't *actually* have anything worthwhile to say. Maybe check first with some other people to see if the article was actually saying something, but you missed it. But if no one can clearly express what the article was trying to say, then throw it aside as a failure. (Well, not literally – just put it back on the shelf, politely.) It's no good and not worth noting.

You should adopt the same aggressive mentality in making notes on question (4), which requires you to evaluate the arguments that the writer makes in favour of his/her basic point, and seeing whether the writer does a good job of dismissing the arguments against his/her position. Don't let the writer walk all over you with his/her claims. Resist. Ask yourself: Do the writer's arguments stand up? Are they circular? Are they based on a false premise? Are they illogical? Don't *assume* the arguments are any good. Be aggressive: test the writer's arguments out, and see if they collapse under scrutiny. Don't be afraid to say, 'That ain't it . . . that ain't it either . . .' to the author, no matter how revered they might be.

● An exception to the rule

The one kind of legal article that is ill-adapted to this kind of hustling, aggressive approach is an article that tries to reach a particular conclusion through a very long chain of reasoning.

An example would be an article that started, 'In this article I want to show that even libertarians – who believe that people should be allowed to do what they like so long as they do not violate other people's rights – should favour legal controls on people's ability to take crack cocaine.' Then what follows is a long argument that goes through the following steps:

1 Let's assume that libertarians are right to believe that people should be allowed to do what they like so long as they do not violate other people's rights . . .

2 If this position were correct, there must be something valuable in allowing people to do what they like, and something damaging about violating other people's rights . . .

>

3 There are three plausible accounts as to what might be valuable in allowing people to do what they like. They are: (i) . . . (ii) . . . (iii) . . .

4 We can safely assume that libertarians would not agree with the first two accounts and would therefore agree that what is valuable about allowing people to do what they like is (iii) . . .

5 There are three plausible accounts as to what might be damaging about violating other people's rights. They are: (i) . . . (ii) . . . (iii) . . .

6 We can safely assume that libertarians would not agree with the first two accounts and would therefore agree that what is damaging about violating people's rights is (iii) . . .

7 So libertarians believe that what is valuable about allowing people to do what they like is . . . and they believe what is damaging about violating other people's rights is . . .

8 However, if this is right, then a libertarian must concede that there is nothing valuable about taking crack cocaine, and in fact taking crack cocaine is just as damaging as violating other people's rights.

9 This is because [cue graphic descriptions of what the effects of taking crack cocaine are] . . .

10 It seems then, that even libertarians – on the most faithful and sympathetic account of what they believe – must favour legal restrictions on the consumption of crack cocaine.

Phew! If you get an article like that to read, you *know* you are in for a long night! The reason is that there are so many steps in the reasoning, and each one has to be looked at with great care to see if the overall argument stands up. These articles – despite being incredibly time-consuming to read – *can* be valuable to read because: (1) they tend to end up at an interesting conclusion, and it's worth knowing whether you can end up at a conclusion that interesting; and (2) reading each step of the argument, and thinking for yourself whether each step is justified, is a great way of educating yourself how to argue effectively. *However*, it's highly unlikely that an argument such as the one above, that tries to reach such a paradoxical conclusion ('A libertarian favouring restrictions on the taking of crack cocaine? Very strange!') and by such an elaborate route (ten stages in the reasoning), will actually stand up. The author *will* almost always make a slip somewhere along the way (either by accident, or by deliberately trying to pull a fast one). And once you've spotted the error in the reasoning (generally, any proposition which starts 'We can safely assume . . .' is *highly* likely to be wrong), there's normally no point in going on with the article.

● Tricks

In going through an article for the first time, be particularly on the look out for *tricks* designed to fool you into thinking either that the writer has something to say, or that his/her arguments in favour of his/her position stand up to scrutiny. Here's a representative list:

Jargon

Academics use jargon – obscure words that are never used by ordinary people – to make themselves look intelligent when they don't actually have anything intelligent to say. Jargon makes an article look like it is deeply profound, whereas 99 times out of 100, the article has absolutely nothing to say that is of any interest to anyone – and were the article to be written in plainer language, that would become obvious. Words and terms that should make you suspicious that you're wasting your time are: heuristic, ontological, interrogate (as in 'This article will interrogate . . .'), interdisciplinary, praxis, structuralist, holistic, semiotic, reflective equilibrium, hermeneutic, conceptual, autopoeisis, sociological, associative, disassociative, problematise, reification, critical theory, modernist, post-modern, signifier. Any time you come across a legal article containing even one of these words, you have my permission to switch off.

Quotes

Quotes have their place in an article. If A has made the same point you are making, but much more eloquently or succinctly than you

>

could, then it's crazy not to quote what A has to say in making that point. But what a quote can never do is establish that a particular point is correct. The fact that A once said *x* does not, and cannot ever, prove that *x* is true. It's amazing how often this point is overlooked by academics, who think that if they can show that Aristotle took a particular position on (say) the nature of justice, that tells something about the nature of justice. It doesn't tell us anything: it just tells us what Aristotle thought, and what Aristotle thought wasn't necessarily correct. Similarly with articles that just amount to one long extended quote, such as articles that pick over what Albert Venn Dicey thought was required by the 'rule of law' or what Wesley Newcomb Hohfeld thought the term 'right' denoted. Such articles are of very limited usefulness – all they tell us is what Dicey or Hohfeld thought (or, rather, what someone thinks they thought) was meant by a particular term or concept, and that doesn't tell us anything about what that term or concept *actually* means, other than it *may* (but equally may not) mean what Dicey or Hohfeld thought that term meant.

Untestable propositions

An untestable proposition is one that cannot be established to be false because it literally has no meaning – so it can only be established to be false by giving it a meaning. So, for example, the proposition 'The law aims to maximise the wealth of society' is untestable because the concept of 'maximising the wealth of society' has no obvious meaning. So there is no way of telling whether this proposition is true or not unless we define what 'maximising the wealth of society' means. Academics like making untestable propositions because they can look impressive and they are safe to make: there is simply no way of proving that an untestable proposition is incorrect and that the academic making it has screwed up. If you attempt to prove that a particular untestable proposition is incorrect by giving it a meaning and then showing that, on that interpretation, the proposition is incorrect, the academic advancing that proposition is always free to say that your interpretation of the proposition is incorrect (or 'unconvincing') and so your criticism fails.

>

Wrongly decided

This is a favourite trick of academics advancing a particular inter-pretation of the caselaw – for example, in arguing that the cases give effect to a particular principle. An example: 'The cases on when someone can sue for a reasonable sum for work that he has done at another's request give effect to the principle that if A has been un-justly enriched at B's expense, B is entitled to sue A for the value of that enrichment.' If you point to a number of a cases where B has been allowed to sue A for a reasonable sum for work that he has done at A's request even though that work cannot be said to have en-riched A in any way, advocates of the above proposition will usually dismiss those cases as 'wrongly decided'. But this is circular: they are only 'wrongly decided' if the proposition above is correct, and that is precisely what is at issue. (Other academics argue that in these cases B's work did, in fact, enrich A in some mysterious way, thereby making the above proposition meaningless, and thus untestable, which is just fine by them.)

● The second run-through

Okay – let's assume you've read a particular article, and made a note on it on a piece of A4 paper, summing up the basic point of the article and the key arguments made in favour of that point. Now you can go through the article again, this time looking to see whether it has any points to make about particular cases that you have already made a note on in your case file. What you are looking for are:

- (good) accounts of what happened in the case and how it was decided;
- explanations why the case was decided the way it was;
- criticisms of the decision in that case, or the way it was decided.

It may also be that the article mentions a particular case that you have not made a note of in your case file. If the case seems interesting enough, then use what the article has to say about that case as the basis for a note about that case in your case file.

Once you've completed the second run-through, you can put the article aside and not bother looking at it again. You've got what you need from it, and it's time to move on to something else. If you come across a subsequent article that trashes the article you've just noted, then obviously go back to your A4 note on the original article and make a note of the subsequent article's criticisms (also making a note of whether you think those criticisms are valid or not), so that all the relevant notes on that article are all in the same place.

● Finding more articles to read

Don't confine yourself to reading just the articles that you've been told to read on your reading list. There is a huge number of legal articles published nowadays, and your teachers won't have had time to read and digest all of the articles that might be relevant to your studies. So the chances are pretty high that there are some good and relevant articles 'out there' that you won't have been referred to on your reading list. So do Google searches for terms relevant to the area of law you are studying to see if there any useful-looking papers, or references to useful-looking papers, on the Internet.

Festschriften

A lot of good and interesting papers on the law can be found in what are called '*festschriften*' (literally, 'celebration writings'). These are books that honour a particular academic or judge by collecting together a number of original essays written by academics on subjects with which the academic or judge in question has or had some connection. Papers published in a *festschrift* are especially likely not to get onto your reading list because your teachers may not even know about the existence of the *festschrift*, let alone have the time to get around reading all the papers contained in it. Fortunately for you, there now exists a searchable database of papers published in legal *festschriften*. Go to http://magic.lbr.auckland.ac.nz/festschrift/, enter into the 'keywords' search engine any terms that are relevant to the particular area of law you are studying, press return, and see what comes up.

You can also search for relevant articles on Westlaw (if you have access to it), though there is always a danger of getting a bit swamped by the number of articles that Westlaw will come up with that are relevant to your search terms. It's also worth looking at the collections of reprinted articles issued by Dartmouth Publishing – under various different subject titles (including two volumes of *Contract Law* articles, four volumes of *International Law* articles, and two volumes of *Family Law* articles) – to see whether there is anything interesting in them that you haven't been referred to on your reading lists.

Hope this is helpful. Mentioning the database of legal *festschriften* makes me think I should give you a list of websites that will be useful to you in your studies. I'll do that next letter.

Best wishes,

Nick

Using the Internet

- From: Nicholas J. McBride [dearnick@pearson.com]
- To: Brown, Jo
- Subject: Using the Internet

Dear Jo,

Obviously, the Internet is a hugely important source of legal information nowadays. In this letter, I'll give you a list of very useful websites that you can access to help you with your studies. However, a word of warning first. The fact that you can access so much information online makes it very tempting to make your room the main place you study law, and your computer your main vehicle for studying law. Try to resist this temptation. Studying for long periods in your room is a bad idea – it isolates you from your fellow students, and as a result you miss out on the companionship, solidarity and intellectual stimulation that they can provide. And all the distractions available in your room (not least all the non-law related sites that you can access on the Internet) mean that you're unlikely to make the most effective use of your time if you study in your room. Making your computer your main vehicle for studying law is also a bad idea. While you can access a lot of information online nowadays, there is a lot of valuable information out there as well (notably, the information in textbooks and monographs, and journals that are not available online) that can only be accessed by going into the Law Library. So use the Internet, but don't let it take over your studies.

Subscription-only websites

There is a large number of excellent websites that give you online access to a huge range of law reports and law journals, such as JUSTIS, Westlaw,

Lawtel, LexisNexis Butterworths Direct Services, and HeinOnline. Unfortunately, you have to pay to access these sites. It may be that your Law Faculty maintains subscriptions to these sites, which will allow you and your fellow law students to access them. If so, your law faculty will tell you how to access and use these sites – so I don't need to say any more about these.

● Reports of cases (UK)

You can find free-to-access reports of cases decided in the UK at the following sites:

Supreme Court/House of Lords decisions

Supreme Court: www.supremecourt.gov.uk/decided-cases/index.html. House of Lords: www.publications.parliament.uk/pa/ld/ldjudgmt.htm or (for older House of Lords decisions) www.bailii.org/uk/cases/UKHL/

British and Irish Legal Information Institute (BAILII)

Go to: www.bailii.org. You can find a lot of cases reported here, including decisions of the Court of Appeal. This site includes, at www.bailii.org/openlaw/, lists of the leading cases in various areas of the law, with links to almost all of the cases listed.

Decisions of the Privy Council

Go to: www.privy-council.org.uk/output/Page31.asp or (for older Privy Council decisions) www.bailii.org/uk/cases/UKPC/. (The Judicial Committee of the Privy Council decides appeals from Commonwealth countries that still acknowledge the Privy Council's ultimate authority to decide what their law says. Nowadays this only applies to countries in the Caribbean.)

The English Reports

Before an organised system of reporting cases was instituted in England in 1865, various different individual law reporters would

>

gather together reports of cases that had been decided by the courts and publish them in volumes of reports known by the name of the law reporter, such as Peake, or Campbell, or Ellis and Blackburn. After 1865, these volumes were gathered together and published in what are called the 'English Reports'.

So, for example, two different law reporters – Campbell and Espinasse – each published a report of a very famous English case called *Stilk* v *Myrick*, which held that a promise to pay someone more for doing something they are already required to do for you is not binding. Campbell's report appeared in the second volume of a series of reports called 'Campbell's Nisi Prius Reports' and is cited as (1809) 2 Camp. 317. Espinasse's report appears in the sixth volume of a series of reports that he published under the title *Espinasse's Nisi Prius Reports* and is cited as (1809) 6 Esp. 129. When the English Reports were published, both of these reports ended up in the 170th volume of the English Reports, with Espinasse's report appearing on page 851, and Campbell's report appearing on page 1168. So if you want to read *Stilk* v *Myrick* you have to look it up in both (1809) 170 ER 851 and in (1809) 170 ER 1168.

Nowadays you can read this case and any other case that appears in the English Reports by going to www.commonlii.org/int/cases/EngR/. To find the report of a particular case, it's simplest to click on the letter representing the first letter of the name of the case, and then scroll down to the actual name of the case, and then click on the name of the case to access a pdf reproduction of the report of that case. Incidentally, if you are ever mystified by a particular abbreviation on a reading list that you are given (for example, you don't know what 'ER' stands for), a very handy site for telling you what you should be looking for is the Cardiff Index to Legal Abbreviations: www.legalabbrevs.cardiff.ac.uk.

○ Statutes (UK)

The texts of statutes passed by the UK Parliament since 1837 can be found at: www.opsi.gov.uk/acts.htm. A statutory instrument is a piece of legislation that is created by a minister in the UK government under powers delegated to him by the UK Parliament. Texts of all statutory instruments that have been created since 1987 can be found at www.opsi.gov.uk/stat. You won't have to worry about statutory instruments too much in your studies, though – as with the Unfair Terms in Consumer Contracts Regulations 1999 – they will sometimes be relevant. If you want to find a particular statute and how it has been amended since then, much the best site to go to is www.statutelaw.gov.uk.

● Law journals

A large number of law journals (mostly based in the United States) make themselves available online on a free-to-access basis. There are too many to list here, but you can access a complete list of free-to-access online law journals by going to the relevant page of the Cambridge University website at www.law.cam.ac.uk/legal-resources/law-journals-on-the-internet.php#ad. Unfortunately, most British law journals make themselves available online on a subscription-only basis, so free-to-access law journals will be of limited usefulness to you, at least at the start of your studies. If you go to www.tictocs.ac.uk, you can look up the tables of contents for the most recent issue of a huge number of law journals (including the *Cambridge Law Journal*, *Modern Law Review*, and *Oxford Journal of Legal Studies*) – just enter 'Law' beside the 'Subject' box under 'Search for TOCs'. This provides a handy way of finding out what has just been published on areas of law of interest to you, without ever leaving your desk.

● Subject websites

There is a large number of free-to-access websites that deal with specific areas of the law. You should have these to hand when studying the following areas of law:

Tort law

The best tort law website is one run by me and Roderick Bagshaw, the co-authors of a textbook on tort law. You can find it at www.mylawchamber.co.uk/mcbride. You'll find there summaries of, and

>

comments on, all the major tort cases decided since 2001, as well as some model answers to tort law problem questions of the kind you might get in your exams. If you go to: www.pibriefupdate.com and sign up for the 'PI Brief Update', you will receive via e-mail a monthly newsletter that will keep you up to date with recent developments in personal injury law (which is an area of tort law).

Criminal law

Go to www.crimeline.info and sign up to receive regular updates via e-mail on recent developments in the criminal law. Note that a lot of developments in criminal law deal with criminal procedural issues and therefore will not actually be that relevant to your studies.

Constitutional law

There are quite a few campaigning websites that will give you lots of useful information about recent developments in the area of constitutional law and civil liberties. Four of the best are:

1 The website of the University College London Student Human Rights Programme (www.uclshrp.com).

2 The 'recent news' section of JUSTICE's website (www.justice.org. uk/inthenews/index.html) (JUSTICE is an organisation that campaigns to promote and protect human rights through the law).

3 The website of the Campaign for Freedom of Information (www. cfoi.org.uk).

4 The website of Statewatch, which is an organisation concerned to protect civil liberties across Europe (www.poptel.org.uk/state-watch).

Contract law

Useful is www.oup.com/uk/orc/bin/9780199207169/, the companion website to Mindy Chen Wishart's textbook on contract law. It provides users with updates on recent developments in contract law, as well as a lot of other useful information and suggestions on issues and questions relating to contract law.

>

Restitution law and property law

The law of restitution is concerned with situations where A has obtained a benefit either from B, or by committing a legal wrong to B, and B wants to sue A for the value of that benefit. By far the best website on this area of law is Steve Hedley's restitution law website: www.ucc.ie/law/restitution/restitution.htm. If you click on the 'Articles' section on the website, you'll find an entire section devoted to articles on property law. Everyone has to study property law (in the guise of land law, and the law on trusts), so even if you don't study restitution law proper, this site will still have something for you.

International law

An American website called 'International Law Update' provides a monthly newsletter on recent developments in International Law. You have to pay to receive their monthly newsletter, but their archives of newsletters are completely free to access: www.internationallawupdate. com/archives.html. It's also worth keeping an eye on 'Opinio Juris': a forum for discussions on international law and international relations between nine academics. See http://opiniojuris.org/.

Family law

The following website ('Family Law Week') provides free-to-access updates on recent developments in family law (click on 'Articles' and 'Judgments' on the left hand side of the screen): www.familylawweek. co.uk/ site.aspx?i=ho0. There is a blog that accompanies the website which is quite useful: http://flwblog.lawweek.co.uk. The website 'Family Lore Focus' is also helpful: www.familylorefocus.com. Also have a look at the articles on 'Restitution and Family Law' in the 'Articles' section of Steve Hedley's restitution website: www.ucc.ie/ law/restitution/restitution.htm.

Criminology

There are a huge number of useful links on the Internet for someone studying the criminal justice system. Instead of listing them, I'll

>

simply refer you to the British Society of Criminology's list of links at www.britsoccrim.org/links.htm. Also keep an eye on http://coppersblog. blogspot.com/ for insights into what policing in the UK is really like.

European Union law

Go to http://eulaw.typepad.com/eulawblog/ for regular updates and incisive commentary on recent developments in EU law. You can also get information about recent European-related news from http://euobserver.com/. A huge amount of information about European Community law, and the workings of European Community institutions can be found at: http://europa.eu/index_en.htm.

Jurisprudence

You should have a look at the companion website to Raymond Wacks' *Understanding Jurisprudence*, if only for his tips on studying jurisprudence (www.oup.com/uk/orc/bin/9780199532124/). A couple of blogs worth keeping an eye on for useful updates on recent articles and books on jurisprudence are run respectively by Larry Solum (http://lsolum.typepad.com/legaltheory/) and Brian Leiter (http://leiterlegalphilosophy.typepad.com/leiter). While Wikipedia won't be of any real help to you for most of your legal studies (because it won't tell you anything that you can't find in your textbooks – and in almost all cases it will tell you a lot less than you can find in your textbooks), it is worth regularly consulting http://en.wikipedia.org/wiki/ while studying Jurisprudence. Wikipedia can give you a lot of useful and clearly written information on the legal philosophers and political/economic/legal concepts that you have to work with in studying Jurisprudence, when plunging straight into the set reading can make you feel disorientated and lost. For the same reasons, it's also worth consulting the Internet Encylopedia of Philosophy (www.iep.utm.edu) and the Stanford Encyclopedia of Philosophy (http://plato.stanford.edu/search/searcher.py) – though the latter is only free to access over a University network.

● Update websites

A lot of the above websites will give you updates on specific areas of law, but there are also some websites which will provide you with updates on recent developments in the law generally. Particularly good is www. lawupdates.co.uk – you should definitely keep a regular eye on that site. It is also worth registering with www.linexlegal.com – doing so allows you to receive updates via e-mail on UK law (and also EU Competition Law, if you happen to be studying that). While it's mainly aimed at professionals, some of the material it carries will be of interest to students. If you are studying tort law or contract law it is a good idea to apply to join the 'Obligations Discussion Group': www.ucc.ie/law/odg/home.htm. A lot of academics belong to this discussion group, and every time anyone posts up a comment on a recent case, or a particular issue affecting contract law or tort law, everyone belonging to the discussion group receives the comment via e-mail. It's a good way of keeping up to date on recent developments in private law, and sometimes (if a discussion gets going) you can get a lot of interesting information and ideas about particular areas of private law from very distinguished academics. But don't abuse the discussion group! If you are allowed to join, do NOT bother everyone else with posts saying things like: 'Hi guys! Got to do an essay on liability for omissions. Any suggestions?'

● UK government websites

The following law-related websites are maintained by the UK government, or bodies funded by the UK government:

The Law Commission

Go to: www.lawcom.gov.uk. The Law Commission is charged by the government with the job of recommending statutory reforms to the law where the law has become out of date or inconsistent or unprincipled. Its website provides a useful source of summaries of, and comments on, the law as it is at the moment.

>

The Charity Commission

Go to: www.charity-commission.gov.uk. The Charity Commission ensures that charities in the UK are properly run. The Charities Act 2006 gives the Charity Commission the effective power to confiscate the assets of any charity that cannot satisfy the Charity Commission that it is run for the 'public benefit'. It remains to be seen whether this terrifyingly totalitarian power will be exercised wisely.

The Equality and Human Rights Commission

Go to: www.equalityhumanrights.com/en/Pages/default.aspx. The Equality and Human Rights Commission attempts to ensure that institutions and employers comply with human rights and anti-discrimination legislation, as well as recommending improvements to that legislation.

Office of Fair Trading

Go to: www.oft.gov.uk. The Office of Fair Trading, which is concerned to ensure fair competition in the marketplace, as well as having the power under the Unfair Terms in Consumer Contracts Regulations 1999 to instruct companies to remove terms that are 'unfair' from their standard form contracts with consumers.

◉ Reports of cases (non-UK)

Cases decided in Commonwealth countries

Cases decided in Commonwealth countries like Australia or Canada can be of great interest to English lawyers, as the legal systems of countries that used to belong to the British Empire (including the United States) are rooted in English law. A huge number of Australian cases are free to access on www.austlii.edu.au/databases.html. Judgments of the Supreme Court of Canada can be accessed here: http://scc.lexum.umontreal.ca/en/. For other Canadian cases, try www.commonlii.org/databases.html#country:canada.

>

Decisions of the European Court of Human Rights

Under s. 2(1)(a) of the Human Rights Act 1998, whenever a UK court has to decide whether UK law violates, or a public body has violated, someone's rights as set out in the European Convention on Human Rights (ECHR), the court is required to take into account the decisions of the European Court of Human Rights (ECtHR). So these decisions are of fundamental importance in determining whether someone can complain that their rights under the ECHR have been violated. You can access the decisions of the ECtHR here: www.bailii.org/eu/cases/ECHR/.

EU law

If you are studying EU law (or European Community law), you have to read cases decided by the European Court of Justice (ECJ), which determines what EU law requires of the various member states of the European Union. You can access decisions of the ECJ here: www.bailii.org/eu/cases/EUECJ/. The official website of the ECJ is http://curia.europa.eu/en/transitpage.htm and contains reports of all decisions of the ECJ, as well as information on where you can find casenotes on those decisions.

International law

It's not generally a good idea to read cases on international law in undigested form, as they are usually huge. But just for completeness, here's the link to judgments of the International Court of Justice (which has the power to decide disputes between states that consent to be bound by its judgments, and the power to determine issues of international law that are referred to it by the United Nations): www.icj-cij.org/homepage/index.php?lang=en.

○ Online lectures

A lot of universities now video their lectures and put them up on free-to-access websites. If you go to http://lecturefox.com/, it will give you a list of links to online lectures on a huge number of different subjects. There aren't currently any legal lectures listed on this website – but there are lectures on issues in political theory that may give you a deeper understanding of law in general, and topics in jurisprudence in particular. And if you want to broaden your mind and cultivate or keep up an interest in a subject that has nothing to do with law – such as nuclear physics – then going onto this website is a very good way of doing it.

● *Festschriften*

I mentioned in my previous letter that there is now a searchable database of papers published in legal *festschriften* ('The Index to Common Law Festschriften') that is always worth using to hunt down papers that have been published on a particular subject you are studying. Here's the address again: http://magic.lbr.auckland.ac.nz/festschrift/.

So those are all the relevant free-to-access websites that I know about, and that will help you with your studies. My advice would be to go onto the Internet, create some new 'Favourites' folders using the above headings, and then enter all of these websites into the appropriate folders so that they will be just one click away if you want to get hold of them at some point in the future. It will take you about 30 minutes to do this, and save you a huge amount of time in the future.

Best wishes,

Nick

Getting the Most Out of Your Teachers

- From: Nicholas J. McBride [dearnick@pearson.com]
- To: Brown, Jo
- Subject: Getting the Most Out of Your Teachers

Hey Jo,

This is the final letter I'll write to you about how to study law. We've already covered how to use textbooks, read cases, look at statutes, make notes on articles, and use the Internet. So the only thing that remains for me to write to you about is how you should approach lectures and having small group teaching sessions with your teachers.

● A preliminary point

Before I get onto that, I want to emphasise one point. I once read somewhere that the difference between school and university is that at school you are a *pupil* and at university you are a *student*. Pupils learn by being *taught*, while students learn by *studying* – by finding out things for themselves. The distinction holds especially true of law students – as I said in a previous letter, law is probably the most self-taught subject that you can study at university. So you shouldn't rely too much on lectures and small-group teaching sessions as a vehicle for finding out about the law. You should rather regard lectures and small-group teaching sessions as providing you with opportunities to pick up useful titbits of information and to test out your blossoming legal skills.

But you mustn't misunderstand me. I don't want to encourage you to skip lectures and the small-group teaching sessions that have been laid on for you. While they are not an essential component of your legal education, they provide a very useful service that you should take full advantage of. But please remember that it is how much work you put in on your own – or in conjunction with your fellow students – that will determine how well you do in your exams, not how many lectures you have been to. If you are spending 60 per cent of your 'working time' as a law student at lectures and small-group teaching sessions, and only 40 per cent of the remaining time working on your own or with your fellow students – then you are in trouble. You are not giving yourself enough of an opportunity to develop as a law student by working away at the law yourself, rather than having it spoon-fed to you by your teachers. A healthier distribution of your working time that you should aim for is: spend 70 per cent of your 'working time' studying on your own, or with your fellow students, and only 30 per cent of your time attending lectures or small-group teaching sessions. If your university has laid on so many lectures for you to attend that this is impractical, think about splitting up the lectures with your fellow students so that you can cut down on the number of lectures you have to attend in person.

◉ Lectures

Okay – let's get on with some guidance as to what you should be doing in lectures. Basically, you should be looking to make notes of points that will make useful additions to your secondary materials and your cases and statutes files. So keep your ears open for:

> ### Summaries of cases
>
> These can be really useful, particularly if the lecturer is talking about a case which is very difficult to understand. Lecturers will usually work really hard to make cases comprehensible to the students that they are lecturing to – if only because it's really embarrassing for a lecturer to speak to an audience that is looking at her with blank incomprehension. If a lecturer is explaining a case and some aspect of his or her explanation seems particularly obscure, *do not hesitate*
>
> >

to stick your hand up and ask him to express himself more clearly. Some lecturers don't like to be interrupted by questions (though personally I welcome it – as I have already made clear, asking questions is much the most effective way of finding out about a subject). But you shouldn't care about that – your lecturers are working for you, not the other way around. If you want to ask a question, you have a right to ask it and have it answered.

Summaries of articles

Again, these are very useful – a really good summary of what an article says can make the actual article a breeze to read through subsequently. I should emphasise that if an article has been summed up very effectively in a lecture, I wouldn't advise skipping the article in your subsequent reading, on the basis that you already know what it says. However effective the summary, it is only a summary and there may be more in the actual article that you may find worth taking a note on – perhaps a summary of a case, or an interesting argument.

Evaluations of the law

It is always useful to note what your lecturer thinks of a particular area of the law – and what arguments she makes in support of her views.

Hints as to what will be in the exam

Obviously these are *very* useful – but hard to pick up. No lecturer is going to stand up and say, 'There is going to be a question on this subject in the exam'. However, if your lecturer is involved in setting the paper, and spends a lot of time talking about a particular subject or issue, then it's worth making a note of that fact and giving that subject or issue special attention in your revision.

Aids to remembering cases

You should also be looking to take notes on any 'story lines' that you can make use of to remember a string of cases, following the advice I gave you in my letter on 'Reading Cases and Statutes'. So – make notes of any general principles that the lecturer has identified as underlying a number of cases, or any speculations that the lecturer has as to why a number of cases were decided the way they were.

You *shouldn't* be looking to make notes on the following:

1 *Statements of basic legal rules.* Suppose your lecturer says, 'A defendant will have the *mens rea* of murder if he has an intention to kill or an intention to cause grievous bodily harm.' There's absolutely no point in your making a note of that. Your textbook reading will tell you that – so why wear out your hand trying to scribble this piece of information down in the middle of the lecture? It would be better to put your pen down and give your hand a rest and wait for the lecturer to tell you something that you won't necessarily find in a textbook.

This takes me onto a more general point. If your lecturer on a particular subject isn't telling you anything that you couldn't find in a textbook, then you should stop going to her lectures. This is for a very simple reason: you can read faster than your lecturer can talk. So you would make better use of the hour that the lecture will last reading a textbook rather than attending the lecture. You will find out more in that hour by reading the textbook than you will by attending the lecture.

2 *History.* Lecturers often like to preface their discussion of a particular area of law with a quick run through of the history of that area. So, for example, if you are being lectured by your tort law lecturer on the law on 'Occupiers' Liability', he may well spend a bit of time talking about what the law said before the Occupiers' Liability Acts of 1957 and 1984 were enacted. Making notes on this is a complete waste of time. You are interested in what the law says *now*, not in what it said 50 or 20 years ago. You are interested in what reforms should be made to the law as it is *now*, not in what reforms were made to the law as it was 50 or 20 years ago.

Having said that, history does have its place. As I've said before, it can help you to remember a string of cases if you see them as part of some historical trend or pattern. Arguments that a particular reform to the law has proved unsuccessful and that the law should return to where it was before that reform was implemented are always interesting and worth noting. But if the lecturer is talking about the history of a particular area of law for no other reason than as a way of introducing that area of law, or because he or she is loath to abandon a set of carefully composed lecture notes that have been made completely redundant by a recent reform, then put your pen down and give yourself a rest.

When a lecture is over, take the notes that you have made on the lecture and use them to make fresh notes in the appropriate places in your case files and in your secondary materials files. This will serve a number of useful purposes:

- Your lecture notes are likely to be quite scruffy and messy – making fresh notes will mean you don't have to rely on your lecture notes.

- Making fresh notes will help you remember in the long-term what was said in the lectures.

- Making fresh notes will give you a chance to look over your lecture notes and see how many of the lecture notes you made actually seem, on reflection, worth entering into your files. If the answer is 'Not many', you are taking too many notes in the lectures and you need to be more discriminating in your note taking.

Small group teaching sessions

That's all I have to say about taking notes in lectures. What about small-group teaching sessions? Any university will arrange for these to take place throughout the year, in parallel with the lectures, as a way of checking the progress you are making as a law student and giving you an opportunity to raise any concerns or questions that you might have about the subjects you are studying. The advice I can give you on these sessions is quite limited because I have no idea what format they will take. However, whatever format they take, the following advice should always hold good:

Be prepared

You won't get anything out of your small-group teaching sessions if you aren't prepared for them. If you're not prepared for a small-group teaching session, then it will turn into a small ordeal for you.

>

You'll be lost, confused, and praying desperately that you aren't called upon to speak – and every minute of the session will seem like ten minutes. Why put yourself through that kind of torture? Come prepared and then you can make the most of the session and actually get something out of it. And if you're not prepared – for whatever reason – it's far better to admit that and ask if you can come along to a later session than put yourself through the agony of sitting in the session, pretending to be better prepared than you are.

Ask questions

Try and take advantage of any small-group teaching session that you attend to get whoever's holding the session to answer your questions about the area of law that you'll be focusing on in the session. So come to the teaching session armed with a list of questions that you want answered. Make sure you have actually got a list – don't rely on your memory to tell you that you have such-and-such a question to ask. The pressure of a small-group teaching session means that your memory will often fail you.

Take your books and notes along

That last point takes me onto a separate point. A small-group teaching session isn't a memory test – so take your textbooks and your notes along to the session so that you can consult them in the course of a general discussion of a particular legal point.

Make notes

When I hold small-group teaching sessions with first-year students, I notice that a lot of them don't take notes when I'm talking to them. This could be because they think that what I'm saying is rubbish. However, I find that hard to believe. More likely explanations are *either* (i) they think that they'll be able to remember what I'm saying without making a note of it; *or* (ii) they think that I'd be offended if they took their eyes off me and started writing in their notebook while I was talking.

Neither of these things are true. On (i), unless a student is blessed with an absolutely exceptional memory, he or she will not be able to remember very much of what was said in a small-group teaching session unless he or she has made good notes of what was said. On (ii), there is no way any of your teachers will be offended if you make notes on what they are saying as they are saying it – they are far more likely to be offended if they make some really brilliant argument and their students just stare at them and don't make any notes to help them remember the pearls of wisdom that have just been scattered before them.

As to what you should be making notes on, what I said in connection with lectures also applies here – you should be looking to make notes of points that will make useful additions to your topic and case files. And when the small-group teaching session is over, you should take your notes and use them to enter a set of fresh notes at appropriate points in your topic and case files.

Exercise your right of freedom of speech

I've already made this point in an earlier letter, but I'll repeat it here: *do not* be inhibited about speaking up in small-group teaching sessions. If there is some point you are unclear on, do say: I don't understand this, could you help me? You're not going to get another opportunity to get some help on clearing up that point – so why not take advantage of it?

Don't be put off asking a question because you think, 'I'll look like an idiot if I ask about that'. You probably won't: your question is likely to be a really good one, and everyone else in your teaching group will profit from having your question answered. And even if you do look like an idiot, so what? It's good for you to make yourself look like an idiot once in a while. It'll stop you being arrogant, which is never an attractive quality. It'll make everyone else feel better about themselves – they'll think, 'Oh, at least I'm not doing as badly as Jo'. And it'll make everyone else feel a bit more comfortable about asking questions themselves – they'll think, 'Well, it might be a bit embarrassing to ask this question, but at least I won't be embarrassed as badly as Jo was.' *Don't ever* leave a small-group teaching session thinking, 'Oh, I wish I'd asked that.' Nothing is worth that kind of regret.

>

Make the most of the opportunities that small-group teaching sessions give you

This is pretty obvious advice, but worth giving nonetheless. Make the most of your small-group teaching sessions.

Suppose that you are being taken for small-group teaching sessions in a particular area of law by Professor White, who is a renowned scholar in that area of law. Use your time with Professor White to get her to talk about her views – not only her views about the area of law she specialises in, but also her views of what other academics have to say about that area of law.

Suppose alternatively that you'll be expected to submit an essay in advance of a particular small-group teaching session with Professor Black – the session will then be used to talk about people's essays and how they might be improved. Try and make your essay the best it can possibly be so you can take full advantage of any feedback you will get from Professor Black in the session on how your essay might have been improved. Don't come up with an average piece of work which will be returned to you with some really obvious criticisms that even you knew could be made of your essay.

Again, suppose that in a small-group teaching session with Professor Green you'll be considering what the law says in a particular fact situation. Prepare well for the session by thinking of as many points as you can that might be made about that situation. Then in the session, make those points – and learn from what Professor Green has to say about them. Also use the opportunity provided by the small-group session to get some guidance from Professor Green about how one should approach the task of writing about problem situations in the exams – what are the examiners looking for you to do? What are they not looking for you to do?

Remember that the more you put into a small-group teaching session, the more you will get out of it. Even if you are being taught by an academic who has *zero* interest in teaching you, he or she will not fail to respond to the interest you show in getting the most out of your session with him or her. He or she will soon 'warm up' and start giving of his or her best for you.

>

Be nice

This is a point that I've made before, but I'll make it again – be warm, bubbly and enthusiastic in your small-group teaching sessions. No one enjoys teaching a surly or uncommunicative student and even the most dedicated teacher will soon lose interest in doing anything for you if you persistently come to his or her small-group sessions with a bad attitude. Of course, if you're feeling down on a particular day when you have a small-group teaching session, it's okay to make that clear – but your normal attitude in going into a small-group teaching session should be positive, friendly and outgoing.

That's enough advice from me. Hope your studies are going well. Keep in touch – I hope you'll let me know how you are getting on.

All the best,

Nick

PART 4

Preparing for Your Exams

How to Write an Essay

19

- From: Nicholas J. McBride [dearnick@pearson.com]
- To: Brown, Jo
- Subject: How to Write an Essay

Hi Jo,

Thanks very much for the copy of your first ever legal essay! I'll try to get round to commenting on it in a bit, but in the meantime, here are some rules for writing essays that you should always observe.

● Don't be lazy

This is the most fundamental rule. Writing good essays involves a lot of effort. A really good essay will look as though it was effortless to write – but that is an illusion, produced by the fact that a really good essay will be effortless to read. Being able to write a good essay is a skill, just like being able to play the piano is a skill – and just as you can't learn to play the piano overnight, neither can you write good essays just like that. Learning to write good essays takes time, and self-discipline, and constant practice – and all that *is* hard. And that is the single most important reason why a lot of students never learn to write good essays – they are not willing to take the time and put in the work required to acquire that skill. But it is vital for your long-term future that you not follow their example. How you do in your exams will depend crucially on how good you are at writing essays. And how you do in your exams will affect everything about your future – what sort of job you can get, how happy you will be in your work, how much money you will earn, who your friends will be in the future, whether you will get married and, if so, to whom. It's incredible to think that all of that depends on whether you are, or are not, willing to observe the rules set out below. But it does.

● Answer the question

This is the second most fundamental rule. It seems such a simple and straightforward rule, and such an obvious one as well – but it is amazing how often students fail to observe this rule. I was talking some time ago to a colleague of mine about her experience marking essays that students had written for a particular exam. She must have marked over 200 students' papers. She told me that only *three* of those students actually tried to answer the question in writing their essays. Incredible, but true. But the fact that so few students actually bother to answer the question in writing an essay gives you a big advantage: if you make the effort in writing an essay to actually answer the question, your essay will automatically look really good compared with everyone else's.

So – suppose you are given the following essay to write:

> 'The law on homicide is in a mess.' Discuss.

This is what we call a **discursive** essay – an essay that asks you to evaluate a particular area of the law. This is the most common sort of essay you might be asked to write. (The other kind of essay that you might be asked to write is a **descriptive** essay – an essay setting out the key elements of a particular area of the law. An example of a descriptive essay would be: 'When will one person be held liable in tort for failing to rescue another?') So, this essay is asking you to say whether or not the law on homicide (which deals with when someone will be criminally punished for causing another's death) is in a mess or not, and to present some arguments in favour of your view. And that's precisely what you should do – make up your mind whether or not you are going to say that the law on homicide is in a mess, and then come up with some arguments in favour of your point of view. But many students don't do that – they don't answer the question. Instead they turn their essay into a descriptive essay and spend

90 per cent of their time setting out what the law on homicide says. (They usually excuse themselves for doing so by first saying, 'Before we can address this issue, it is first necessary to set out the law on homicide . . .' *Whenever* you find yourself writing 'it is first necessary . . .' ask yourself: Am I drifting off the point here? The answer will almost always be 'yes'.) They then realise that actually they were supposed to be writing a discursive essay on whether the law on homicide is in a mess and try to rescue the essay by saying in the very last paragraph 'So, as we can see, the law on homicide is [is not] in a mess . . .' when that is the very last thing we can see from what has been said so far. *Of course*, in writing an essay on whether the law on homicide is in a mess, you are going to have to talk about what the law on homicide currently says, but *in the context* of a discussion of whether the law on homicide is in a mess. So a good response to the following question might start:

> The law on homicide is in a mess – it is unclear, inconsistent, and serves no rational purpose.

And then all you need to do for the rest of the essay is come up with *examples* of the law on homicide's being unclear, inconsistent and serving no rational purpose. You don't need to set out the *whole* of the law on homicide to do this – you just have to switch a flashlight on *elements* of the law that help demonstrate your overall point.

This second most fundamental rule – that in writing an essay, you should answer the question – has a sub-rule: in writing an essay, you should *only* answer the question. Don't drift off the point for a second. If you are set an essay on a particular topic, and given some reading to do on that topic, there is a great temptation to try to refer to *all* the things that you have been told to read on that topic in your essay. Resist that temptation: only bring into your essay cases and articles that are relevant to the point you are making in your essay. If you approach an essay thinking, 'I *should* mention the case of *X* v *Y*, and I *must* get in somewhere a reference to Professor X's interesting argument that . . .' then you are flirting with disaster: it's very likely that your essay will just turn into an unfocused, messy hodge-podge of observations and arguments. When you are writing an essay on a particular topic, work out what you are going to respond to the question that has been set and then focus like a laser on making out what you want to say. It doesn't matter if a lot of interesting stuff that you've read about is left unsaid – the agony of not being able to show off to the reader just how much you know about your subject is the price you have to pay for writing a really good essay.

○ Write clearly

Again, this is such an obvious rule, but it is very rare for students to make the effort to observe it. An infallible way of telling whether you are writing clearly enough is to employ what I call the '**friend test**'. Imagine that a friend has asked you the question that you are responding to in writing your essay. Would your friend understand what you are saying? If the answer is no, you have failed the 'friend test' and you are not writing clearly enough.

The two most common causes of unclear writing are: being in a hurry, and over-complication. Students often fail to write clearly because they are in too much of a hurry to take the time to make some sense of what they want to say. This is *particularly* the case, I find, when students write about cases. For example, consider the following:

> An example of the courts forcing people to act in good faith is the *Interfoto* case, where the defendants did not have to pay the extra charge because they had not been warned about it.

Would anyone reading this have much of a clue as to what happened in the *Interfoto* case? What makes this sort of bad writing completely unforgiveable is that it is just so unnecessary – there is absolutely no reason why the student who wrote this had to rush over the facts of the *Interfoto* case. They could easily have written:

> There are many cases which can be interpreted as examples of situations where the courts have required people to act in good faith
>
> >

when contracting with other people. For example, in the case of *Interfoto Picture Library* v *Stiletto Visual Programme*, the defendants hired some slides from the claimants. The small print in the claimants' standard terms said that if the defendants did not return the slides on time, they would have to pay the claimants £5 per slide for every extra day they kept them. This term was not brought to the defendants' attention. The defendants returned the slides 13 days late and were sent a bill for £3,000 as a result. The Court of Appeal held the defendants did not have to pay the bill. One way of looking at this case is that the Court of Appeal took the view that the claimants had acted in bad faith in failing to draw such an onerous term to the defendants' attention, and should not be allowed to profit from this.

Isn't that much clearer? But don't think it's clearer just because I wrote it. You don't need to be particularly clever to write as clearly as this: the only reason our student didn't write this is that he/she wasn't willing to take the time to do so.

As I've just said, the second reason why students often fail to write clearly is that their essays are over-complicated. They try and make points that are far too subtle and difficult to make out convincingly. The best essays are quite simple in what they have to say. You should be able to reduce what you want to say in your essay down to a five or six sentence 'soundbite'. If you can't, then your essay is too complicated to be worth writing, and you should rethink your essay. Some academics might be horrified at this advice, but they aren't trying to do what you have to do. They have the luxury of writing an article on a particular topic, or an entire book. In an exam, you will probably have about 45 minutes or an hour to write a convincing essay on a particular issue. You can't afford to act like an academic in that sort of situation. The following advice – given by an Oxford Fellow, Bruce McFarlane, to a student in 1956 who was just about to sit his history exams – has always struck me as completely correct:

It's no use treating an examination as if it were the Last Judgment; your scrupulous weighing of the pros and cons, your unwillingness

>

> to decide, would be admirable . . . if you were writing serious history. [But you're] not supposed to be doing that; you're supposed to be showing how clever you are or aren't, and it's absolutely suicidal to be modest, unsure, diffident or muddled . . . You've got to have a fairly simple, fairly plausible, intelligible 'attitude' and you've got to plug it confidently.

So, if you have to write a discursive essay on a particular topic, try and think of a simple and straightforward 'line' (but still interesting) that you can take in response to that essay question and avoid like the plague any temptation to depart from that line or overcomplicate it. Similarly, if you have to write a descriptive essay on a particular area of the law, try to think of a very straightforward and simple way of setting out the law – for example, presenting the law as the product of a clash of two competing principles or philosophies, or presenting the law as giving effect to one or two very simple ideas.

And when you write your essay, do everything you *possibly* can to make your essay easy to follow. Make sure that the first paragraph makes it clear what you are going to say in the rest of the essay. Don't make your essay into the equivalent of a conjuring trick where what you are saying is only revealed (ta-da!) at the end of the essay. If you have three points to make, number them: (1) . . . (2) . . . (3). And make sure it's clear that these *are* three *different* points, and that points (1) and (2) aren't the same points just written in different ways – don't force the reader to do the work of figuring out why points (1) and (2) are actually different points. If your essay has a number of different parts (for example, one part of your essay sets out a number of different arguments in favour of the overall point you are making, while another part considers an argument that is commonly made against the point you are making and shows why that argument doesn't stand up), then use headings to distinguish the different sections of your essay.

○ Use concrete examples

A great aid to writing clearly – and also writing succinctly – is to use concrete examples. For example, suppose you have been set the following essay:

> 'There is no reason why constitutional conventions should not have the force of law; in fact, some constitutional conventions already do.' Discuss.

(Just in case you haven't covered constitutional conventions yet, examples of constitutional conventions are:

1 that the Monarch will only dissolve Parliament 'early' on the advice of the Prime Minister;

2 that the Monarch will not refuse assent to a Bill that has been passed by both Houses of Parliament;

3 that the Prime Minister will resign or seek a dissolution of Parliament if his party loses a vote of confidence in the House of Commons;

4 that a member of the Cabinet will not question the correctness of a decision reached by the Cabinet as a whole without first resigning his position as a member of the Cabinet;

5 that the Prime Minister will not disclose to other people the advice he/she has received from the Monarch at one of his/her weekly meetings with the Monarch;

6 that if the current Speaker of the House of Commons is a Labour MP, the next Speaker will not be a Labour MP.)

Suppose, in writing the descriptive part of the essay (whether some constitutional conventions have the force of law), which I would advise you to do first (there's no reason why, in considering the issues raised by an essay title, you should consider them in the order in which they have been raised by the essay title if it would make more sense to do them in a different order), you want to argue:

> 1 constitutional conventions do not have the force of law because the courts will not award any remedy or impose any kind of sanction in response to the *mere* fact that a constitutional convention has been departed from; and
>
> >

> 2 if the courts do award a remedy or impose a sanction when a constitutional convention is departed from that is because the person who has departed from that convention has in doing so breached some independent rule (such as that statutory powers should not be exercised in a way which is wholly unreasonable, or that people should not disclose information imparted to them in confidence) that does have the force of law.

This is pretty abstract stuff that can be made a lot easier to understand by bringing it down to earth through a concrete example. For example, you could consider what could happen if the Prime Minister leaked to a newspaper information about what the Queen had told him at their last weekly meeting, and make the point that if the Prime Minister was successfully sued for damages by the Queen, that would not be because he had breached a constitutional convention in leaking the details of their conversation to the newspapers, but because in leaking that information he breached an independent legal rule that says that if A tells B something in confidence, then A is not allowed to disclose that information to a third party unless it is in the public interest to do so.

Again, suppose in writing the discursive part of the essay (whether constitutional conventions should have the force of law) you want to argue that constitutional conventions should not have the force of law, because:

> 1 if the courts were to award a remedy or impose a sanction in response to the breach of a constitutional convention, there are only four different kinds of remedies/sanctions that they could award/impose: (i) criminal punishment; (ii) an award of damages; (iii) an injunction; (iv) a declaration that failing to observe the convention was unlawful;
>
> 2 it would be unthinkable – for various constitutional reasons – for the courts to respond to the breach of a constitutional convention in ways (i), (ii) or (iii); and
>
> >

3   if the courts merely responded to the breach of a constitutional convention by issuing a declaration that failing to observe the convention was unlawful, the courts would be brought into disrepute – it would look like the courts were powerless to back up their words ('this action is unlawful . . .') with concrete action ('. . . and we forbid you to do it on pain of being sent to prison if you disregard our order'), or did not seriously mean what they said ('we're saying that this action is unlawful, but not so unlawful that we want to do anything about it').

This is quite a complex point to get across, but focusing on some concrete examples could really help to make what you are saying a lot clearer. For example, you could make out point (2), above, by considering a hypothetical situation where the Prime Minister has refused to resign on losing a vote of confidence in the House of Commons, and show that even if constitutional conventions did have the force of law, the most the courts could possibly do in that situation would be to issue a declaration that the Prime Minister was acting unlawfully in refusing to resign.

The essay on constitutional conventions demonstrates another reason why concrete examples can be so useful. You can sometimes make a particular concept or idea immediately intelligible by drawing an **analogy** with a real-world situation. For example, students sometimes find it difficult to understand what a 'convention' is and what it might mean for a 'convention' to have the 'force of law'. But this difficulty can normally be immediately solved by pointing out that in football, there is a custom that if your team has kicked the ball out to allow an injured player to be treated, once play has resumed with the opposing team taking a throw-in or a goal kick, the opposing team will give the ball back to your team. This custom is like a constitutional convention – it is a practice that is normally observed, and on the few rare occasions that it is not observed, the failure to observe it is severely disapproved of by everyone else. And the question of whether a constitutional convention should have the force of law is analogous to the question of whether the referee in a football game should have the power to punish a side that fails to give back the ball to the other team after the other team has kicked the ball out of play in order to allow an injured player to be treated. So using homely concrete examples like this can be a very good way of making the points you want to make a lot clearer to the reader.

○ Write something interesting

To get a really good mark for an essay, particularly an essay written in an exam, you will *have* to write something interesting. Boring may get you a 2.1 – but it won't get you a First.

So if you are writing a descriptive essay, make the effort to come up with an interesting way of setting out the area of law you've been asked to write about. Think about:

- centring your description of the law around a concrete example that you can constantly refer back to;
- using a table or tables to set out the key elements of the law;
- organising your description of the law around some core principles that (you will argue) the law gives effect to.

But whatever you do, *don't* just repeat what is in the textbook. That is boring – you have *got* to come up with something that is *better* than what is in the textbook. (Which is actually not as hard as it sounds.)

And if you are writing a discursive essay, make the effort to come up with an interesting 'line' in response to the question. In doing so, it's worth thinking about adopting a *contrarian* position, where you adopt a line of argument which goes against the current, fashionable trend of thinking. An essay that takes that kind of line will automatically be much more interesting than an essay which just repeats the well-worn arguments that everyone else has been making for years, and as a result have a much better chance of getting a First than the second kind of essay. (If you don't believe me, I strongly recommend you either read Alan Bennett's play *The History Boys* or watch the DVD.) But don't be contrarian just for the sake of it. Only adopt a line of argument that goes against the current orthodoxy if you actually believe in that line of argument – if your essay lacks conviction, that will be pretty clear and your essay will suffer for it. Also be aware that the person marking/reading your essay may well be a true believer in the current orthodoxy, and will take some convincing that your argument is correct. So make sure, if you do adopt a contrarian position in your essay, that you take time to consider the strongest possible arguments *in favour* of the current orthodoxy and then show how those arguments do not stand up. Note that I said: 'the *strongest* possible arguments . . .' If you try to pull a fast one and put up some really weak (what are called 'straw man') arguments against your position, that isn't going to impress anyone and your easy knock-outs will be rewarded with a pretty poor mark.

Two qualifications need to be made to what I've just said. First, don't adopt a contrarian position in writing an essay if doing so will require you to do the impossible. For example, let's go back to the essay on whether the law on homicide is in a mess. Okay – now everyone thinks that the law on homicide is in a mess, so it *would* make for an interesting essay to argue that the law on homicide is, in fact, in perfect working order. However, it's impossible to argue that effectively, because to do that you would have to go through the entire law on homicide and argue that every single element of the law makes perfect sense. It's just not possible to do that in an essay. You could maybe do that in a book – but in an essay there simply isn't the space to make your essay convincing. So if you are going to do an essay on whether the law on homicide is in a mess, you won't have a choice about what line you will take in response to that question. You will *have* to argue that the law is in a mess – and make your essay interesting through the points you come up with to show that the law is in a mess.

Secondly, don't adopt a contrarian position in an exam essay if the exam essay expressly excludes you from adopting such a position. For instance, a few years back, I was pretty confident that my tort students would get an essay asking them to talk about what's called the 'rule in *Rylands* v *Fletcher*' (which basically says that if you bring a dangerous thing onto your land, and it escapes, and does damage to your neighbour's land, you'll be liable for that damage even if you weren't at fault for the escape) – there had been a very big and recent case on that rule, and examiners often set questions around recent developments in the law. (We'll talk about that some other time.) Not many people think very much of the rule in *Rylands* v *Fletcher*, so I gave the students some arguments *in favour* of the rule, so that they could write an interesting essay on it if it came up, instead of a boring '*Rylands* v *Fletcher* is rubbish' essay. So – come the day of the exam, there was indeed an essay on *Rylands* v *Fletcher* on the paper, but it was a quote from an Australian judge saying that the rule in *Rylands* v *Fletcher* should be abolished and then after that, the question said something like, 'In light of this, critically assess the decision of the House of Lords in *Transco plc* v *Stockport MBC*' (which decision had upheld the existence of the rule in *Rylands* v *Fletcher* in English law). So anyone wanting to say that the rule in *Rylands* v *Fletcher* was a good thing was left nowhere to go – the examiner was basically saying, 'I want you to trash the rule in *Rylands* v *Fletcher* (and the decision of the House of Lords in *Transco*) for 45 minutes.' So it just wasn't possible to write a contrarian essay in response to that particular question.

If your essay is going to be non-contrarian in nature and argue in favour of a position that pretty much everyone agrees with, you can still make it interesting enough to stand out from the crowd by making as strong a case in your essay as you can *against* the position you are arguing for, and then demolishing that case. So, for example, suppose that you are writing an essay which is aiming ultimately to argue that prison doesn't work (whatever that means). The most interesting way of doing this essay is to set out as carefully as you can the strongest arguments that can possibly be made *for* the position that prison works, and then do a really great demolition job on those arguments. Again, remember that this kind of essay will only be as strong as the arguments that you set out to demolish, so don't succumb to the temptation to confine yourself to considering the weakest arguments against your position.

One final point about writing interesting essays: if you are writing a discursive essay to be marked by a supervisor or a tutor, or simply for practice, it's essential that you *go beyond* the reading list, and have a look to see whether there are any other articles or short books that you haven't been referred to, but which are relevant to the essay. The more ideas and arguments you expose yourself to, the more likely it is that you will be able to come up with an interesting line in response to the essay question that you have been set. If you just stick with what you've been told to read, then it's not very likely that you will have anything interesting to say in response to the essay question – you'll just be repeating what you've read in articles that are really well-known and familiar. So the very first thing you should do when you've been asked to write a discursive essay on a particular topic is do a Google search of terms relevant to the essay and see what's 'out there' on the Internet that might be relevant to your essay. Of course, you'll turn up a lot of irrelevant stuff – but just an hour's searching should turn up some very useful material. And following all the other advice I gave you, in my letter on reading articles, on how to find other articles relevant to your studies should help you turn up further material that is relevant to the essay you are planning to write.

● The first paragraph is *vital*

Your first paragraph has a bigger influence on what final mark you get for an exam essay than any other part of the essay. To see why this is, you've got to understand a bit about how essays are marked.

The final mark you get for an exam essay will be a percentage mark – usually, 70 per cent or more is a First Class mark, between 60 and 70 per cent is a 2.1, between 50 per cent and 60 per cent is a 2.2, and beyond that it will depend on the particular university you are at what the boundary is between a Third and a Fail. (Of course, I hope you'll never have to worry about where that boundary is.) Now – while the mark you get is a percentage mark, the examiner *won't* mark your essay by giving you points as he/she reads your essay, and then give you a percentage mark by seeing how many points you got compared with a notional maximum number of points that you might have got for your essay. No – this is how it works.

The examiner will form a view on reading your essay whether it is a First Class essay, a 2.1 essay, a 2.2 essay, or worse than that. Having formed this view, the examiner will then ask him/herself: was it a high or a low First/2.1/2.2/whatever? And if he/she thinks it was a First Class essay (it answered the question, was interesting, had good arguments), but not a high First (but it didn't blow my mind), you'll get 71 or 72 per cent. If on the other hand, he/she thinks it was not only a First Class essay but a really high First (it was the best essay I've ever read on this subject), you could get 80–85 per cent for an essay like that. (Only God gets more than 85 per cent for an essay – don't ask why; that's just the way it is.) Similarly if he/she thinks it was a 2.1 essay (it was okay, not very interesting), but a low 2.1 (the arguments seemed to be a bit flimsy, failed to mention a couple of relevant cases) then you'll get 62 or 63 per cent for that. If, on the other hand, he/she thinks it was a high 2.1 (the arguments were pretty solid, and the essay mentioned the relevant cases) then you could get 68 or 69 per cent for that.

Now – note that there is an *absolute gulf* between getting 70 per cent and getting 69 per cent for an essay. Someone who gets 69 per cent for an essay might think – argh, I only just missed a First. Wrong: you didn't *just* miss a First; you were never in with a chance of getting a First. And that's because the overall impression that the examiner got from your essay was that it was *not* First Class quality. It was a 2.1 *at best*. It was a really good 2.1 essay – but it was *never* going to be a First. So whether you get a First or not depends on what overall impression the examiner forms of your essay. And the first paragraph is the most important paragraph of your essay in shaping the overall impression that the examiner forms of your essay.

To see why this is so, let's go back to the essay on whether the law on homicide is in a mess. Let's just look at two alternative first lines:

> A 'The law on homicide is in a mess – it is unclear, inconsistent and serves no rational purpose.'
>
> B 'To address this issue it is first necessary to set out the law on homicide.'

I can tell you for a fact that an examiner reading line (A) will immediately think: 'This is going to be a First Class essay.' And an examiner reading line (B) will immediately think, 'Ugh – 2.1 at best.' It should be pretty obvious why this is. Line (A) tells the examiner: this candidate is going to answer the question, they know what they want to say, and they are going to give me some good arguments in support of their answer. Line (B) tells the examiner: this candidate doesn't really know what to say in response to the essay question and is trying to avoid having to answer it by fleeing to the safety of a boring description of the law.

Now, first impressions are hard to budge. If the examiner starts off thinking that your essay is a First Class essay, then you'll have to do something
seriously wrong somewhere in the rest of the essay to dislodge that first
impression and end up getting a 2.1. If you keep your nose clean and do
what you promised to do in your first line – that is, highlight some elements of the law on homicide that establish that it is unclear, and inconsistent, and serves no rational purpose – then you will get a First at the
end of the essay. (Whether it's a high First or a low First depends on how
great the execution of the essay is.) If, on the other hand, the examiner
starts off thinking that your essay is a 2.1 essay, then you're going to have
do something seriously impressive in the rest of the essay to dislodge that
first impression and get him/her to start thinking that maybe your essay
is a First Class essay after all.

That's why the first paragraph is absolutely vital. And that's why most of
the time you spend writing practice essays should be spent on learning
how to write impressive opening paragraphs – that is, an opening paragraph that makes it clear how you are going to respond to the essay title
and sets the stage for the rest of the essay by introducing the key ideas that
will underlie your response. Some examples:

'The doctrine of consideration is in need of reform.' Discuss

The philosophy underlying the doctrine of consideration is simple
enough: only promises that form part of a commercial deal – what we
can call 'bargain promises' – should be enforced. It is essential that the
courts enforce bargain promises if our society is to enjoy any kind of
sophisticated market economy. In contrast, a gratuitous promise – for
example, A's promise to pay B £100 on his next pay day, or his promise to pay B £100 a year for the rest of her life to reward her for saving
his life, or his promise to waive part of a debt that B owes him – is eco-
nomically 'sterile' and there is consequently no public policy reason
why it should be enforced. Critics of the current state of the doctrine of
consideration reject the idea that only bargain promises are worth en-
forcing. They fall into three camps. (1) 'Social critics' argue that gratuitous promises that have been relied upon should be enforced, in
certain circumstances. (2) 'Libertarian critics' argue that gratuitous

>

promises that were intended to be legally binding should be enforced. (3) 'Economic critics' argue that there are some gratuitous promises that it is important to enforce for the purpose of ensuring the smooth running of our market economy. I will argue that none of these criticisms of the current state of the doctrine of consideration are valid.

'Prison works.' Discuss

The catchphrase 'prison works' is capable of being interpreted in a number of different ways. (1) The prospect of being imprisoned is a more effective deterrent to crime than any other form of punishment available to us. (2) Imprisoning people for serious offences is a more effective way of cutting crime rates than any other form of punishment available to us. (3) Imprisoning people for serious offences is a more cost-effective way of cutting crime rates than any other form of punishment available to us. I will argue that while claim (1) is true, it is also immaterial whether or not (1) is true. I will go on to argue that while claim (2) is untrue, that is also immaterial. What actually matters is whether claim (3) is true. I will argue that claim (3) is not likely to be true. So while prison may 'work' at some level, it does not work at the level that matters to us – cutting crime rates in the most cost-effective manner possible.

When will one person be held liable in tort for failing to rescue another?

The normal rule in English law is that if I fail to save you from harm, you will not be able to sue me in tort for compensation for that harm – no matter how easy it might have been for me to rescue you. However, there are a number of well-established exceptions to that rule. If: (1) I put you in danger of suffering that harm, or (2) I stopped someone else saving you from that harm, or (3) you were harmed by a child or an animal that was initially in my control, or (4) I 'assumed a responsibility' to you to save you from that harm, or (5) you were on my land at the time you suffered that harm, and you suffered that harm because my land was in a dangerous condition, then I will be held liable to compensate you for the harm you suffered if I failed to take reasonable steps to

>

protect you from that harm. There have been attempts to expand the categories of exceptions to the 'no liability for omissions' rule to cover the case where: (6) it was my job, as an employee of the State, to save you from harm. So far there is only tortious liability in situation (6) where I intentionally chose not to save you from harm, knowing that I was required to do so under the terms of my employment: in such a case you could sue me for committing the tort of misfeasance in public office. But in cases where I *carelessly* failed to save you from harm, the current state of the law is that there is no tortious liability (though there may be liability under the Human Rights Act 1998) in situation (6): the general rule of 'no liability for omissions' applies.

○ Make sure your essay stands up to scrutiny

Again, a pretty obvious rule which is routinely ignored by students. Don't make any old point or argument in your essay – make sure that the points and arguments that you do make do not suffer from any obvious flaws. Always ask yourself – Is what I am saying true? What objections could be made to what I'm saying? Do those objections stand up?

For example, take the interpretation of the case of *Interfoto Picture Library* v *Stiletto Visual Programme* that I talked about before.[1] According to this interpretation, in that case the Court of Appeal refused to allow the claimants to charge the defendants £5 a day per slide for returning their slides late because the claimants had acted in bad faith in inserting that charge for late return into their contract with the defendants. But if you were relying on that interpretation of the case to argue that the courts require contracting parties to act in good faith towards each other, you should be asking yourself: Is that interpretation of the *Interfoto* case correct? What objections could be made to it? Do those objections stand up?

So someone who objected to the above interpretation of the *Interfoto* case might argue, 'The Court of Appeal in the *Interfoto* case didn't say to the claimants, "Well – you sure pulled a fast one on the defendants sneaking that term into the contract; but we're not going to allow you to get away with that – we're going to find that that term is unenforceable and of no effect."

---

[1] See pages 258–9.

Instead, they said, "Sadly for you, you never even managed to get the term as to payment for late return of the slides into your contract with the defendants. That term wasn't actually validly incorporated into your contract with the defendants because the defendants didn't think that such a term would be part of their contract with you: while they were happy to deal with you on your standard terms, they never thought that such an onerous term would be part of those terms, and you never told them that it was." So the *Interfoto* decision had nothing to do with sanctioning bad faith behaviour – the Court of Appeal in that case was giving effect to the much more basic idea that you can't be bound by a contract term which you didn't agree to, and which you didn't give the appearance that you were agreeing to.'

Does this objection stand up? If it does, then you *can't* use *Interfoto* as support for the idea that the courts require contracting parties to act in good faith towards each other. You'll have to cast around for some other, stronger, authorities in favour of that view. And if you think you've found them: test them out. Ask again – is there a more plausible interpretation of these cases? Doing this is hard work, but it is essential that you do this work if you are going to construct a solid argument that will stand up to scrutiny.

In testing the arguments that you are making in favour of a particular position that you are taking, look out in particular for whether they are *circular* or *incomplete* or based on a *false premise*. (You may want to look again at my letter on logical arguments at this point.) For example, suppose that you are criticising the law for saying that a teacher does not have a duty to take any steps to stop a child being bullied as she goes home from school. To try to make your discussion of the issue clearer, you wisely follow my earlier advice and introduce a concrete example where B is being consistently bullied on her way home by other people in her class, and A, the class teacher, knows about this but has done nothing to reprimand or discipline the bullies. Now you want to find a way of criticising the law for not holding A liable for failing to protect B. Don't just seize on any old argument in favour of saying the law is deficient. Try to find one that isn't flawed in some obvious way.

Suppose, for example, that you are thinking of arguing: 'The law in this area is deficient because the law should say that A has a duty to take steps to stop B being bullied.' Unfortunately, that's a circular argument. It simply assumes that the point you are trying to establish – that A should have a legal duty to protect B – is correct.

Alternatively, you might think of arguing: 'The law in this area is deficient because B has a right not be bullied.' However, this argument is incomplete. B does have a right *against the bullies* not to be bullied, but that does not establish that she should have a legal right that A take steps to protect her from being bullied.

What if you try to argue, 'The law in this area is deficient because A should protect B from being bullied'? Sadly, again, that argument is incomplete because while we can accept that A should protect B from being bullied, that does not – all on its own – establish that the law should step in to encourage A to do the right thing by imposing a legal duty on her that requires her to take steps to protect B from being bullied.

Trying a different approach, you could try to argue, 'The law in this area is deficient because A should protect B from being bullied, and the law should encourage us to do the right thing.' However, that argument seems to rest on a false premise. It is not at all clear that the law should *always* encourage us to do the right thing. We don't have laws against adultery, or being rude to people, or letting your children down, or failing to rescue strangers who are drowning.

Finally, we come to an argument that actually seems to work: 'The law in this area is deficient. The law should encourage us to do the right thing where doing so will not have any seriously adverse consequences. That is the case here: A should protect B from being bullied, and encouraging A, and other teachers, to do the right thing in this sort of situation will not have any seriously adverse consequences.' This argument isn't circular or incomplete. However, you still have to test it out to see whether it rests on a false premise. You've got to ask yourself whether imposing a legal duty on someone like A to protect someone like B from being bullied may in fact have some seriously adverse consequences.

● Don't avoid a fight

Students sometimes seem to think that if they mention any arguments that run counter to the point that they are trying to make in their essay, that will somehow undermine and weaken their essay. So they just concentrate on the arguments that support their case, and ignore any opposing voices. The truth is quite different: if you don't mention any obvious arguments that run counter to the general thrust of your essay, that will look like a sign of weakness. It will look like you are avoiding dealing with those arguments because you know you have no response to them. A strong essay will make the arguments in favour of its position, and then consider the arguments against its position and demolish those opposing arguments. And again – don't try to pull a fast one by introducing some weaknesses into your opponent's position that will make it much easier for you to dismiss him/her. Doing so will only weaken your essay.

● Pay attention to the details

There's a saying: 'Don't sweat the small stuff.' That is: don't get worried about small things. Please, please do sweat the small stuff when you are writing an essay. Little slips in spelling, grammar and punctuation can create a terrible impression and result in your getting a lower mark than the content of your essay deserves.

So – it's 'Act of Parliament' not 'act of parliament'. And 'it's' always means 'it is' or 'it has'. So never write 'it's' if you *don't* mean to say 'it is' or 'it has'; write 'its' instead. It's the European Court of Human Rights that ultimately decides whether someone's rights under the European Convention on Human Rights have been violated, not the European Court of Justice. Avoid run-on sentences – sentences that squash together two or more different sentences into the same sentence – they make you look illiterate. (See what I did there?) Don't refer to Hoffmann LJ's decision in *Stovin v Wise* – his decision in that case was given in the House of Lords, not the Court of Appeal, and so it was Lord Hoffmann's decision, not Hoffmann LJ's. If you want to refer to the major reason for the decision in a case, talk about the *principal* reason for the decision. If you want to refer to the idea or theory underlying the decision in a case, talk about the *principle* underlying the decision. Defendants in tort cases are *sued* – they are not *prosecuted*. An unsuccessful defendant in a criminal case is found *guilty* of committing a particular offence; he is not held *liable* for committing that offence.

● Don't plagiarise

I can't believe I have to say anything about this, but as plagiarism is a growing concern for university authorities, I guess I should. Plagiarism involves stealing someone else's ideas and passing them off as your own. The 'someone else' is normally an academic who has published a book or an article. Plagiarising an academic's work usually involves either: (1) copying out chunks from his/her book or article into your essay without acknowledging that those chunks did not come from your head, but came from someone else's published work; or (2) setting out an idea or concept that he/she came up with without acknowledging the source of that idea or concept. Plagiarising someone else's work is just dumb, dumb, dumb – and not just because you might be caught out and embarrassed, or worse.

Let's take the first form of plagiarism – writing an essay by copying out chunks from a book or article that someone else has written. This is not going to help you in the long run. As I said before, writing essays is a skill that requires a lot of time and practice to acquire. Copying out chunks from someone else's work is not going to help you acquire that skill. So any essay that you write that contains substantial sections from someone else's work is just a waste of time – you may have saved yourself some effort by lifting someone else's work, but you are guaranteeing that when you are asked to demonstrate your essay writing skills in the exams, you will have nothing to show.

As for the second form of plagiarism – stealing an idea or concept from someone else's work and passing it off as your own – again this is just pointless. No one is expecting you to write something wildly original in an essay. There is absolutely no reason for you to want to pretend that some idea or concept came from you, rather than someone else. You will get just as much credit for acknowledging that you came across that idea or concept in an article or book written by some academic – at the very least, it shows that you have done some reading around the subject and been able to appreciate someone else's work.

So those are my rules for writing essays. But before I stop, three more pieces of advice.

Handwriting

The first I can't claim any credit for (no plagiarism here!) – it was actually a suggestion of a colleague of mine here at Pembroke College, Dr Loraine Gelsthorpe, which struck me as being very sensible. She suggested that in writing practice essays for exams, students should not write them on computers, but should instead write them longhand. The idea behind this is that writing essays in longhand is a very different skill from writing essays on a computer. If you write an essay on a computer, you can write a sentence, see what it looks like, delete bits of it if you are unhappy, and try it again. You can also insert text into the middle of an essay, if you think a particular point needs expanding, or you suddenly realise that you should have mentioned a particular case at a particular point in the essay. And you can move text around the essay if you think that it would be more appropriate to have a particular section appear earlier or later on in the essay than it currently does. You can't do ANY of this if you write an essay longhand. You have to work out what you want to say, and how you want to say it, before you start writing – because once you start writing, there is no going back. So you have to make sure that your essay plan is a good one before you put pen to paper. Writing an essay on a computer doesn't encourage you to acquire this skill – you don't need to have a particular plan when starting writing an essay on a computer: you can just start writing, see how it goes, let a plan emerge as you go along, and revise the text in light of your emerging understanding of what the essay should look like. But it's essential that you do acquire this skill because you're going to need it for the exam, where – unless you have special circumstances – all your essays have to be written longhand. However, for the time being I would suggest that you continue to write your essays on a computer to enable you to get into the habit of writing some really good, effective essays. Once you've shown yourself able to do that, then I would advise abandoning the computer and writing your essays longhand to acquire the special skills required to write really good, effective essays in exam conditions.

>

Model writing

The second suggestion does come from me. It would be a good idea for you to get into the habit of reading some really good legal writing. The writing doesn't have to be on any subject that you are studying: good writing is good writing, whatever subject the writer is writing about. My recommendation would be that you read anything by Peter Birks – probably the greatest private lawyer of the twentieth century, and also the best legal writer I have come across. His writing is a real model for everyone else to live up to, and you can't fail to benefit from soaking up some of his style. Although not a legal writer, you would also benefit a lot from reading anything (well, maybe not *anything* – some of his papers can be very subtle and abstruse) by a philosopher called Derek Parfit. His major work is a book called *Reasons and Persons* but you can access some of his writings (including a draft of a major new book called *On What Matters*) for free at: http://users.ox.ac.uk/~ball2568/parfit/bibliography.htm. He is such a clear writer you would again get a lot out of reading anything he has written.

Make the most of your opportunities

My third piece of advice is – don't waste the chances you get to write essays and have them marked by your teachers. A lot of students when they are set an essay to write will use the essay: (1) to engage in an agonised journey of self-discovery where they only find out what they want to say about a particular topic once they've finished, or almost finished, writing the essay; or (2) to write everything they know about a particular topic, so that when it comes to revising that topic, they will have a ready-made summary of the law on that topic that they can read. Don't do either of these things. If you do, your essay will be rubbish as an essay (for a start, it won't answer the question) and you will have missed a golden opportunity to improve and test your essay-writing skills. Remember what I said at the start of this letter: being able to write well is an art that has to be learned. It doesn't come naturally. So it's just criminal to waste the opportunities you are given to get a professional to look at your essays and tell you how good they are.

If you would like to read anything else on how to write good, effective essays, you should definitely get hold of the excellent *A Short Guide to College Writing* (3rd edn) by Sylvan Barnet, Pat Bellanca and Marcia Stubbs. It's also worth reading George Orwell's essay *Politics and the English Language* (now freely available on the Internet). You should also have a look at chapters 9 and 10 of Thomas Dixon's excellent book *How to Get a First*.

Okay – be in touch soon about the essay you sent me.

Best wishes,

Nick

A Sample Essay

> ○ From: Nicholas J. McBride [dearnick@pearson.com]
> ○ To: Brown, Jo
> ○ Subject: A Sample Essay

Hey Jo,

I've now had a chance to read your essay. I promised to give you some comments on it, and that's what I've done below. I've reproduced your essay, with some footnotes containing my comments inserted into the essay. But as a special bonus for you, I've followed your essay with the essay that *I* would have written had I been set the essay title that you were set. I hope that by comparing your essay with my essay you'll see a bit more clearly in what respects your essay might have fallen short of what your teachers want from you.

Okay – here goes: here's your essay, with my (highlighted) comments inserted into your essay.

'The mens rea of murder – leave it alone'
(Glanville Williams). Discuss

A defendant will commit the crime of murder if he performs the actus reus of murder with the mens rea. The actus reus of murder is causing the death of another life in being. The mens rea of murder is 'malice aforethought'. The law is clear that a defendant will have 'malice aforethought' if he acted with an intention to kill or an intention to cause grievous bodily harm. So the mens rea of murder is – intent to

---

kill or intent to cause grievous bodily harm. Before we can assess whether the mens rea for murder should be changed, it is first necessary [Why is it necessary? Make it clear to the reader where you are going] to discuss when the courts will find that a defendant had an intent to kill. [Not a great first paragraph – what point are you going to be making in this essay? Also use headings to make it clear where you are going in your essay]

This issue has long troubled the courts. In *Hyam* v *DPP* it was held that the defendant was guilty of murder. She was held to have had the necessary intent to kill because she foresaw at the time she acted that it was probable that someone would die as a result of her actions. [What were the facts in *Hyam*?] But this was criticised in the later case of *Moloney* where the defendant shot his stepfather with a shotgun and was charged with murder. The House of Lords held that the defendant should not be held to have an intent to kill just because he knew it was probable or likely that his stepfather would die as a result of his pulling the trigger. Lord Bridge held that was something that should be taken into account in judging whether the defendant had an intent to kill, but foresight on its own did not necessarily amount to an intention. What sort of foresight is needed before you can find that the defendant had an intent to kill was made clear a year later in the case of *Hancock and Shankland*. In that case the defendants were two miners who threw a concrete block from a bridge and killed the driver of a taxi which was travelling under the bridge at the time the concrete block was thrown off. The defendants were charged with murder. The House of Lords held that they could only have been held to have had an intent to kill the taxi driver if they knew when they threw the concrete block off the bridge that there was a very high probability that the taxi driver would be killed as a result. [All this is accurate (except you nowhere mention that a defendant will obviously be held to have had an intent to kill if he or she acted with the *aim* or *purpose* of killing). But where are you going with this? Why are you telling us all this? What point are you making? Only bring in cases if they help you to make a point – and make it clear before you bring in the case what point you are making.] In *Nedrick* the Court of Appeal looked at all these cases and held that a jury would only be entitled to infer that a defendant had an intent to kill if he foresaw that it was virtually certain that someone would die as a result of his actions. In *Woollin* the House of Lords agreed with this, but held that the rule should be that a jury would only be entitled to 'find' [There's some debate over what the House of Lords meant by substituting 'find' for 'infer' in the *Nedrick* direction: are you going to go into that? If not, why not?] that a defendant had an intent to kill if he foresaw that it was virtually certain that someone would die as a result of his actions.

So the end result of all this is that if a defendant has intentionally [What does this mean?] shot someone, for example, he will be found guilty of murder – he clearly had an intent to kill. But if a defendant caused someone else's death without wanting that to happen, he could still be found to have had an intent to kill if he foresaw at the time that the victim was virtually certain to die as a result of his actions. But the jury does not have to find that he had an intent to kill: whether they will or not will depend on all the circumstances. [This is debatable – but you haven't made that clear.]

I feel that this is a satisfactory state of affairs. Obviously, there are going to be some cases where we will find that a defendant had an intent to kill because he foresaw that death was virtually certain to occur as a result of his actions. The plane bomber case is one example. [What is the plane bomber case?] But equally obviously, there are going to be some other cases where a defendant will obviously not have had an intent to kill even though he knew that death was virtually certain to happen. The conjoined twins case is an example of this. The doctors in that case knew that Mary would definitely die if she was separated from Jodie – but that didn't mean they had an intent to kill Mary. [Your discussion of this case isn't very well written – you could have done a better job of setting out the facts, explaining them in a less rushed way.] As the law stands at the moment, it allows juries to make up their minds in these difficult cases whether there was an intent to kill – it doesn't force them into making the wrong decision by laying down any rules about when they can find that someone had an intent to kill. [How are juries meant to know *when* to find that someone had an intent to kill if they aren't given any direction on that issue? You don't seem concerned about this obvious point.]

However, some have criticised the existing state of the law, Lord Goff being the most prominent example. He suggests that the mens rea for murder should be changed and that a defendant should be held guilty of murder if he was 'indifferent' to the risk of death that his actions created. This would not really make much difference in a lot of cases. The plane bomber would still be found guilty of murder and the doctors in the Jodie and Mary case would not be found guilty of murder. Adopting Lord Goff's proposal might mean that drunk drivers would be found guilty of murder. [Does Lord Goff agree? How might he deal with this point?] This would not be acceptable. So Lord Goff's proposal should be rejected. But I agree with him that the rule that a defendant has the mens rea of murder if he had an intent to cause grievous bodily harm needs to be changed. It produces too many cases of unfairness and injustice. [Concrete examples of such cases to help make out your point?] I would agree with the Criminal Law Revision Committee that a defendant who intended to cause grievous bodily harm should only be found to have the mens rea of murder if he knew that there was a risk that his actions might cause death. [Fatal error! Never *ever* agree with an official law reform proposal – it's just too boring to get you a good mark.]

So subject to this one point, I agree with Glanville Williams that the mens rea of murder should be left alone. [Overall – a bit flat, and far too short. It doesn't really say anything that interesting, and is not that well executed. There's no real mention of any of the academic debates in this area, apart from Lord Goff's views. Has no one else said anything of any interest?]

Now – here's the essay I would have written.

'The mens rea of murder – leave it alone' (Glanville Williams). Discuss.

A defendant will have the mens rea for murder if he or she acts with an intent to kill or an intent to cause grievous bodily harm. There is

>

widespread agreement that the rule that a defendant will have the mens rea for murder if he or she acted with an intent to cause grievous bodily harm ('the gbh rule') is in need of reform. In this essay I will concentrate my fire on the rule that a defendant will have the mens rea for murder if he or she acted with an intent to kill. I will argue that this rule needs to be reformed. However one interprets the term 'intent', asking 'Did the defendant have an intent to kill?' does not provide an adequate basis for determining whether the defendant should be found guilty of murder.

Four different interpretations of the term 'intent' can be distinguished.

Aim or purpose

On the first view, a defendant can only be said to have acted with an 'intent to kill' if he or she acted with the aim or purpose of killing. This view of intent is endorsed by John Finnis. However, on this view many defendants whom we would want to convict of murder will be acquitted because they will lack the mens rea for murder.

Consider the example of the Bad Doctor, who extracts a patient's heart with the aim or purpose of experimenting on it. The Bad Doctor knows that the patient will die if he takes out the patient's heart, but he does not care about that. The patient does die and the Bad Doctor is charged with murder. On this first view of when we can say that someone had an 'intent to kill' the Bad Doctor did not act with an 'intent to kill'. He did not extract the patient's heart with the aim or purpose of killing the patient. If the patient could have survived without his heart, the Bad Doctor would have been perfectly content. So on this first view of when we can say that someone had an 'intent to kill' the Bad Doctor lacks the mens rea for murder and is entitled to be acquitted of murder and convicted of manslaughter. This is surely unacceptable.

John Finnis' view of intention has equally unpalatable consequences in the case of the Plane Bomber, who plants a bomb on a plane which is designed to blow the plane up when it is in mid-air. The Plane Bomber has some insured cargo on the plane, and when the plane blows up, destroying the cargo, he plans to collect on the insurance. The plane blows up as planned, and all the passengers

>

and crew on the plane are killed. The Plane Bomber is caught and charged with murder. On John Finnis' view, he should be acquitted and found guilty of manslaughter instead because the Plane Bomber had no intent to kill when he planted the bomb on the plane. It was no part of his aim or purpose to kill the passengers or crew. Had they all – by some miracle – survived, the Plane Bomber would have been perfectly happy. But to acquit the Plane Bomber of murder would be just as unacceptable as acquitting the Bad Doctor of murder.

Aim or purpose or 'oblique intent'

Glanville Williams argues that a defendant can be said to have acted with an 'intent to kill' if:

(a) the defendant acted as he did with the aim or purpose of killing; or

(b) the defendant acted as he did realising that it was virtually certain that someone would die as a result of his actions.

On this view, the Bad Doctor and the Plane Bomber would both be found guilty of murder. Both realised when they did what they did that it was virtually certain that someone would die as a result of their actions. However, adopting Glanville Williams' view is not free from problems. Consider the following three cases:

1 *The Conjoined Twins case.* In *Re A (conjoined twins)*, doctors proposed to save the life of one Siamese twin (Jodie) by separating her from her weaker twin (Mary). The doctors in this case realised that it was virtually certain that doing this would result in Mary's death – Mary was dependent on her link with Jodie to live. So on Glanville Williams' view, the doctors in *Re A* had an 'intent to kill' and would therefore need to rely on a defence to avoid a murder conviction if they carried out the operation.

2 *The Mountaineer case.* A Mountaineer is climbing a mountain with a companion when the companion (who is below the Mountaineer and is linked with him by a rope) slips and falls into a deep crevasse. The Mountaineer's companion is left dangling in the crevasse and the Mountaineer is trapped on the mountain, unable to move or call for assistance. He cannot pull the rope up because the weight on the

>

rope is too heavy and he dare not move his feet for fear of being pulled into the crevasse by the weight of his companion on the rope. Night approaches and both the Mountaineer and his companion are in severe danger of dying of exposure. The Mountaineer decides to cut the rope and his companion falls to his death. On Glanville Williams' view, the Mountaineer has the mens rea for murder and will need to rely on some kind of defence to escape conviction.

3 *The Good Doctor case.* A Good Doctor administers a dose of morphine to a cancer patient in order to relieve the agonising pain being experienced by the patient. The dose given to the patient – who only has a few days to live – is just enough to relieve the pain (a smaller dose would have had no effect on the patient's level of pain) but at the same time is so large that the Good Doctor realises that the patient is now virtually certain to die within a few hours. On Glanville Williams' view, the Good Doctor had an 'intent to kill' when he administered the morphine – he realised at the time he acted that it was virtually certain that his doing so would accelerate the patient's death. So, on Glanville Williams' view of intent, the Good Doctor will need to rely on a defence to avoid a conviction for murder.

No one seriously thinks that any of the defendants in these cases should be labelled 'murderers' – but adopting Glanville Williams' view of 'intent' creates the danger that precisely this will happen. Glanville Williams would doubtless have responded, 'But the danger can be averted by providing these defendants with defences.' But this response is less than satisfactory. The reason for this is that if the defendants in these cases are provided with defences, those same defences might then be exploited by defendants who acted with the aim or purpose of killing – defendants who no one wants to see acquitted of murder.

So, for example, if we allow the Good Doctor a defence on the ground that he was acting in order to relieve his patient's pain, what is to stop Bad Doctor II taking advantage of the same defence when he euthanases a cancer patient in order to bring that patient's pain to an end? Similarly, if we allow the doctors in the Conjoined Twins case or the Mountaineer a defence on the basis that they had to do what they did in order to avoid two people dying, as opposed to

>

one, what is to stop Bad Doctor III taking advantage of the same defence when he kills a terminally ill patient in order to extract the patient's heart and give it to another, otherwise healthy patient, who is in desperate need of a heart transplant? Adopting Glanville Williams' view of 'intent' has the effect of putting strains on the law of murder with which it simply cannot cope.

Aim or purpose or 'oblique intent' subject to a proviso

In its 2005 Consultation Paper on *A New Homicide Act for England and Wales?* the Law Commission sets out a possible approach for finding when someone had an intent to kill. Under this approach, a defendant will be held to have had an intent to kill if, subject to the proviso set out below –

1 the defendant acted with the aim or purpose of killing; or
2 when the defendant acted, he knew that death was virtually certain to result from his actions; or
3 when the defendant acted, he acted with the aim or purpose of achieving a particular goal and he knew that death was virtually certain to result if that goal were achieved.

The proviso is this: a defendant cannot be deemed to have acted with an intent to kill if he or she acted as he did with the specific purpose of avoiding killing anyone.

This approach has the virtue of making it clear that Plane Bomber II – who uses a bomb that he knows is unreliable – will be held to have had an intent to kill if the bomb goes off and kills the passengers and crew. While at the time he planted the bomb he did not appreciate that it was virtually certain that the passengers and crew would be killed, he did appreciate that if things worked out as he hoped and the bomb went off, it was virtually certain that the passengers and crew would be killed.

This approach also has the virtue of saving the Good Father – who, in desperation, throws his baby from the top of a burning building knowing that it is virtually certain that the baby will be killed but desperately hoping that the baby will not be – from being found to have had an intent to kill. The proviso will apply in his case: as he

>

LETTER 20 A SAMPLE ESSAY

acted with the specific purpose of avoiding killing anyone, he will not be found to have had an intent to kill.

However, the fundamental problems that afflict Glanville Williams' approach to the issue of intention also afflict the Law Commission's approach. The proviso will not apply to save either the Mountaineer or the doctors in the Conjoined Twins case or the Good Doctor from being found to have had an intent to kill. None of these can be said to have acted with the specific purpose of avoiding killing anyone. Their *only* purpose in acting in the way they did was to achieve some quite different goal: relieving pain in the case of the Good Doctor, saving the stronger twin in the Conjoined Twins case, and saving himself in the Mountaineer's case. The Law Commission concedes as much in its Consultation Paper in discussing the case of the Good Doctor. It concludes that the Good Doctor will be found not guilty of murder not because he did not have an intent to kill, but because he has a defence based on the weak ground that what he did has always been regarded as legitimate.

So if we adopt the Law Commission's proposed approach to intention, the only way to save people like the Mountaineer, and the doctors in the Conjoined Twins case, and the Good Doctor from being convicted of murder will be to supply them with defences, thereby creating unacceptable strains within the criminal law.

Common sense

On this view – which may be the one currently adopted by the judiciary – a jury in a murder case should simply rely on its common sense to determine whether, given all the circumstances, a defendant can be said to have acted with an 'intent to kill'. Obviously, if the defendant acted with the aim or purpose of killing then they should find that he had an 'intent to kill'. But if the defendant did not act with the aim or purpose of killing but instead realised that it was virtually certain that death would result from his actions, then the jury will still be entitled to find that the defendant had an 'intent to kill'. But they will not *have* to find that the defendant had such an intent. They should simply use their common sense and look at all the circumstances to determine whether the defendant had an 'intent to kill' in this situation.

>

This view is not free from problems. In the Bad Doctor case, the Plane Bomber case, the Conjoined Twins case, the Mountaineer case and the Good Doctor case, the defendants did not act with the aim or purpose of killing, but they did realise that death was a virtually certain consequence of their actions. On the view under inspection here, a jury will be 'entitled' to find that the defendant had an 'intent to kill' in some, all or none of these cases. How is a jury meant to determine in which of these cases there *was* an 'intent to kill'? Consistency would seem to demand that they either find that there was an 'intent to kill' in *all* of these cases or an 'intent to kill' in *none* of these cases. Either result is unacceptable, for the reasons set out above in criticising John Finnis' and Glanville Williams' views of 'intent'. If the jury only finds an 'intent to kill' in *some* of these cases, they can only be doing so by taking into account factors which are irrelevant to the issue of whether there was an 'intent to kill' – such as whether the jury thinks the defendant deserves to be found guilty of murder. This is an equally unacceptable result. Defendants are entitled to expect that juries do not, in answering the questions put to them, take into account considerations that are irrelevant to those questions.

So adopting the 'common sense' view of 'intent' can only result in difficulties.

Depraved indifference: the way forward

So – whichever view one takes of 'intent', asking in a murder case whether a given defendant had an 'intent to kill' will in certain cases give rise to problems. Either a defendant who deserves to be convicted of murder will be acquitted on the ground that he did not have an 'intent to kill'. Or a defendant who does not deserve the label 'murderer' will have to rely on a defence to avoid a murder conviction – which defence may well be denied to him because of the problems that providing him with such a defence will entail for cases where a defendant acted with the aim or purpose of killing.

Given this, there is a good case to be made for sweeping away the idea that a defendant will be found to have had the mens rea for murder if he had an intent to kill – and with it, the 'gbh rule'. A new start must be made. What is needed is for the mens rea for murder to be

>

defined in such a way that the Assassin (who acts with the aim or purpose of killing, usually as a means to achieving some other end such as earning money), the Bad Doctor and the Plane Bomber will all be held to have had the mens rea for murder; while at the same time, the doctors in the Conjoined Twins case, the Mountaineer and the Good Doctor will not. Lord Goff suggests that the Scottish concept of 'wicked recklessness' provides a way of discriminating between these cases; I would prefer to employ the American concept of 'depraved indifference'. The word 'depraved' connotes a degree of inhumanity that the word 'wicked' does not. A knowingly drunk driver who mows down and kills a pedestrian might be said by some to be 'wickedly reckless'; but no one could say that he is 'depraved'.

So – I suggest that the mens rea of murder be changed so that a defendant who has caused another's death will be held to have had the mens rea of murder if, at the time he acted, he demonstrated a 'depraved indifference' to the value of human life. Implementation of this proposal would have the effect we desire. The Assassin, the Bad Doctor and the Plane Bomber would all be held to have had the mens rea for murder – all showed a 'depraved indifference' to the value of human life at the time they did what they did. At the same time, the doctors in the Conjoined Twins case, the Mountaineer and the Good Doctor will not be held to have had the mens rea for murder – none of them showed a 'depraved indifference' to the value of human life at the time they did what they did.

An objection

It might be objected that if the law of murder were reformed in the way proposed, it would become intolerably uncertain. Whether a defendant was convicted of murder would depend on a jury's wavering and varying intuitions as to what amounts to 'depraved indifference' to the value of human life. There would be no guarantee that like cases would be treated alike. The objection is overstated.

The fact that a high degree of consensus exists on the issue of when someone shows a 'depraved indifference' to the value of human life is shown by the fact that everyone would agree that the Assassin, the Bad Doctor and the Plane Bomber show a 'depraved indifference' to

>

the value of human life; and everyone would agree that the doctors in the Conjoined Twins case, the Mountaineer and the Good Doctor do not. Admittedly, there are cases where reasonable people could disagree over whether a given defendant showed a 'depraved indifference' to the value of human life. For example, consider the case where a Terrorist plants a bomb in a shopping mall and then in good time telephones a warning to the police. The police do not clear the mall in time and someone is killed by the bomb going off. In such a case, arguments could be made both in favour of, and against the view that the Terrorist showed a 'depraved indifference' to the value of human life when he acted as he did. On the one hand, the Terrorist actively wanted to expose other people to the *risk* of being killed; on the other, it was part of his plan that no one should actually be killed by the bomb. But in such doubtful cases, juries could be instructed to acquit the defendant of murder and convict him of some lesser offence.

Conclusion

Glanville Williams is wrong. The mens rea of murder needs to be changed. Asking whether a defendant in a murder case had an 'intent to kill' does not provide a satisfactory basis for determining whether he should be found guilty of murder. This is so whatever view one takes of the meaning of the word 'intent'. The law needs to be changed so that it says that a defendant who has caused the death of another will have had the mens rea for murder at the time he acted if, at that time, he showed a 'depraved indifference' to the value of human life.

You can see immediately that there are a number of key differences between my essay and yours. My essay uses *a lot* of concrete examples to make its points. My essay only mentions *one* case – and I only mention that case because it helps me make a point. My essay shows a greater awareness of the academic arguments in this area than yours did. My essay uses headings to help break up the essay and help show the reader where I'm going. My essay is less rushed than your essay – I take as much time as I need to make the point I want to make, and then the essay stops. There is no 'padding' and no drifting off the point. In my essay I make it clear from the start what I am going to be saying – and for good measure, I conclude by restating what I have already said. In my essay I try and make interesting points, instead of getting hung up on boring or obvious points (such as that the 'gbh rule' should be abolished).

I'll stop comparing our essays now because I'm scared that if I go on you'll become extremely depressed. That's not my intention (in the sense of 'aim or purpose'). I'm simply pointing these things out to you because I want to help you write excellent essays in the future. If you adhere to the advice I've given you in this letter and the previous letter, there's absolutely no reason why you shouldn't in time start writing top class essays.

Remember what I said in my previous letter. There's an art to writing good essays, and it's not one which is really practised nowadays until you get to university – and even then not much attention is paid to it. So you shouldn't beat yourself up over the fact that you aren't very skilful at writing good essays at the moment – and you shouldn't expect to become very skilful overnight. But with time and practice, there's no reason why you shouldn't succeed eventually. So, don't get down – make the most of every opportunity you get from now on to write essays.

Best wishes,

Nick

Answering a Problem Question

- From: Nicholas J. McBride [dearnick@pearson.com]
- To: Brown, Jo
- Subject: Answering a Problem Question

Hey Jo,

Having spent so long on advising you on writing essays, it would be re-miss of me if I didn't also give you some advice on answering problem questions. So here goes.

● Three types of problem question

There are basically three types of problem question that you might be asked to answer:

1 An essay disguised as a problem

Let's call this a 'Type A problem question'. Here's an example:

> Peter Smith is the leader of a political party that secured a majority of 80 MPs in the House of Commons at a general election held six months ago. Peter Smith duly became Prime Minister. He immediately offended the Queen by cancelling the Prime Minister's weekly audiences with her. When the newspapers reported that 'associates of the Queen' had criticised Peter Smith for being 'arrogant', Peter Smith announced that his government would submit to Parliament a Bill that would allow a referendum to be called over whether the
>
> >

> Queen should continue to act as Head of State or should be re-placed by an elected President.
>
> Fred Jones – the Chancellor of the Exchequer and Peter Smith's deputy – was incensed by this announcement as he was an ardent monarchist. He contacted the Queen to tell her that if he were Prime Minister, his government would not dream of seeking to remove her as Head of State. He also told the Queen that if he were invited to form a government, he was confident he could command a majority in the House of Commons as he had always been more popular than Peter Smith among MPs in their party. On receiving this news, the Queen summoned Peter Smith to see her and dismissed him as Prime Minister. She then invited Fred Jones to form a government, which he is in the process of doing.
>
> Peter Smith has now applied to the courts for a judicial review of the Queen's decision, asking that they declare that the Queen acted un-lawfully in dismissing him as Prime Minister.
>
> Discuss.

This problem question is really inviting you to write a *descriptive essay* that:

1 explains the scope of the courts' powers to review exercises of what is called the **royal prerogative** (that is, powers that are exercised by the Monarch; these powers include the power to dissolve Parliament and the power to appoint the Prime Minister); and

2 uses that explanation as a basis for offering an opinion on what the prospects are of Peter Smith's application for judicial review succeed-ing in this case.

2 A genuine problem

Let's call this a 'Type B problem question'. This sort of question raises one or more issues that are genuinely problematic. What the law says on these issues will be very uncertain, and you will be expected to expose that uncertainty and discuss how it might be resolved by the courts were they ever confronted with the problem question you are answering. An example of a Type B problem question is:

Alf was employed by Bean plc. He owned a house worth £200,000, on which there was outstanding mortgage of £150,000. He also had an insurance policy with Crusty Insurers, under which Crusty undertook to pay off Alf's mortgage if – while the insurance policy was in force – Alf was diagnosed as suffering from one of a number of illnesses, including cancer.

In September 2003, Alf went for a medical check-up with Dr Dim. This check-up was arranged and paid for by Bean plc to ensure that their employees were healthy, and occurred every year. Dr Dim carelessly failed to spot that Alf had a number of symptoms indicating that he had testicular cancer. Dr Dim also wrote in his report on Alf, 'He clearly shows signs of being an alcoholic'. In fact, Alf did not drink alcohol at all. On seeing Dr Dim's report, Bean plc sacked Alf. Alf had to sell his house because he could not keep up the mortgage repayments – thus allowing his insurance policy with Crusty to lapse – and moved back in with his parents.

It is now two years later. Bean plc is insolvent. Alf is still unemployed and his doctors have just diagnosed him as suffering from testicular cancer. His doctors tell him that if he has chemotherapy, there is a 20 per cent chance that the cancer will be cured. They also tell him that if his symptoms had been diagnosed two years ago and he had received chemotherapy then, there is an 80 per cent chance that the cancer would have been cured.

Advise Alf as to what, if any, claims in tort he can bring against Dr Dim.

You won't know this at the moment because you haven't studied tort law in sufficient depth, but it is genuinely uncertain whether Alf can bring a claim against Dr Dim in this situation. There are arguments on both sides and in answering this problem question you would be expected to show an awareness of this fact.

3 A 'shoot the ducks' problem

Let's call this a 'Type C problem question'. Here's an example:

> Albert was HIV+. No one other than Albert and his doctor was aware
> of that fact. Albert had always fancied Britney, who was engaged to
> Charlie. One night Albert and Britney were at a party together, and
> Albert spiked Britney's orange juice with very strong alcohol. Britney
> got very drunk and told Albert that she was scared that Charlie had
> been unfaithful to her. Albert lied to Britney, telling her that he had
> found out that Charlie had slept with Britney's best friend, Debra, a
> week ago. Albert suggested that Britney get her revenge by having
> sex with him. Britney said, 'Okay – but only if you use protection and
> pay me £300 cash in advance.' Albert didn't have the money, but ap-
> proached his very rich friend Ernest, who was also at the party, and
> told him, 'Look – I'm in a tight spot. I sold some cocaine to a friend
> of mine and he was caught by the police, and he's threatening to tell
> them I was his supplier unless I pay him £500 tonight.' This was un-
> true. Ernest – who has often bought drugs from Albert – went to a
> cashpoint and withdrew the £500 needed, which he then gave to
> Albert back at the party. In the meantime, Albert bought a pack of
> condoms from a machine, using counterfeit coins to buy them.
> Albert then gave Britney £300, telling her, 'Don't tell Ernest I gave you
> this – I borrowed some money off him recently by telling him I was
> strapped for cash, and he wouldn't like it too much if he heard I'd
> been flashing this much money around.' Britney then had sex with
> Albert. Unfortunately, the condom they used was defective and
> Britney is now HIV+.
>
> What crimes, if any, have been committed in this situation?

This question isn't genuinely problematic – the law on what crimes have
been committed in this situation is pretty clear. What *you* have to do in
answering this question is identify *all* the crimes that have been committed in this situation – the more crimes you spot, the higher your mark. So
a Type C problem question is more of a memory test than anything else –
can you remember enough of your Criminal Law to be able to pick out all
the offences that have been committed in this situation?

In what follows, I'll give you some tips on answering Type B and Type C problem questions; the advice I gave you in the previous two letters on writing essays should give you sufficient guidance on how to answer Type A problem questions. Unless I make the contrary clear, you should take it that my tips apply to answering both Type B and Type C problem questions.

● Some tips

Issue spotting

One of the most common reasons why students fail to do well in answering problem questions is that they fail to spot, and discuss, *all* of the relevant issues raised by a problem question.

To avoid this failing, when you are *thinking about* a problem question, try first of all to look at the problem question from the point of the view of the person or persons who will be *initiating proceedings* in that situation. This will be the claimant or claimants if the problem is a contract problem or a tort problem; the applicant for judicial review if the problem is a public law problem; the prosecutor if the problem is a criminal law problem; and so on. Ask yourself: What sort of arguments will this person or these persons be making in this situation? So if it's a criminal problem you are considering, you'll be asking yourself: What sort of offences will the prosecutor be saying have been committed in this situation? What points will she be making to support her contention that those offences have been committed in that situation?

Having done that, try then to look at the problem question from the other side – from the perspective of the person or persons who will be *defending proceedings* in that situation. This will be the defendant or defendants if the problem is a contract problem or a tort problem; the public body against whom judicial review is being sought if the problem is a public law problem; the defendant or defendants if the problem is a criminal problem; and so on. Ask yourself: What sort of arguments would I be trying to make if I were acting on behalf of the persons defending proceedings in this situation? How would I try to knock out the case that is being made against them by the person initiating proceedings? So if it's a criminal problem you are considering, you'll be asking yourself: Is there any way of establishing that the defendants did not commit the offences they are going to be charged with? Is there any element in the definition of those offences that creates a weak point in the case against those defendants?

Now, of course, if you are doing a Type C problem it will often be the case that nothing can be said on behalf of those defending proceedings in the situation you are considering. A particular defendant *is* simply liable, or guilty. But it's essential that whenever you are looking at a problem question that you look at the problem from *both* sides. Doing this should help you identify all the relevant issues raised by the problem, and put you in an excellent position to write a good answer to the problem question.

Adopt a direct approach in writing a problem answer

Having said all that, I must emphasise straightaway that this process of looking at a problem question from both sides should be engaged in as a *an exercise* – whether in your mind or on a bit of rough paper – when you are considering the problem question for the first time and thinking about what to say in response. When you *write* your final answer to – say – the Type C problem set out above, you must *not* write things like:

The prosecution will argue that Albert committed the crime of rape when he had sex with Britney. They will argue that Britney did not consent to have sex with Albert when she had sex with him. They will argue that section 76(2)(a) of the Sexual Offences Act 2003 applies here. They will argue that Britney cannot be said to have consented to have sex with Albert because he intentionally deceived her 'as to the nature and purpose of' what they were going to do together – either by deceiving her about the fact that he was HIV+ or by deceiving her about whether Charlie had been unfaithful to her.

On the other hand, Albert will argue that section 76(2)(a) will not apply here because: (1) the fact that he was HIV+ did not make his and Britney's having sex totally different in nature from what Britney thought it would be; (2) he did not intentionally deceive her about the fact that he was HIV+, he merely failed to tell Britney about that fact; and (3) the fact that he lied to Britney about Charlie being unfaithful

>

> to her did not mean he deceived her about 'the nature and purpose of' what they were going to do together.
>
> If the prosecution is unsuccessful on this point, they will argue that section 75(2)(f) of the Sexual Offences Act 2003 operates here to raise a presumption that Britney did not consent because Albert administered to her a substance that was capable of stupefying her at the time she had sex with Albert. On the other hand, Albert will argue that this presumption is rebutted in this case because, despite the fact that he gave her the alcohol, Britney did genuinely consent to having sex with him: a drunken consent is still consent.

This is a terrible way of answering a problem question. It makes you look like you don't know what to think. Alternatively – and even worse – it makes it look like you are deliberately being cagey in order to avoid taking a position that might be incorrect. Looking at a problem question from both sides is merely meant to help you identify the issues raised by a problem question. You should adopt a quite different approach when actually writing your answer to the problem question.

I think the best problem answers adopt a very *direct* style. They always tell the reader where they are going before they get there. So I *wouldn't* recommend that you say, in answering the type C problem set out above:

> I will now consider whether Albert was guilty of rape when he had sex with Britney. In order to establish that Albert was guilty of rape, it must be established that: (1) Albert had sex with Britney without her consent; and (2) Albert had no reasonable grounds for believing that Britney was consenting to have sex with him.
>
> On the first issue, Section 76(2)(a) of the Sexual Offences Act 2003 provides that Britney could not be said to have consented to have sex with Albert if he intentionally deceived her as to the 'nature and the purpose' of what they were going to do. But this probably does not apply here because Albert did not intentionally deceive her as to the 'nature and purpose' of what they were going to do. The fact that he
>
> >

was HIV+ did not change the 'nature and purpose' of what they were going to do; and in any case Albert did not intentionally deceive Britney about his HIV status. Albert did deceive Britney about the fact that Charlie had been unfaithful to her but that did not change the 'nature and purpose' of what they were going to do. Section 75(2)(f) of the Sexual Offences Act 2003 provides that there is a presumption that a complainant in a rape case is not to be taken to have consented if 'any person administered to . . . the complainant, without the complainant's consent, a substance which . . . was capable of causing the complainant to be stupefied or overpowered at the time' the complainant had sex. This section applies here because before having sex with Britney, Albert administered a substance to her that was capable of causing her to be stupefied at the time she had sex with Albert. But the presumption that Britney did not consent that is raised by section 75(2)(f) is rebutted in this case because Britney was not, in fact, stupefied when she had sex with Albert and did, in fact, genuinely consent to have sex with him. So it seems that Albert will not be found guilty of rape because Britney will be found to have consented to have sex with him – so the first element of rape will be missing here.

This is a big improvement on the 'sitting on the fence' answer to this problem that I set out above; and it is probably a good idea for beginners to adopt this very 'careful' style in answering problem questions, so that they don't miss anything. But you should ultimately be aiming to write something much more direct in your problem answers:

Albert was not guilty of rape when he had sex with Britney: she genuinely consented to have sex with him. Section 76(2)(a) of the Sexual Offences Act 2003 does not apply here to raise a conclusive presumption that Britney did not consent to have sex with Albert. Albert did not intentionally deceive Britney about whether he was HIV+ (he merely failed to tell her he was HIV+) and even if he did, his deception did not relate to the nature and purpose of what they were going to do together: sex with a man who is HIV+ is no different in nature or purpose to sex with a man who is not. Albert did intentionally deceive

>

Britney about whether Charlie had been unfaithful to her, but that deception did not relate to the nature and purpose of what they were going to do together. Because Albert administered to Britney a substance that was capable of stupefying her at the time she had sex with him, section 75(2)(f) of the 2003 Act does apply here to raise a presumption that Britney did not consent to have sex with Albert. But it is submitted that that presumption is rebutted here because Britney was not, in fact, stupefied at the time she had sex with Albert and fully knew what she was doing. The fact that she would probably not have had sex with Albert had she not been drunk is, of course, irrelevant: a drunken consent is still consent.

This answer is much less ponderous than the 'careful' answer that immediately preceded it. It is therefore much easier to read and – crucially – uses far fewer words to make the same points. This can be absolutely vital when you are doing a Type C problem question in an exam and have to make lots of points in very little time.

Even when you are doing a Type B problem, I would recommend adopting a direct style. So in answering the Type B problem set out at the start of this letter, I *wouldn't* recommend – except to beginners – that one write:

In order to sue Dr Dim in negligence, Alf will have to establish: (1) that when Dim examined him and made his report to Bean plc, Dim owed Alf a duty of care; (2) that Dim breached that duty of care; (3) that Dim's breach of that duty of care caused Alf to suffer some kind of loss; and (4) that that loss is actionable.

On the first issue, it is difficult to say whether Dim owed Alf a duty of care in examining him and making his report to Bean. The authorities on this issue are in an uncertain state. On the one hand, *Spring* v *Guardian Assurance Ltd* established that an employer will owe an exemployee a duty of care in writing a reference for him because of the impact a bad reference might have on the ex-employee's job prospects. This case could be extended incrementally to cover this one: there seems little difference between writing an unfairly bad reference for

>

an ex-employee which causes the ex-employee not to get a job; and writing an unfairly bad observation on a medical report which causes an employee to be sacked. Indeed, the second act is much worse than the first. However, in *Kapfunde* v *Abbey National*, the Court of Appeal ruled that a doctor who conducts a medical inspection of a prospective employee will not owe the prospective employee a duty to take care not to 'doom' the prospective employee's employment prospects by making an inaccurate diagnosis of the prospective employee's health. On balance, it is possible to argue that *Kapfunde* was either wrongly decided or does not apply here . . .

A much more direct approach will save time and allow one to go into the issues in more depth if writing under a time constraint:

Alf will want to bring two claims against Dr Dim in this case. The first is for compensation for the fact that had Dim inspected him properly, Alf's testicular cancer would – in all probability – have been cured. The second claim is for compensation for the losses suffered by Alf as a result of losing his job – including the insurance payment that he did not receive from Crusty when his cancer was finally diagnosed because he had had to sell his house on losing his job. The first claim will probably fail; the second claim will probably succeed.

The problem with Alf's first claim is that it is doubtful whether Dim owed him a duty to examine him properly. After all, Dim was working for Bean plc when he examined Alf and he did not tell Alf – when he examined him – that Alf had a clean bill of health, thus lulling him into a false sense of security. If Dim did not – as I contend – owe Alf a duty to examine him properly, Alf cannot sue Dim for the losses he has suffered as a result of Dim's failure to examine him properly. In particular, he cannot sue Dim for the fact that in all probability he would not now have testicular cancer had Dim examined him properly.

Alf is much more likely to be successful in bringing his second claim for compensation against Dim. Alf will be able to claim that Dim owed him a duty to take care not to misrepresent his medical condition to Bean; that Dim breached that duty; and that Dim is liable for the loss

>

of employment and consequential losses that Dim's breach caused Alf to suffer. The main authority in favour of the proposition that Dim owed Alf a duty to take care not to misrepresent his medical condition to Bean is *Spring v Guardian Assurance Ltd.* In that case . . . Admittedly, the decision of the Court of Appeal in the *Kapfunde* case seems to indicate that Dim did *not* owe Alf a duty of care in this case. In that case . . . However, the decision in *Kapfunde* was flawed by a misinterpretation of the basis of the House of Lords' decision in *Spring* . . . In any case, even if *Kapfunde* is good law, it can be distinguished here: there is a big difference between stopping a prospective employee getting a job by giving him a bad medical report and getting a prospective employee sacked by giving him a bad report.

Do you see the difference? The direct style is much more assured and controlled. It makes you look more of a 'star' and therefore much more likely to impress whoever is reading your answer. At the same time, adopting a direct style doesn't stop you acknowledging uncertainties or ambiguities in the law – something which is crucial when doing a Type B problem. But instead of being paralysed by those uncertainties and ambiguities, you are acknowleging them in order to clear them up.

Of course, you can't adopt a direct style in answering a problem question unless you *know where you are going*. So it is essential before you write out your final problem answer, that you scribble down on a piece of rough paper the points or issues raised by the problem question and consider how those points or issues are likely to be resolved by the courts. Once you've done that, you can then start to plan how you will set out your answer.

In doing a problem question in an exam, give the examiner what he or she wants

Here is a small part of a problem question set in a criminal law exam:

. . . Jeremy walked out of the bar in a drunken state and got into his car. He drove off at 60 mph and five minutes later accidentally ran over and killed Kyle, who was crossing the road . . .

You are asked to discuss what offences, if any, have been committed in this situation. Should you discuss whether Jeremy is guilty of murder in this situation? The answer is 'no' – it's so obvious that he's not guilty of murder (he didn't intend to kill anyone when he was driving drunk down the road at 60 mph), there's really no point in discussing it. You should consider instead whether Jeremy is guilty of some lesser homicide offence, such as manslaughter or causing death by dangerous driving.

Now, here's another small part of a problem question set in a criminal law exam:

> . . . Kyle suggested to Jeremy that they play a game of Russian Roulette. Kyle took a revolver with six chambers and placed a bullet in one of the chambers, leaving the other five chambers empty. Kyle spun the chambers, pointed the gun at Jeremy and pulled the trigger. The gun 'clicked' harmlessly. Kyle handed the gun over to Jeremy and invited him to play. Jeremy spun the chambers, pointed the gun at Kyle, and pulled the trigger. The gun fired and Kyle was shot dead instantly . . .

Again, you are asked to discuss what, if any, offences have been committed in this situation. Should you discuss whether Jeremy is guilty of murder? The answer is 'yes' – even though, just as in the previous situation, it's obvious he is not guilty of murder (because, again, Jeremy could not be said to have intended to kill Kyle when he pulled the trigger). So why should you consider whether Jeremy is guilty of murder in this situation, but not in the previous situation?

The answer is that in answering a problem question in an exam, *you should discuss whatever issues the examiner wants you to discuss.* Now, it's highly likely that the examiner who set the second problem question wants you to discuss whether Jeremy is guilty of murder, so as to make you demonstrate that you understand that someone will only be guilty of murder if he causes death with an intent to kill, and that you understand when someone will be held to have had an intent to kill. So if you *don't* discuss whether Jeremy is guilty of murder and just go straightaway to consider whether Jeremy is guilty of a lesser homicide offence, the examiner will wonder, 'I wonder whether this candidate didn't discuss whether Jeremy is guilty of murder because he or she knew that he's not guilty – or because he or she just didn't think about the possibility.' And the examiner will mark you down just in case the latter is true.

So in doing a problem question in an exam, give the examiner what he or she wants. Discuss the issues that the examiner had in mind in setting the problem question. You may be wondering: How on earth am I going to know what the examiner wants? Well, if you do the issue spotting exercise that I gave you earlier, you won't fail to see any issues that are raised by a problem question. And then you've just got to use your judgment to weed out the issues that the examiner can't have meant you to discuss when he or she set the problem question. Whatever is left at the end of this weeding out process, you should discuss.

Presume that everything is relevant

Let's consider a small part of the Type C problem that was set out at the start of this letter:

> Ernest – who has often bought drugs from Albert – went to a cash-point and withdrew the £500 needed, which he then gave to Albert back at the party. In the meantime, Albert bought a pack of condoms from a machine, using counterfeit coins to buy them.

In considering how to answer a problem question, you should *presume* that *all* the details in the problem question are going to be relevant to your answer. Asking yourself 'Why's that detail been inserted into the question?' can often help you identify issues that you might otherwise have missed.

So, for example, why has the person who set the above problem gone out of his way to say that Albert used counterfeit coins to buy the condoms? Thinking about this helps you to see that there's an issue here which the problem setter wants you to discuss: Whether Albert is guilty of committing the offence of fraud.

But you should only *presume* that all the details in a problem question are going to be relevant to your answer. If you blindly assume that every detail in a problem question *must* be relevant, it can seriously unhinge your answer. For example, the above problem question goes out of its way to say that Ernest has often bought drugs from Albert. Does this mean that the person who set this problem wants you to discuss what offences Ernest might have committed in buying drugs from Albert and what offences Albert might have committed in selling drugs to Ernest? This is highly unlikely. (How do I know? Again, it's just a matter of good judgment.) It's more likely that this detail has been inserted to keep the problem going along. It helps to explain why Ernest believes Albert's story and why Ernest is willing to help Albert out. It follows that if you spend lots of time explaining what offences were committed by Ernest and Albert in buying and selling drugs, you will be just wasting time that could be more profitably spent on discussing other issues raised by the question.

So in doing a problem question you've simply *got* to trust your judgment and your knowledge of the law. If a problem question contains a particular detail and you've concluded that: (1) it's not relevant to your answer and (2) you're not meant by the person who set the question to discuss why it's not relevant, then just ignore it.

Using cases in answering problem questions

In answering problem questions, you should follow this rule:

> Support *every* legal statement you make by referring to a case or a statute unless the legal statement in question is so well known to be true among lawyers it doesn't need to be supported.

This needs a bit of explanation.

A legal statement is one which only a lawyer is qualified to make. 'The sun is shining' is obviously not a legal statement – anyone might be qualified to make that kind of statement. 'Someone will be guilty of murder if they cause someone's death by acting in a particular way and when they acted in that way they had an intent to kill or an intent to cause someone to suffer serious bodily harm' is a legal statement – only someone who knows something about the law, a lawyer, is qualified to make that kind of statement.

Some legal statements are so well-known to be true that you can make them without providing any support for them. Examples of such statements are: 'A defendant will have had the *mens rea* for murder if he acted with an intent to kill or an intent to cause grievous bodily harm'; 'A promise is not contractually binding in English law unless it is supported by consideration or made in a deed'; 'A defendant will only be held liable to pay damages in negligence to a claimant if he has breached a duty of care owed to that claimant'.

Now – in providing support for a legal statement that you have made, it's usually sufficient to refer simply to the name of a case in which that statement was endorsed, either by putting the name of the case in brackets after your statement or by putting a colon after your statement and then the name of the case. Like so:

> An employer will owe an ex-employee a duty of care in writing a reference for him (*Spring* v *Guardian Assurance*).
>
> An employer will owe an ex-employee a duty of care in writing a reference for him: *Spring* v *Guardian Assurance*.

You need do no more than refer to the name of the case. Setting out the facts of the case and discussing how it was decided won't add any more support to your statement, so doing so would just be a waste of time.

But if you are making a legal statement that is more controversial and which finds no direct support in the cases, then you will need to do a lot more to support your statement than simply refer to the name of a case. Take, for example, the statement that:

> Dim owed Alf a duty to take care not to misrepresent his medical condition to Bean plc.

Now – there is no case that *directly* supports this statement. So how can we back it up? Well, we might be able to use the House of Lords' decision in *Spring* v *Guardian Assurance Ltd* [1995] 2 AC 296 as support for the idea that Dim owed Alf a duty of care in reporting on Alf's state of health to Bean plc. In order to do this, we have to show that the House of Lords' decision in *Spring* rested on some *principle* and that this principle applies in Alf's case and indicates that Dim owed Alf a duty of care not to misrepresent his medical condition to Bean plc.

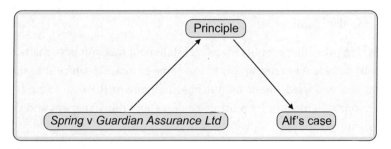

So, for example, in my textbook on tort law, I argue that the decision in *Spring* rests on a 'dependency principle', which says that if A takes on a job (such as giving a reference) knowing that B's future welfare is almost entirely dependent on A's doing that job properly, then A will owe B a duty to do that job with a reasonable degree of skill and care. If this is right, then that would indicate that Dim owed Alf a duty of care not to misrepresent his medical condition to Bean plc. After all, when Dim took on the job of examining Alf, he knew that Alf's future employment prospects with Bean plc were almost entirely dependent on his examining Alf with a reasonable degree of care and skill. So if the decision in *Spring* does rest on this 'dependency principle', then the decision in *Spring* does provide some support for the statement that Dim owed Alf a duty to take care not to misrepresent his medical condition to Bean.

But in order to make out that the House of Lords' decision in *Spring does* rest on the 'dependency principle', you would have to refer in quite a lot of detail to the facts of the case and what the judges said in that case, showing how the 'dependency principle' provides the most *appealing explanation* of why the judges came to the decision they did in the *Spring* case. So in order to provide effective support in your problem answer for the proposition that Dim owed Alf a duty to take care not to misrepresent his medical condition to Bean, you will have to discuss the decision in *Spring* in some depth. Certainly, it wouldn't be enough simply to say:

> Dim owed Alf a duty to take care not to misrepresent his medical condition to Bean plc: *Spring* v *Guardian Assurance Ltd.*

Nor would it be enough to say:

> Dim owed Alf a duty to take care not to misrepresent his medical condition to Bean plc: see *Spring* v *Guardian Assurance Ltd*, which holds that if A takes on a job knowing that B's future welfare is almost entirely dependent on A's doing that job with a reasonable degree of skill and care, then B will owe A a duty to do that job with a reasonable degree of skill and care.

Instead, you would have to say something along the following lines:

> Some support for the proposition that Dim owed Alf a duty to take care not to misrepresent his medical condition to Bean plc is provided by the case of *Spring* v *Guardian Assurance Ltd*. In that case . . . [insert summary of the facts here]. The House of Lords found that the defendant had owed the claimant a duty to take care not to supply him with an unfairly damaging reference for him.
>
> Lord Goff argued that a duty of care was owed because the defendant had 'assumed a responsibility' to the claimant. This seems implausible: at no stage did the defendant promise to supply the claimant with a fair reference, and indeed the reference was not even supplied at the claimant's request. There is some suggestion in the subsequent caselaw (see the decision of the Court of Appeal in *Kapfunde*) that the source of the duty of care in *Spring* was that the claimant and the defendant were at one time in an employer–employee relationship and that the decision in *Spring* does no more than establish that employers will owe ex-employees a duty to take care not to provide them with unfairly damaging references. However, a close examination of the facts in *Spring* shows that the claimant and the defendant were never in an employer–employee relationship, and the House of Lords went out of its way to indicate that this issue was
>
> >

immaterial to their decision. Moreover, it seems implausible to suggest that the House of Lords would have reached a different decision in *Spring* had, say, the claimant been an ex-student and the defendant a university tutor; or if the claimant had been applying for a research position and the defendant had been an independent referee brought in to assess the quality of the claimant's work.

The better view, it is suggested, is that the duty of care in *Spring* arose out of the high degree of dependency that existed between the claimant and the defendant, where the claimant's future job prospects – as the defendant well knew when he took on the job of writing a reference for the claimant – were almost entirely dependent on the defendant's taking care not to supply the claimant with a rea-sonable degree of skill and care . . . [refer to any helpful *dicta* in the *Spring* decision that support this interpretation here]. If that is right, then it possible to argue that the decision in *Spring* provides some support for the proposition that Dim owed Alf a duty of care in this case. Just like the defendant in *Spring*, when Dim took on the job of examining Alf, he knew full well that Alf's future employment prospects with Bean were almost entirely dependent on Dim's taking care not to misrepresent Alf's medical condition to Bean. As a result, it can be argued that Dim owed Alf a duty to take care not to misrepresent Alf's medical condition to Bean.

This is the sort of thing you would be expected to write if you wanted to get a good mark for your answer. (I hope what I've just written also makes it clear, if it wasn't clear already, why just making a note of the headnote of the cases you are told to read will leave you hopelessly unprepared to do well in the exams.)

Headings

Make sure to use headings to divide up your problem answer. This has a number of advantages. First, it will make your answer much easier to read and follow. Secondly, using headings will help you see at a glance what issues you have already covered – and as a result what issues remain to be discussed. So using headings can help ensure that you don't inadvertently fail to discuss some vital issue raised by the problem question. Thirdly, using headings can be a great time saver. Instead of saying:

> I will now consider whether Albert has committed the offence of rape . . . I will now consider whether Albert has committed the offence of fraud . . . I will now consider whether Albert has committed the offence of theft . . . I will now consider whether Albert has committed the offence of maliciously inflicting grievous bodily harm . . .

You can simply say:

> **Offences that may have been committed by Albert**
>
> **Rape**
>
> . . .
>
> **Fraud**
>
> . . .
>
> **Theft**
>
> . . .
>
> **Maliciously inflicting grievous bodily harm**
>
> . . .

I recommend that in doing *criminal problems*, you should normally use a heading for each possible defendant, and then sub-headings for each crime that that defendant might have committed. In doing *tort problems*, you should use a heading for each possible claimant, and then sub-headings for the defendant that that claimant might be suing, and sub-sub-headings for each cause of action the claimant might have against a particular defendant, if he or she has more than one.

In the case of problems in other subjects, which can't be so neatly structured as criminal problems or tort problems, your headings should identify each of the issues that stand in the way of whoever is initiating the proceedings succeeding in his or her action or prosecution or application, as the case may be.

Tort problems

Talking of tort problems, you can get further specific guidance from me on how to do such problems – as well as a number of model answers to sample tort problems – by going to the website that accompanies my *Tort Law* textbook. Go to www.mylawchamber.co.uk/mcbride and then click on 'Companion website support' and then click on 'Help on answering tort problem questions'.

Abbreviations and note form

In order to save time in the exams, many students write problem answers using abbreviations and a note form style of writing. For example:

> A not glty of rape: B consented. Irrebuttable presumption of no consent (SOA, s.76(2)(a)) does not apply here: no intentional deception of B as to 'nature and purpose' of act (deception about HIV does not count because sex with HIV+ man no different from sex with HIV− man; deception about C not relevant). May be presumption of no consent under SOA, s.75(2)(f) because A spiked B's drink, but presumption rebutted here because B – despite spiking – still consented to sex.

Abbreviations are fine and I would have no problem with you using them – but ensure that you introduce them properly. If you are going to be using the letter 'A' for 'Albert' then the first time you refer to 'Albert' write his name out in full followed by, in brackets, the abbreviation you will be using for 'Albert'. Like so: '. . . Albert ('A') . . .' Similarly, if you are going to be using an abbreviation for an Act of Parliament like the Sexual Offences Act 2003. The first time you refer to the Act, refer to it by its proper name

and then follow it, in brackets, with the abbreviation you are going to use for that Act from now on. Like so: '. . . the Sexual Offences Act 2003 ('SOA') . . .'

So far as using note form and shortened words to write a problem answer is concerned, I would recommend that you try to avoid doing this in an exam. If you are under severe time pressure then okay – but otherwise you should try and turn in something that is more polished and elegant. Why? Simply because note form answers are hard to read, and examiners don't like having to be made to work harder than necessary when they are marking exams – and they are liable to punish students who go out of their way to make their lives difficult.

Essay or problem question?

My students sometimes ask me, 'If we have a choice in the exam between doing an essay or a problem question, which should we go for?' It's tricky.

I think it's easier to write an essay that will get a high mark than a problem answer that will get a high mark. (I'm talking here about **discursive** essays, which are the principal kind of essays you might get asked to write in an exam.) The reason for this is that the general standard of essay writing among students is so low that an essay that is well-written, interesting and well-argued will be seized on by the examiner with tears of gratitude and awarded with a very high mark.

In contrast, to get a high mark for a problem answer – in particular, an answer to a Type C problem question – it's essential that you cover all the issues raised by the problem question and don't make a mistake in discussing those issues. If you miss even one issue or misstate the law on one point, that will drag your mark down. So I often compare writing a problem answer with defusing a bomb – one false step and it's all over. And when I'm marking a problem answer that has started off well, I often find myself holding my breath – I'm in such suspense to know whether the writer is going to be able to get to the end of the answer without it all going horribly wrong. In contrast, if you make one weak argument in an essay that is otherwise of a high standard, the examiner will usually be indulgent and think, 'Well, so what if he or she gave one weak argument? The overall standard was so good, this should definitely get a high mark.'

Given that, you might think my advice to my students would be to choose to do an essay over a problem answer every time. But there is a downside to that choice. It's this: marking an essay involves a lot more *judgment* on the part of the examiner than marking a problem answer. So if you write an essay, you're always taking a bit of a chance with what mark you get for it. It may be that your essay is, objectively, really good – but it's given a poor mark because it rubbed the examiner up the wrong way or because the examiner was in a bad mood when he or she marked it. In contrast, if you write a problem answer that covers all the issues raised by the question, does so in an intelligent way, doesn't misstate the law, backs up every legal statement by reference to a case or a statute – you can be sure you are going to get an excellent mark for your answer whoever the examiner is.

To sum up, then:

> It's easier to *guarantee* a high mark for a problem answer than it is for an essay – you can *never* be sure that an essay you write will get a high mark. But, on the other hand, it is easier to *get* a high mark for an essay than it is for a problem answer.

So, what should you do if you have a choice between writing an essay and a problem answer? If you are confident that you could write a better essay than a problem answer (or *vice versa*), then obviously go for the essay (or problem answer, as the case may be). If you are so talented that you think you could do *both* really well, go for the essay *if* you don't think there's much chance that what you say will rub anyone up the wrong way. (You'll just have to take a chance on the examiner not being in a bad mood when he or she marks your essay.) If, on the other hand, what you have to say is quite controversial and might annoy the examiner if he or she takes a different view, there's no point in taking a chance – do the problem answer instead.

That's enough advice from me for today! Good luck with your studies and don't hesitate to get in touch if you need any more help.

Best wishes,

Nick

Coping with Stress

○ From: Nicholas J. McBride [dearnick@pearson.com]
○ To: Brown, Jo
○ Subject: Coping with Stress

Hey Jo,

Sorry to hear you've been getting stressed out, worrying about the upcoming exams. Please do bear in mind the following points: I hope they will help you feel a bit better about things.

The first thing I want you to remember is that it's not worth worrying about these exams: even if they don't go well, you're only in your first year at university and will have other chances to make up for how you've done. So try not to build them up in your mind as this huge make-or-break thing, because that's simply not the case.

And *be positive*! Don't run yourself down and start thinking that you're not going to be able to deal with these exams. Of course you are – there's absolutely no reason why you shouldn't be absolutely fine taking these exams, just like thousands of other people up and down the country who will be taking exams very similar to yours this summer. Don't build them in your mind into a bigger, or harder, thing than they are. Reassure yourself of this by having a look at the exam questions that were set in previous years. At first sight, they may look pretty intimidating and un-doable. But on a second look, you should find a way 'in' and figure out a good answer to most of the questions. This should calm you down a bit and help you to see that the forthcoming exams are the equivalent of a steep hill that you have to walk up and over, not a towering mountain.

And if you are feeling stressed out about things, whatever else you do, *don't shut yourself away*. There's a great temptation to think that no one else wants to know, or cares, how you're feeling and that even if they do, there's nothing they can say to you that will help you. Again, that's simply not the case. So it was good that you wrote to me – but also reach out to your personal tutor, and whoever's the main person in charge of your studies and see if they've got anything to say to you that will provide you with some help or reassurance. Also make it clear to your friends how you're feeling – they may feel the same way, and it will make you feel better to know that you're not on your own in this, and it will also make them feel better to know that they aren't alone either.

And *don't forget to relax!* One of the damaging things about stressing about exams is that it makes you feel guilty about taking time off to socialise with your friends, or go to the cinema, or just go mad clubbing. Any time you think about doing something like that, a little stress related voice in your head will say, 'I CAN'T do that – I can't waste my time like that when I've got so much to do.' But you *can* and you *won't* be wasting your time. If, in a desperate attempt to obtain a washboard stomach, I decided to spend an entire day doing sit ups, I wouldn't end up with a decent set of abs – but I would end up doing my abdominal muscles some severe damage. To exercise your muscles effectively, you need to give them a rest every now and then, to allow them to recover from the work you've been making them do. It's the same with your brain – it needs regular periods of downtime, if it's going to work effectively. So it's really important that between now and the exams, you regularly take some time off your studies and do something completely different. Don't allow your feelings of stress to put you off doing this.

Those are all fairly obvious points, all of which I hope you will take on board. But many students do follow all of the above advice, but still feel really high levels of stress. Why is this? I think part of the reason is that they don't understand where stress comes from, and so are ill-equipped to deal with it effectively. So, let's address this issue and see what comes of it. Why do people get stressed? Well, I think the answer is that people get stressed about things that are important to them but that they can't control. Stress is a reflex reaction to feelings of powerlessness over things that are important to you. You can test out whether this is true by simply thinking about your own feelings of stress. You're not getting stressed about whether you'll wake up late on the first day of the exams, or stressed that your pens won't work in the exams. That's because at the moment you are able to do something to stop those things happening: you can set loads of alarm clocks to wake you up on the morning of your first exam, and you can take loads of pens with you into the exam. But you *are* getting stressed over whether you'll 'freeze' in the exams and not do yourself justice, or whether the 'right' questions will come up in the exam. These are things that you have no control over, and that's precisely why you're getting stressed out about them.

This means that stress is a predictable emotion. You will be tempted to feel stressed if you feel powerless over something that is important to you. So stress isn't something that just happens – it happens for a reason. And if that's right, then it follows that you can take steps to avoid getting stressed about things. To demonstrate this point, let's take an easy example: you don't feel stressed *at the moment* about the possibility that you might wake up late on the first day of the exams. That's because you don't feel powerless to do something about that *at the moment*: you still have the chance to buy about five different alarm clocks that will guarantee you wake up at the right time on the first day of the exams. But if you have only one alarm clock in your room *the night before the exam*, then you may well start to feel extremely stressed about the possibility that that alarm clock will let you down and you'll wake up late. So avoid putting yourself in that situation of feeling powerless by buying an extra alarm clock *now* (if you don't have one), as a back-up, so that the night before the exam, you won't have anything to worry about. Similarly, concentrate on doing what you can do *now*, while you still have the chance, to work on things that will help you in the exam, like improving your essay writing and problem answering techniques, or your knowledge of the law. If you work to improve those things *now*, you won't spend the night, or the week, before the exam stressing over the fact that it's too late to learn how to write a decent essay or problem answer, or stressing over the fact that there are still huge holes in your knowledge of the law that you can't now make up because you've run out of time. These particular feelings of powerlessness are easily avoidable if you do something *now* to ensure that you simply won't have an occasion to feel them when the time comes.

Another reason why students feel high levels of stress is that they allow their feelings of stress to grow out of control. There are two main reasons why stress has a tendency to grow over time. The first is that stress encourages you to waste your time. Instead of using the time left to you before the exams to improve your chances of doing well in the exams by working on the things that you still can do something about, you instead spend your time worrying about things that you can no longer do anything about, or about things that you could never have done anything about. The second reason why stress grows is that when you realise how much time you are wasting to stress, if you are unable to let go of your feelings of stress, then you will start experiencing feelings of powerlessness in respect of your stress (it's important to you to get rid of it, because it's using up your time unproductively, but you can't get rid of it), and as a result you'll start getting stressed about feeling stressed. And then you'll get stressed about feeling stressed about feeling stressed. And in this way a vicious upward cycle of stress develops.

Don't allow this to happen to you. Your feelings of stress can only grow if you allow them to distract you from what you have to do right *now*, which is *focus* on the things you can do between now and the exams to improve your position for the exams. So make a list of practical things you can do between now and the exams to help yourself do well in the exams, and concentrate on getting those things done. And, as you are doing these things, try to shut out any voices that may go off in your head, saying, 'But what about . . . ?' and 'There's no point . . .' There *is* a point, and there is *nothing else* that you need to think about other than getting through your list of things that you can do to help yourself. Focus on that, and your feelings of stress won't be a given a chance to grow.

If you follow all this advice, then you should feel *a lot* less stressed, both now and in the future, than you seem to be at the moment. But – and this is the final point I want to make – following the above advice will help you avoid *unnecessary* stress, but it won't mean that you'll *never* feel worried about things. There will always be some things that are important to you, and that you can't control. For example, if a firm offers you a job when you leave university, but makes the offer conditional on your getting a 2.1 in your final year exams, none of the advice above will help you avoid feeling *some* stress about whether you will get the 2.1 you need. That's because whether you get a 2.1 in your final year exams won't be completely under your control: the examiners will have the final say on that. If you want to avoid stressing about that kind of thing, the only way to do that is simply to let go of the worry. Try to train your mind to think along the following lines: 'I can't ultimately control whether the examiners will recognise all my efforts with at least a 2.1, so there's no point worrying about it. If I get a 2.1, all my worrying will have been for nothing. If, in spite of everything I've done to prepare for the exams, things don't work out and I don't get a 2.1, then there will have been nothing I could have done about that, and so again all my worrying will have been for nothing. So – I'll just let go of the worry and try to think of something else.' Some people find it helps while they try to think along these lines to do something symbolic to represent letting go of the worry – like writing the worry down on a piece of paper and burning the paper, or letting it float away on a stream. It sounds crazy I know, but apparently it does help.

So, to sum up:

1   get a sense of perspective: don't get worried about things that actually aren't that important;

2   be positive: don't think of the obstacles you face as being bigger than they are, and don't think of yourself as being smaller than you are;

3   don't lock yourself away: reach out to other people if you are feeling troubled – they want to help you;

4   don't forget to relax;

5   do what you can to improve your position between now and the exams so that you won't feel stress later on over things that you could have done something about earlier, but can't now do anything about;

6   don't feed your feelings of stress by allowing them to distract you from doing the things you can do now to help yourself do as well as you can in the exams; and

7   try to let go of any remaining worry you feel about the things that you absolutely positively cannot do anything to affect: realise that there is no point worrying about the things you have absolutely no control over.

I hope all this helps you a bit. If you want to read anything further that might help you feel a lot calmer about things, I'd recommend the *Discourses* of a Greek philosopher called Epictetus. You may well think that a disabled slave who lived almost 2,000 years ago won't have much to say to you – but you'd be surprised. The US Army makes its soldiers study Epictetus to train them to cope with stressful situations they may find themselves in (such as being captured and imprisoned by the enemy), so you may well get something out of reading him as well. This is from the first chapter: 'What, then, is to be done? To make the best of what is in our power, and take the rest as it naturally happens.' Reading the *Discourses* helps you to do that: I strongly recommend it.

Be thinking of you,

Nick

Tips on Revising

> - From: Nicholas J. McBride [dearnick@pearson.com]
> - To: Brown, Jo
> - Subject: Tips on Revising

Hi Jo,

Thanks for your e-mail. I'm glad you're now feeling a bit less anxious, and determined to get down to some serious revision for the exams. Okay – here are my tips on how to make the absolute most of the time remaining to you. You should be aiming in your revision to do two things:

- get the details of the law, and ideas about the law, into your long-term memory;
- improve your essay writing and problem answering techniques.

Both of these are crucial to your being successful in the exams. If you can't write good essays and problem answers, then you won't do well, no matter how much you might know about the law. If you don't know anything about the law, or have nothing to say about it, you won't be able to write good essays or problem answers, no matter how good your technique is.

You already know from everything I've already told you how to improve your essay writing and problem answering techniques: practice, practice, practice. But what's the best way of getting information about the details of the law, and ideas about the law, into your long-term memory? The answer is: *use* the information, over and over again. This is just common

321

sense. If you think about it for a second, you'll see that using information is the quickest, most painless and most effective way of remembering that information. If you need to learn the layout of a town, you could spend hours and hours staring at a map of the town, trying to burn it into your brain. But why make it so hard on yourself? – Just walk around the town a few times, and you'll learn the layout of the town without even trying. If you need to learn a recipe, you could copy it out a few hundred times, and it may, just may, stay in your head for a year. Or you could simply make the recipe 20 times and you'll never forget it. Why do people who move to France learn in months to speak French far more proficiently than schoolchildren who can spend years trying to learn French and forget everything they've learned in half the time it took them to learn it? The answer is: people who move to France are using the language all the time, and that helps them pick it up so much more quickly than children who are taught French by being made to study it, rather than use it.

So, if you can find ways in your revision of constantly using information about the law, that information will go into your head without your even realising it, or your having to try to remember it. But what ways are there of doing this? Well, that's what I'm here to tell you.

● The primary revision method

Your primary way of revising for the exams should be – writing answers to essay questions and problem questions that have been set in your university's exams in previous years. What you should do is this. If you want to revise a particular topic in, say, criminal law, look at the last five years' criminal law exam papers (they should be available in your University library, if not online), see what sort of questions have been set on that topic, pick a couple of questions that are fairly representative of the sort of questions that tend to be asked on that topic, research the hell out of them both by using your existing notes and looking up new material (either in books in your law library, or online), and then write some really good answers to those questions. As a revision method, this has some huge advantages:

- the past paper questions alert you to what you really need to know about the topic you are revising, and so direct your revision to the most important issues relating to that topic;

- exams in some subjects tend to have the same sort of questions come up year after year – so if you can figure out how to answer a good selection of questions that have been set in previous years, that can really set you up to turn in some brilliant answers to the questions that are set in your exam;

- in researching how to answer the past paper questions that you have chosen to do, you are using the information that your researches turn up because you will be constantly thinking about how the information that you are looking at relates to the questions you are going to answer; using the information in this way should help it get into your long-term memory;

- in writing out answers to past paper questions, you will again be using the information that your researches have turned up, this time in the course of writing your answer, and using the information in this way will again help it get into your long-term memory without your really trying;

- by writing out answers to past paper questions, you will be improving your essay writing and problem answering techniques.

This last point illustrates why answering past paper questions should be your primary revision method. No other revision method combines the two things you should be aiming for in your revision – to get information about the law into your long-term memory, and improve your essay writing and problem answering techniques.

◉ Supplementary revision methods

Doing past paper questions is an effective way of getting information about the law into your long-term memory, but it's not the only way. I'd also recommend that you think about employing some of these other methods in the course of your revision. You'll note that all of them are geared around the idea of learning information by using it:

Definitions

In some of your subjects, you will need to learn definitions. For example, if you are studying criminal law, you need to learn the definitions of all the offences that you are studying as part of your course. To learn a definition, first of all write it out as clearly as possible. For example, if you are trying to learn the definition of the elements of the offence of maliciously wounding or inflicting grievous bodily harm, contrary to s 20 of the Offences Against the Person Act 1861, this is *not* a clear definition:

> *Actus reus*: wounding or inflicting grievous bodily harm
>
> *Mens rea*: maliciously

This is not clear enough: we all know what wounding means, and we can all have a pretty good idea of what grievous bodily harm means, but what is 'inflicting' and what is 'maliciously'? A clearer definition will go something like this:

> *Actus reus*: wounding or causing grievous bodily harm
>
> *Mens rea*: intending to cause some physical harm, or being subjectively reckless as to whether your actions will cause some physical harm

Once you've got a clear definition, write it down in the middle of a piece of A4 paper (turned on its side), and then get jazzy with it! Have the facts and names of cases coming off the central definition to illustrate and support the key terms (for example, what case established that 'inflicting' means 'causing'? what cases said there was a difference? do these cases survive at all?). Draw the facts of the cases if possible rather than write them down – the added creativity involved in drawing should help fix the facts into your head. Around the edge of the paper, write down (or draw) some hypothetical situations and say whether a s.20 offence would be committed in those situations. Before you know it, and without even trying, the central elements in the definition will be fixed into your head.

Cases

I've already given you some tips on remembering cases. But just to recap briefly, you will most effectively remember cases if you can arrange them into some kind of pattern. So think of issues or ideas relating to a particular subject that you are studying, write the issue or idea down in the centre of a piece of A4 paper (turned sideways), and then try to arrange as many cases as you can around that issue or idea. So, for example, the issue might be 'Is Parliament sovereign?' Write that down in the centre of a piece of A4 paper (turned sideways) and then think about all the cases that you've come across (and look for more that you haven't yet come across) and try to arrange them (with drawings or key words to illustrate their facts, or what they say) under a set of answers to the key question. So think about what cases take the line: 'An Act of Parliament will always be valid unless it is repealed by another Act of Parliament'; and what cases take the line: 'An Act of Parliament will not be valid insofar as it purports to bind future Parliaments, or change the rules governing how an Act of Parliament is passed'; and what cases take the line: 'An Act of Parliament will not be valid insofar as it contains provisions that violate the rule of law'; and what cases take the line: 'An Act of Parliament will not be valid insofar as an earlier Act provides that it will not be valid, and that earlier Act has not been expressly repealed by Parliament', and arrange the cases around the central issue 'Is Parliament sovereign?' according to what answer they support.

Filling gaps in your knowledge

Make a list of issues or questions that you are hazy about, arrange the list into a rough order of importance, research the hell out of those issues or questions starting with the ones at the top of your list, and then write mini-essays or textbook entries about those issues or questions. Again, the process of researching and writing will help get the details relating to the issue or question you are working on into your long-term memory without your really trying.

When you are doing this, concentrate in particular on issues or questions that tend to crop up regularly in the exams (for example, What counts as a non-natural use of land for the purposes of the rule in *Rylands* v *Fletcher*?

or, When will someone's consent to having sex/being touched be so vitiated that they will not be regarded as having consented to have sex/be touched at all?) because they are issues on which the law is very uncertain or problematic. Use the past paper questions as a guide to help you with this.

○ The importance of having a plan

Work out a revision plan for between now and the end of the exams. This is very important, for a number of reasons:

- Having a plan will help ensure that you cover everything you need to cover between now and the exams. Haphazardly revising whatever you're in the mood for on a particular day will likely leave you with some bigs gaps in your knowledge and understanding.

- Having a plan will give you a stimulus to work. You won't be able to put off revising a particular topic to another day if you can see that doing this will have knock-on effects on what else you will have time to revise before the exams.

- Having a plan will help you not to panic about your revision. If you start thinking about *everything* you need to do between now and the exams to prepare for the exams, you will tend to feel overwhelmed and helpless. You need to stop thinking about *everything* you have to do, and just focus in on what you have to do *today* to get ready for the exams. Having a plan helps you to do this – it gets your mind off the bigger picture and helps you just to think about what has to be done today. Plus having a plan is reassuring – it helps you to think that you know what you are doing, you are in control, and the possibility for things going wrong has been minimised.

So: sort out a plan for yourself. But to make a plan, you have to be prepared. You have to think about what topics you want to revise. You have to have gone through the past paper questions, and picked out some representative questions that you are going to attempt. You have to have thought about what other revision methods you are going to employ, and how you are going to use them. So take three or four days to do this, and then spend a day putting together your plan of attack.

In making your revision plan, make sure that you don't overload yourself. Don't give yourself four or five tasks to accomplish each day if you have no chance of getting through that many tasks. And leave yourself some room for things to go wrong. Have some free days scheduled where you can catch up on any aspects of your revision plan for which it turned out that you didn't have time. And on each day of your plan, give yourself some free time that you can cut into if a particular task is taking longer than expected, or more interesting than you might have expected! (Though if you follow my advice, I hope all your time spent revising will be relatively interesting.)

● The importance of taking time off

Remember what I said in my previous letter about the importance of taking time off, and not working your brain all the time. If you spend all your time revising, then you'll burn yourself out, and approach the exams feeling tired, jaded and listless – when you need to feel enthused and sparky. And it's important that when you do take time off, make sure you enjoy it – that you do something nice for yourself, and don't spend the time worrying about the exams, or feeling guilty that you are taking time off from your revision.

Now – the best way of ensuring that you do take adequate time off from your revision, and of ensuring that you have some quality time off that is free from worries or guilt feelings, is to build your time off into your revision plan. Set yourself goals, and plan what rewards, by way of spending some time off revising, you will give yourself for achieving those goals. If you build your time off into your revision plan in this way, you'll help ensure that you do get adequate time off from revision, and your breaks from revision will start to seem like something you are entitled to enjoy in recognition of how hard you've been working, rather than a guilty or worry-filled treat.

● Work together

Where you can, work with other people in your revision:

1 *Picking questions.* Get together with your fellow students to work out together what sort of questions you should be focusing on in your revision.

Two minds are better than one, and they may have some useful advice for you (and you may have some useful advice for them) as to what sort of topics might come up in the exams.

2 *Send your written work around.* If you've written an essay or problem answer, send it to them for their comments and advice. This will help to ensure that you work hard at making the essay or problem answer as good (and, in particular, as clear) as possible, and reading your essay or problem answer and thinking about whether it is correct, and sending you comments on it, will provide your fellow students with another useful (because it involves using information) method of revising.

3 *Share information.* If, in the course of your revision, you've come across a really useful article on a particular subject, then let other people know about it. You'll benefit from your generosity when someone else finds something useful that you haven't heard of.

4 *Ask each other questions.* You and your fellow students should get into the habit of asking each other questions that have cropped up in the course of your work and that you don't know the answer to. Maybe someone else in the group knows the answer. If no one does, then you could collaborate together on looking into it. Either way, your group's knowledge of the law will be improved.

● Predicting what will come up on the paper

Wouldn't it be great if you could get an advance peek at what the questions will be in this year's exam? Well, you can't. But you can make some educated guesses as to what might come up in the exam, and prepare for those questions to come up in your revision. Here are some tips on spotting what sort of questions are likely to come up in the exam.

1 *Past papers.* Look at the past papers that have been set on the subject you are revising over the last few years. Is there an issue that tends, time and time again, to form the basis of a question in the exam? If so, be prepared for a question on that issue to come up again.

2 *Last year's paper.* Pay particular attention to last year's paper. Examiners tend not to set the same sort of essay questions two years in a row, so if there was an essay question on last year's paper on a particular issue, it's not likely you will get a similar essay question this year. So preparing for such a question to come up will normally be a complete waste of time. But only normally. There are some papers where the same sort of questions get set time and time again. In which case, last year's paper will be as good a guide as any as to what is likely to come up in this year's paper.

3 *Recent developments.* Examiners are human beings. When an examiner sits down to write an exam, he or she can often feel very jaded and uninspired. Lacking in ideas for good essay and problem questions, he or she will *often* turn to recent cases and articles for inspiration. So, in your revision, pay *a lot* of attention to recent developments in the subject you are revising.

A case decided in the past year is *far* more likely to form the basis of a problem question in the exam than a case that was decided five years ago. An article that was published in the past year is *far* more likely to supply a quote for an essay question than an article that was published five years ago. An issue that has made the newspapers in the past year is *far* more likely to form the basis of an essay question or a problem question than an issue that was dominating the headlines five years ago.

So make sure that your revision concentrates *a lot* on improving your knowledge of:

- recent cases relating to the subject you are revising (and what academics have to say about them);
- recent articles on the subject you are revising (don't limit yourself to the articles you have been told to read: explore the journals and recently published books for articles that the examiner might have come across);
- recent issues relating to the subject you are revising that have made the news.

● Some common questions

Now to address some questions that my students tend to ask me when I suggest they revise in the above way:

Revision notes

'I've tended to revise in the past by just making summaries of my notes – shouldn't I do the same for my Law exams?' The answer is 'No'. When I was a student, I used to make revision notes, and I hated the time I spent making them, and I'm not sure I got anything out of them. Drawing up revision notes – by which I mean bare summaries of your notes, rather than anything more creative – is a really ineffective way of revising. It's boring, which means your brain isn't taking much, if anything, into its long-term memory, and it doesn't help at all with improving your essay writing and problem answering techniques, which is 50 per cent of the battle so far as getting ready for exams is concerned.

Essay plans

'If I am attempting to write an essay in response to a past paper essay question, would it be okay if I just wrote an essay plan rather than a complete essay?' The answer is 'In an ideal world – no.' If you have time to write a full essay, then do that. There is a huge difference between being able to draw up an essay plan and actually being able to execute it. Writing essay plans won't get you ready for the task of writing full essays in the exam. However, if you don't really have time to write a full essay, then an essay plan is better than nothing – but make sure that you always, *always* write a full first paragraph for the essay. As I've said before in my guidance on writing essays, the first paragraph of an essay is crucial: so make sure you get as much practice in as possible at writing really good, effective, attention-grabbing first paragraphs.

Timed answers

'If I am attempting to answer a question, should I write my answer in the time I'd have to write it if I were doing it in an exam?' The answer is 'Not at the moment.' At the moment, we are looking to improve your essay writing and problem answer techniques. To do that, you need to take time – a lot of time – over your essays and problem answers, trying to make them as good as possible. It would be a good idea to work out how much you can write in 45 minutes or an hour (depending on how long you get to answer each question in your exams) and learn to write to that kind of length – but so far as learning how to write an answer in 45 minutes or an hour is concerned, leave doing that until the run up to the exams. At the moment, we have to focus on quality. So if you are aiming to write an answer to a particular question, give yourself a couple of days to do it – one day to research, one day to write. Really take your time to make it as good as possible.

Scope of revision

'Do I have to revise everything relating to a particular subject, or are there some topics or issues that I can disregard?' The answer is 'It depends.' If the exam in a particular subject will require you to answer four questions, then you only have to know enough to be able to do four questions on the day. To ensure that this is the case, you will generally only have to revise six topics or issues that regularly crop up in the exam – you can dump everything else. However, it may be that a particular exam tends to mix up in its questions a lot of different topics or issues – in which case, you will probably have to cover everything to make sure you are covered in the exam.

Okay – that's enough from me. Good luck with your revision, and let me know how you get on in the exams!

Best wishes,

Nick

Last Advice Before the Exams

From: Nicholas J. McBride [dearnick@pearson.com]
To: Brown, Jo
Subject: Last Advice Before the Exams

Hey Jo,

The very best of luck for your exams! I'll be thinking of you! As for whether I've got any last minute words of advice, I do have a few things I want to say to you – but first, a word of warning. You've probably had loads of advice from your teachers as what to do in the exams. If any of my advice contradicts what they've told you, then ignore my contradictory advice. They will know far better than me what's the best approach for you to adopt in the exams – after all, they are going to be marking them. That said, here are a few tips for you to bear in mind in doing your exams.

● Timing

Spend *equal time* on all the questions you have to do in the exam. Suppose, for example, that you have to answer four questions in three hours, which gives you about 45 minutes for each question. Make sure that you don't spend more than 45 minutes on each question. Do *not* succumb to the temptation to spend 'just five more minutes' on any question. The extra marks you will pick up by spending 'just five more minutes' on the question will be dwarfed by the marks you will lose by spending only 40 minutes on the next question. Be disciplined. If the 45 minutes for doing a particular question are up, finish your sentence and then move on to the next question. Leave about a page space between your answers to allow you to add extra material to any of your answers if you have time at the end of the exam.

Writing essays

I've said this before, but I'll say it again – if you are writing a discursive essay (discussing a particular area of the law's merits or demerits), make sure your essay has a point and that you make that point clear *right* at the start of the essay and that you spend the rest of the essay making that point out. If you find yourself writing things like, 'First, it is necessary to discuss the history of this area of the law' or 'A brief survey of the cases reveals how complicated this area of the law is' or any other phrase that invites you to engage in a boring and pointless run through the case law in the area, *stop and think*: Surely there's a better way of doing this?

Plan your essays

Don't rush into doing any essay. Even if you think, 'Yes, this essay is on something I know about. I can do this essay!' – *stop and think*: What's the *best way,* the *most effective way,* the *most impressive way* of doing this essay? Your first instincts as to how to do the essay are usually going to be wrong. *Stop and think*: Is there a better way, a more effective way, a more impressive way of doing this essay? Five minutes spent thinking and planning at the start of your writing time will pay far more dividends than five extra minutes spent writing.

The importance of first impressions

Remember what I told you in my first letter on writing essays: pay extra special attention to the first paragraph and make sure it's a winner. Make the examiner think, on reading the first paragraph, 'This is going to be a first class essay'. If you can do that, you will be *far* more likely to get a first class mark for your essay than you will if the examiner thinks after your first paragraph, 'This is going to be a second class essay.' I cannot emphasise too strongly how important it is that start your essay in an interesting and arresting way. Just read what Thomas Dixon has to say in his excellent *How To Get a First* (Routledge, 2004):

Speaking from the point of view of someone who regularly marks . . . exam essays, I cannot tell you how welcome it is to pick up a script and find that its author has made an effort to engage your attention, arouse your interest, provide you with a thought-provoking, arresting or unexpected opening paragraph or two. If this attention-grabbing opening is followed by or includes an account of a key scholarly dispute to which the essay relates, and a brief map of the essay itself, then, speaking for myself, I will be so overwhelmingly grateful that I will be predisposed to give the essay a first if I possibly can.

And he is not just speaking for himself: he is speaking for all examiners who mark essays, everywhere.

○ Leave your weakest answer to last

The law of first impressions – that first impressions are hard to dislodge – applies also to the whole of your answer paper. Say you have to do four questions in your exam. You have picked your four questions, but you feel that your answer to one of the questions is going to be significantly weaker than your other answers. Leave your weakest answer to last. If, in your first three questions, you have established yourself in the mind of the examiner as a top student, that might make her inclined to overlook or go easy on any failures or omissions in your last answer. Who knows? Maybe she will surmise that your last answer was weaker than the others because you were exhausted or running into time trouble, and out of sympathy give you a higher mark for your last, weak answer than she would have done had you written that answer first, before any of the others.

Another reason for leaving your weakest answer to last is this. Suppose that at your university a First Class script is one which gets a mark of 70 per cent or above. And suppose that you have to do four questions in your exam, and the exam is marked out of 100, with each question being marked out of 25. Suppose that for your first three questions, you get marks of 18, 19 and 18 – so, 55 in total. This will only leave you needing a mark of 15 on the last question to get an overall First Class mark for your paper. The examiner would have to have a heart of stone to give you a mark of 13 or 14 out of 25 for that last question, when you only needed a mark of 15 to get an overall First. So even if your last question, objectively, deserves a mark of 13 out of 25 because it's so weak, it's likely that the examiner will bump up the mark to 15 to get you over the First Class boundary. So, that's another reason for leaving your weakest answer to last. Your opening strong answers can actually give the examiner an incentive to inflate the mark for your concluding, weak answer.

○ Try and finish with an essay

This was one of the first tips for the exams I was ever given as a student (by Professor Hugh Collins) – but it's a tip that is subject to the preceding bit of advice, that you should always leave your weakest answer last. If your answers to all of the questions on the paper are likely to be equally strong, you should aim to finish with an essay. The reason for this goes as follows. Suppose you have to do four questions in your exam, and you have decided to do two essays and two problems. Try to make one of the essay questions the last question you will answer. The reason is that if you are running into a bit of time trouble, an essay can be compressed to fit the remaining time available without too much loss of quality. In contrast, a problem answer is less susceptible to being compressed. As a result, it's much harder to write a problem answer to a high standard in a shortened period of time.

○ General guidance on problem answers

Don't make your problem answers overcomplicated. Don't make ridiculous assumptions/arguments as to what the actors thought/why the actors did what they did. Always have in mind the sort of answer the examiner would have had in mind when setting the question: relatively straightforward, addressing five or six key issues with reference to the relevant case law, easy to mark when done right.

○ Never stop thinking

I wish I had £10 for every time a student has told me, 'I can't believe the marks I got in the exams. I thought I did really well in the exam on X law, but I got my worst mark for that. And I thought my exam in Y law was a disaster, and I got my best mark in that subject.'

It's so common for students to say this, there must be a reason for it. There must be a reason why students do worst in the papers they think they've done the best in, and why they do best in the papers they think they've done the worst in. After many years of pondering this mystery, I think I've got the answer. How you do in the exams is related to how *hard you think* during the exams.

If you're having a really torrid time in an exam and really having to fight to do well, then you are being made to think very hard. In writing problem answers, you are so desperate to find anything relevant to say that you start seeing points that you might otherwise have missed. In writing essays, you work very hard to make some intelligent points, hoping that your doing so will redeem what is, in your eyes, an otherwise disastrous performance.

In contrast, if you are sitting a paper that seems very straightforward to you, your brain tends to switch onto 'auto-pilot' and you stop really thinking about what you are doing in the exam. In writing your problem answers, you get sloppy and complacent and start to miss some relevant issues. Your essays tend to be more directed towards what you *think* the essay question is about rather than what it is *actually* about.

The end result is that you will get a much better mark for your performance in the exam where you had a really tough time than you will for your performance in the exam that seemed very straightforward to you.

The lesson you should draw from this is not to switch off during the exam. If the exam seems very straightforward, *be on your guard. Stop and think*: Are there some issues I'm missing in doing this problem question? Any relevant cases that I haven't thought about? What is this essay really about? Is there some way I could improve on the essay I was thinking of writing on this topic? *Never stop thinking* along these lines.

● Style

Use headings, numbers and underlining throughout to make your exam as easy to mark and as follow as possible. If you can remember to do so, write on every other line only. This will make it very easy for you to insert corrections into your answers if you need to do so.

⦿ In the exam

Try to remain calm, especially at the start of the exam when you experience the shock of seeing a lot of brand new questions for the first time. When doing a problem question, don't panic. Just think – 'I *have* covered the material that will allow me to do this question. I just have to be calm and I *will* see the issues raised by the question and I *will* remember what cases and statutes are relevant to those issues.' When thinking about how to approach an essay, just think – 'I *have* thought about this before. I just have to be calm and the ideas *will* come as to what points I should make in my essay and how the essay should be structured.'

Jot down any ideas/cases/issues as they come to you on a bit of rough paper: don't rely on your memory to bring them back to you when you need them – under stress you will be particularly prone to the phenomenon of being completely unable to remember something that you were thinking about just two minutes ago. On the same lines, it might be a good idea at the start of the exam to scribble down quickly any key rules or names of cases that you are very likely to need to use in the exam. You then won't have to worry about forgetting these rules or names in the course of the exam.

⦿ After the exam

When the exam is over, *leave the exam paper in the exam hall.* There's absolutely no point in taking it away with you and looking at it and worrying about what you should have said. By then it will be too late. And try to avoid getting into any extended discussions about what you wrote in the exam – again there's no absolutely no point. Just a simple 'It went okay' should suffice. Certainly don't do what I did after my contract law exam in Oxford, when I foolishly went through the paper with one of my lawyer friends who had also sat the exam. He said that he had done a particular question. 'I didn't do that question,' I said. 'It was obvious it was all about *The Super Servant (No 2)* and I hadn't revised that case.' 'What's *The Super Servant (No 2)*?' my friend replied. The rest of his day was ruined – and so was mine.

● Whatever happens, be philosophical

Even the best of students can get unlucky in the exams. You may prepare really well for the exams but then get caught cold by a really unfair exam and end up getting a mark that your efforts simply didn't deserve. This can happen. Examiners are human and can foul up, just like the rest of us. My advice is: try to be philosophical and put it behind you. You've just got to believe that everything will work out well for you in the end, and this bit of what looks like bad luck will at some point in the future turn out to be a real blessing. I've found that to be true in my own life, and that of many people I know – and I have no doubt it'll be true of you as well.

But let's hope it won't come to that and that your examiners will do a good job and you will receive the credit you deserve! Good luck with the exams, Jo – and let me know your results when they come through.

Best wishes,

Nick

PART 5

Thinking About the Future

Moving On

○ From: Nicholas J. McBride [dearnick@pearson.com]
○ To: Brown, Jo
○ Subject: Moving On

Hi Jo,

Congratulations on your exam results! I'm so pleased for you. I'm glad that now those exams are behind you, you're now starting to think about what you might do when you leave university. It's good that you're thinking along these lines – your three years at university will pass by very quickly and it's never too early to start preparing for life outside university.

But don't make up your mind just now what you are going to do when you leave university! Explore your options – find out what you are really interested in doing. Try to get some work experience in a law firm, and in a set of chambers, to help you see whether you are interested in working as a solicitor or a barrister after university. Get hold of the latest *Student's Guide to Careers in the Law* (Chambers and Partners). That will give you a lot of really helpful advice about pursuing a career in law after you leave university. It covers:

● What sort of careers you can pursue in the law after leaving university (solicitor, barrister, in-house lawyer, government lawyer); and in the case of each career, what kind of work it involves and what sort of skills are required to succeed in that career.

● How you go about becoming a solicitor or a barrister.

>

- Where you can go to do the LPC (Legal Practice Course – the vocational training course for solicitors) and the BVC (Bar Vocational Course).

- What the law schools offering the LPC and BVC are like; also how to apply to get into one of them and how to obtain funding to support you in your year doing the LPC or BVC.

- How to apply to get some experience working in the holidays in a law firm (on what's called a *vacation placement*) or in a set of barristers' chambers (on what's called a *mini-pupillage*).

- The various deadlines for applications for vacation placements and mini-pupillages.

- What it's like to work for each of the major UK law firms (and how much you'll earn); also what it's like to be a member of each of the major sets of chambers in the UK.

- The various deadlines to obtain two-year training contracts with law firms and pupillages with sets of chambers.

- What law firms operate in different areas of the country – and what law firms specialise in the various areas of law that you might be interested in working in.

It's an invaluable book. You should be able to find an up-to-date copy (it comes out every year) in your law library. If your law library doesn't have an up-to-date copy, you or your law library can order one (it costs about £17) from www.chambersstudent.co.uk. (You can also use this website to access a lot of useful information on the above issues; though I get the impression the book is more exhaustive than the website.) If you can get a free copy from your university careers centre or law faculty, you should also have a look at the latest edition of *The Training Contract & Pupillage Handbook* (Globe Business Publishing Ltd in association with The Law Society). This is another great source of useful information for aspiring solicitors and barristers. If a free copy isn't available, but you're feeling rich, you can buy a copy (it's about £25) by going to www.tcph.co.uk.

If you are seriously interested in becoming a barrister, I strongly recommend that you buy the following books, each of them written (or co-written) by an ex-student of mine: Alexander Robson and Georgina Wolfe, *The Path to*

Pupillage (Sweet & Maxwell), and Adam Kramer, *Bewigged and Bewildered: A Guide to Becoming a Barrister in England and Wales* (Hart Publishing). Both of them provide really excellent advice for anyone thinking of becoming a barrister.

Here are some more websites that you might find useful in exploring the possibilities of working as a lawyer after you leave university:

www.lawcareers.net – this is a very good, straightforward site which contains a lot of useful information for people proposing to become solicitors or barristers.

www.rollonfriday.com – this is a really fun site for solicitors, with lots of gossip, jokes and insider information. Move your cursor over 'inside info' and then click on 'city firms', and you will instantly access a table comparing salaries at all the big London law firms. If you want to get some information as to what it's like to work at one of the law firms in the table, just click on the name of the firm. Also check out the discussion forums at 'community' for tips on applications and interviews.

http://l2b.thelawyer.com – a good source of legal news and information about law firms. If you are being interviewed for a training contract by a particular law firm, it's good to show that you know a lot about the law firm and any recent developments it's been involved in. This site allows you to pick up that kind of knowledge very quickly – just type into the search engine the name of the law firm that you are applying to, click on 'go' and then start reading.

www.gls.gov.uk – this site tells you all you need to know about what is involved in working for the Government Legal Service (GLS), and how to get a job working for the GLS.

www.cps.gov.uk – this site does the same thing for the Crown Prosecution Service (CPS). (You should note, though, that while you can enter the GLS straight out of university, and get a pupillage or a training contract with the GLS, in order to become a Crown Prosecutor working for the CPS, you have to already be qualified as a barrister or a solicitor.)

Of course, you should also think about careers outside the normal solicitor/barrister paths. Quite a few of my ex-students are now making careers for themselves working for international organisations such as Amnesty International or the United Nations.

If you are interested in following their example, the normal career path seems to be:

1 get an internship at an international organisation so as to improve your cv, get some experience of what working in such an organisation is like, and develop those all important contacts that might be able to get you a permanent job later on;

2 do a one-year or two-year postgraduate Masters degree in law or economics or social work, without which you simply wouldn't be considered for a decent job at the sort of organisations I'm talking about;

3 apply, apply, apply for positions!

In order to give yourself the best possible chance of being successful in pursuing this kind of career, you need to do as much as you can now to make yourself into the kind of person that organisations such as Amnesty or the United Nations would be interested in taking on. It will be important that you have at least one other language – and the more languages you know, the better. The Michel Thomas language courses are brilliant introductions to virtually any European language you can think of: but in order to become completely confident you need to use your summer holidays to travel abroad and talk as little English as possible. It will be important that you show a long-standing interest in human rights and political issues: so join any university societies that focus on these kinds of areas, and if there aren't any, then form some. See if there are any opportunities to do voluntary fund raising work in your holidays for any international charities. Sad to say, personal contacts are absolutely crucial to getting ahead in the 'third sector' – so make as many personal contacts as you can. If you can get a mini-pupillage at a set of chambers specialising in human rights issues, then that would be a great way of getting to meet people who could open some doors for you. Attend any talks at your university on international law, and try to talk to the speakers afterwards. Try to start writing for your university newspaper, and see if you can get an interview with any 'big shots' in the international sphere. If your university offers you the option of spending a year abroad in the middle of your law degree, think about taking it – both to improve your languages, but also for the opportunity of meeting new people in a new

country who may also be interested in working for international organisations. Read as many books as you can about the work that international agencies and other non-governmental organisations do and write to the authors, or anyone you've read about who you've particularly admired.

I think that's enough advice from me about your future career plans. It's up to you now to start researching, thinking, and applying! In the end, only you will be able to tell what is the right career choice for you, and only you can do the spade work that will enable you to pursue that career once you leave university.

This is the last time you will hear from me for a little while. Just in case a 'little while' turns out to be quite some time, I wanted to give you some general advice that I think you should bear in mind whatever legal career you end up pursuing. Unlike all the other advice I've given you in the time we've known each other, I won't attempt to explain or justify the advice below. You are free to accept it or reject it, as you please. Having said that, here's my advice:

1 If you end up working as a lawyer, be kind to your clients. Treat them as you would like to be treated if they were in your shoes and you were in theirs. But don't let your desire to advance your clients' interests lead you to adopt a 'win at all costs' mentality. Never forget that you have a responsibility to treat your opponents fairly, showing a decent regard for their legitimate interests.

2 Never be proud or self-righteous. Remember that however worthy and just your cause is, it is *your cause* that is worthy and just, not *you*.

3 President Richard Nixon's farewell speech to his staff – delivered the day after he had resigned the Presidency of the United States in disgrace – is one of *the* great speeches of the twentieth century. In delivering that speech – apparently without any preparation – he achieved a level of wisdom and insight that had signally eluded him up until then. One of the final lines of the speech strikes me as being particularly wise and worth remembering: 'Always give of your best, never get discouraged, never be petty; always remember, others may hate you, but those who hate you don't win unless you hate them, and then you destroy yourself.'

>

4 Another quotation, this time from the Christian preacher John Wesley: 'Make all you can, save all you can, give all you can.' He's talking about money, which is something you'll probably be earning quite a lot of if you end up working as a practising lawyer. I don't think you'll have any problem taking Wesley's first two pieces of advice; but I'll hope you'll take the third as well. Give away as much of your money as you can afford.

5 Don't think about your self-interest. It's a trap always to be thinking about your career, or your position, or how much money you have got. Forget about all that. The only thing that should matter to you as a lawyer is that you be a *good* lawyer. If being a good lawyer brings you advancement and lots of money, then that's great. If it doesn't, then don't worry about it. It's better to lose your job or forgo a promotion if saving your job or getting that promotion requires you to sell out your principles and do something unethical. After all, 'What does it profit a man if he gains the whole world and loses his soul?'

6 It's sometimes said that while the English eat to live, the French live to eat. Try to approach your work in the same spirit as the French eat their food. Don't work simply because you get paid a good salary for doing the work you do, and this allows you to live a good life outside of work. Work because you live to do the work you do, because you love to do it. So if you've become bored and resentful of the sort of work you do as a lawyer and the only reason you can see for carrying on with it is the money it pays, *stop* doing that kind of work and find a different line of work as a lawyer that you will find more satisfying and fulfilling.

7 Having said that, don't let the work you do as a lawyer take over your life. While the work you do as a lawyer will be important, there will always be other things that are, and should be, more important and have to take priority.

That's it from me – I'm done. Good luck with everything, Jo! I'm always here for you if you ever want to talk.

All best wishes,

Nick

Appendix

● Preface: The tort wars

(from McBride and Bagshaw, *Tort Law*, 3rd edn (Pearson Education, 2008))

The current division

The academic community of tort lawyers is now divided into two rival camps.[1] Much the larger camp is made up of academics who take what we might call the *modern* view of tort law. According to this view of tort law,[2] in tort cases the courts determine whether A should be held liable to compensate B for some loss that A has caused B to suffer. According to this view, then, tort law is simply the law on compensation – it tells us when one person will be held liable to compensate another for some loss that he or she has caused that other to suffer.

Throughout the 1960s and 1970s, it was assumed without question among academic tort lawyers that the modern view of tort law was correct.

---

[1] Or possibly three. There is a school of thought that, unlike any other area of law one can possibly think of (such as contract law, or family law, or company law, or international law), tort law does not actually refer to anything in particular. According to this *nihilistic* view of tort law, nothing unites the various legal rules and principles that are customarily discussed in tort law textbooks. For some reason, this view seems quite popular among academics from the University of Cambridge: see Weir 2006, ix ('Tort is what is in the tort books, and the only thing holding it together is the binding'); Howarth and O'Sullivan 2001, 1 ('[it is] particularly difficult to present a rational or logical classification of [tort law]'); M&D, 90 ('Expecting structure, order or theoretical consistency from our courts or any underlying theory for tort recovery is perhaps asking too much from them'). It is hard to know whether these authors intend such statements to be taken seriously: why would they spend their time writing about a subject which – according to them – does not exist?

[2] Stevens 2007, at 2, calls this view of tort law, the 'loss model' of tort law.

There was universal agreement that, in the words of Lord Bingham, the 'overall object of tort law is to define cases in which the law may justly hold one party liable to compensate another.'[3] There were, of course, disagreements among the tort academics as to *why* people were held liable 'in tort' to pay compensation to someone else. Some argued that the object of such awards was to pass losses that were suffered by individuals onto business and insurance companies, so that those losses could then be spread throughout the community through price rises and premium increases, thus minimising the social impact of those losses. Others argued that in holding people liable to pay other people compensation, tort law was concerned to minimise the 'cost of accidents' by encouraging people who could most cheaply avoid an accident occurring to take the precautions required to stop that accident occurring. And a third group argued that in making compensation awards, tort law was simply concerned to protect those who had suffered a loss which they did not deserve to suffer. But these disagreements masked an underlying consensus – a universal agreement among tort academics that the modern view of tort law was correct.

That consensus began to break down in the mid-1980s – round about the time the authors of this book went to Oxford to study law. In Canada, a legal philosopher called Ernest Weinrib wrote a series of articles arguing that tort law was concerned with *corrective justice* – which, for our purposes, can be taken as a fancy name for 'remedying *wrongs*'.[4] At roughly the same time, the greatest modern scholar of English private law – Professor Peter Birks, Regius Professor of Civil Law at the University of Oxford – started to take an interest in the classification of legal obligations, as part of his work on the law of unjust enrichment. He began to argue that tort law, as a subject, is not centred around a particular *response* – that is, compensation.[5] Rather, tort law focuses on a particular *event* – the commission of a *civil wrong* – and describes the varying ways in which the law

---

[3] *Fairchild* v *Glenhaven Funeral Services Ltd* [2003] 1 AC 32 at [9].
[4] See Weinrib 1995 for the most complete statement of Weinrib's views on tort law, and law generally.
[5] It is noticeable that the first part of the US Third Restatement of Tort Law is explicitly centred around a response: 'Liability for Physical and Emotional Harm'. (The second part, 'Economic Torts and Related Wrongs', also seems based on the response of compensation for economic harm.) It is not clear how successful this approach will be: Peter Birks regarded any response-based approach to describing the law of tort as doomed to be incoherent, repetitive, and incomplete.

responds to that event.[6] Out of the work of these two academics emerged a very different view of tort law from that which held sway in the legal academy in the 1960s and 1970s, and one which is now endorsed by a significant minority of tort academics.[7] According to this view of tort law, in tort cases, the courts determine whether A has committed a wrong in relation to B, and if he has, they determine what remedies will be available to B. To put it another – exactly equivalent – way, in tort cases, the courts determine whether A has violated B's rights in acting as he did, and if he has, they determine what remedies will be available to B.

We can call this view of tort law, the *traditional* view of tort law.[8] Traditional, because up until about 40 years ago, it had *always* been thought that tort law was all about protecting people who had suffered a wrong, people whose rights had been violated.[9] Up until about 40 years ago, Lord Hope's statement in *Chester* v *Afshar* that 'the function of the law [of tort] is to enable rights to be vindicated and to provide remedies when duties have been breached'[10] would have been regarded as a statement of the obvious. But no longer: those who endorse the modern view of tort law would in all likelihood dismiss a statement such as Lord Hope's as narrow and naïve.

Why this disagreement matters

It is as impossible for a tort law textbook to be neutral on the issue of whether the modern or traditional view of tort law is correct as it is for a science textbook to be neutral on the issue of whether the Earth is flat or spherical. The issue is too fundamental for neutrality to be an option. Whether the modern or traditional view of tort law is correct affects:

1 *The reach of tort law.* One of the reasons for the popularity of the modern view of tort law among tort academics is that it makes their subject

---

[6] See Birks 1983, 1985, 1995, 1997a.

[7] See Goldberg and Zipursky 2001, 2006; Coleman 1993, 2001; Calnan 2005; Stevens 2007; Beever 2007.

[8] Stevens 2007, at 2, calls this view of tort law, the 'rights model' of tort law.

[9] For example, the full title of the 13th edition of Sir Frederick Pollock's *The Law of Torts* (published London, 1929) was 'The Law of Torts: A Treatise on the Principles of Obligations Arising From Civil Wrongs in the Common Law'. See also Goodhart 1938.

[10] [2005] 1 AC 134, at [87] (endorsed by Baroness Hale in *Gregg* v *Scott* [2005] 2 AC 176, at [216]).

so excitingly huge. On the modern view of tort law, tort law has the potential to intervene and provide a remedy in *any* situation where A has caused B to suffer some kind of loss. That is, after all, the function of tort law – to determine whether it would be 'fair, just and reasonable' to allow B to sue A for compensation, and if it would be, to allow B to sue A for compensation. So, on the modern view of tort law, any situation where one person causes another to suffer some kind of loss is one which tort academics are entitled to discuss with a view to deciding whether a remedy should be granted or not in that situation.

In contrast, the traditional view of tort law places severe constraints on the scope of tort law's jurisdiction. On the traditional view, if A has caused B to suffer some kind of loss, B will not be entitled to sue A in tort for compensation for that loss unless she can first show that A violated her rights in acting as he did. If she cannot do this then tort law has nothing to do with her and it cannot be invoked to help her out. As we will see later on in this Preface, this hurdle – of having to show that A's conduct violated B's rights – can be very difficult to surmount. And if it cannot be surmounted, that is the end of B's case so far as tort law is concerned. No matter how beneficial it might be to grant B a remedy in this situation, there is nothing to talk about so far as tort law, and the tort academics, are concerned.

2   *What goes into tort textbooks.* On the modern view of tort law, the task of a tort textbook is to set out *all* the situations where B is entitled to sue A for compensation for a loss that A has caused her to suffer. In contrast, if the traditional view of tort law is correct then a tort textbook need only concern itself with cases where B is entitled to sue A for compensation because A has violated her rights. On the traditional view of tort law, cases of what we will call 'compensation without wrongdoing' – that is, cases where B is entitled to sue A for compensation for a loss that A caused her to suffer without, however, violating B's rights – fall outside the scope of a tort textbook.

3   *How we think about the way cases are decided.* As anyone who has ever read a few tort cases will know, the way judges decide cases supports the traditional view of tort law. In a case where A has caused B to suffer some kind of loss and B is seeking some remedy against A as a result,

the judges do *not* say – 'Well, let's weigh up and pros and cons of awarding B a remedy here. On balance, we find that it would be desirable to allow B to sue A for some compensation here, so it is duly ordered that A should pay B £10,000.' Instead – just as the traditional view of tort law would lead us to expect – the judges first of all look to see if A violated B's rights in acting as he did. If he did then they will normally grant B a remedy; if he did not, B's claim will fail. *Ubi ius, ibi remedium* – where there is a right, there is a remedy. If there is no right, there is no remedy (so far as tort law is concerned).

This fact about the cases creates a problem for the modern view of tort law. How can the modern view of tort law be correct when the way tort law cases are decided makes it so obvious that the traditional view of tort law is correct? The preferred solution for those academics who adopt the modern view of tort law is to argue that when the judges *say* that they are granting B a remedy in a given case because A violated her rights, that is not the *real reason* for their decision. In order to discover the real reason, one must discard all the nonsense in the cases about 'rights' and 'duties' and 'unmask' the real 'policy concerns' that motivated the courts' decision.[11] This is another reason why the modern view of tort law is so exciting, and therefore popular among tort academics.

---

[11] Two notable examples of this kind of thinking were provided in two consecutive issues of the *Cambridge Law Journal* by the tort academic turned politician, David Howarth. In *Gorringe* v *Calderdale MBC* [2004] 1 WLR 1057, the claimant was injured when she drove her car into a bus. Had she been driving more slowly, she would have avoided the bus. The claimant sued the defendant local authority for failing to put up a warning sign by the side of the road, telling her to slow down. Lord Hoffmann, giving the leading judgment, dismissed the claimant's case on the ground that the defendant local authority had not owed her a duty to save her from the consequences of her own foolishness. According to Howarth 2004, at 548, the real reason for the decision was Lord Hoffmann's 'extremist hostility to the very idea of negligence liability.' In *Sutradhar* v *Natural Environment Research Council* [2006] 4 All ER 490, the claimant was poisoned from drinking water contaminated with arsenic. He sued the defendants in negligence for compensation – they had surveyed the water in the area where the claimant lived but did not test it for arsenic; had they done so, the arsenic would have been detected and steps would have been taken to protect people like the claimant from suffering arsenic poisoning. The House of Lords upheld the Court of Appeal's decision to throw out the claim, on the ground that the defendants – not having had any kind of contact or developed any kind of relationship with the claimant – had not owed him a duty to take steps to save him from suffering arsenic poisoning. According to Howarth 2005a's note on the Court of Appeal's decision, at 25, 'The court's real worry in *Sutradhar* seems to have been the 699 other claimants waiting in the wings and that their success might put a large hole in Britain's international development budget.'

It *is* exciting to think that you have found out what is really going on – that the courts are pursuing a secret agenda in the cases and you know what that agenda is. But it must always be remembered that exciting is not necessarily true. It may be exciting to think that President Kennedy was assassinated by the CIA and the Mafia. But it is not necessarily true.

At any rate, whether the traditional view of tort law is correct or not should have a big impact on the way we think about the way tort cases are decided. If the traditional view is correct, then we have no reason not to take the judges seriously when they deny a claimant a remedy in a tort case on the ground that the defendant did not violate her rights in acting as he did. If the traditional view of tort law is wrong, and tort law is not in fact concerned with vindicating a claimant's rights, then in tort cases where a judge denies a claimant a remedy on the ground that the defendant did not violate the claimant's rights in acting as he did, that cannot be the real reason for the judge's decision. The fact that the defendant did not violate the claimant's rights cannot be sufficient reason to deny her a remedy in tort. Something else must be going on – and we need to find out what it is.

4   *How we judge whether a case was correctly decided.* Finally, whether the traditional or modern view of tort law is correct will have a big impact on how we approach the issue of judging whether a given tort case was correctly decided. For example, in *Bradford Corporation* v *Pickles*,[12] the defendant blocked off a stream of water flowing under his land so that the water could not flow into the claimants' reservoirs. The claimants sued the defendant in tort. They lost: as they had no right to receive the water that flowed under the defendant's land, the defendant did nothing wrong to the claimants in blocking that water off. Was this case correctly decided?

If we adopt the traditional view of tort law then we will approach this issue by asking whether the House of Lords in *Bradford Corporation* v *Pickles* was right to say that the claimants had no rights over the water flowing under the defendant's land. If the House of Lords' decision on this issue was correct, then *Bradford Corporation* v *Pickles* was correctly decided: the defendant did not violate the claimants' rights in acting as

---

[12] [1895] AC 587.

he did, and so the claimants could not have been entitled to a remedy in tort against the defendant. If, on the other hand, we adopt the modern view of tort law, then that cannot be the end of the matter. So what if the defendant did not wrong the claimants in acting as he did? The traditional view of tort law is wrong: recovery in tort is *not* conditional on its being shown that the defendant violated the claimants' rights in cutting off the water to their reservoirs. Instead, we should look at the pros and cons of awarding a remedy here, taking *all* the circumstances of the case into account.

What we think

So it is simply impossible to write a tort textbook without either endorsing the modern view of tort law or the traditional view of tort law. Too much depends on which view is correct. So where do we stand? We endorse the traditional view of tort law, and wholly reject the modern view of tort law. We do so for two reasons.

1 *Process.* As has already been observed, *the way* tort cases are decided supports the traditional view of tort law. In a negligence case, the courts ask: did the defendant breach a *duty* of care owed to the claimant? In a case where a claimant is suing a defendant in nuisance because the defendant blocked something from coming onto the claimant's land, the courts ask: did the claimant have a *right* to receive the thing that the defendant obstructed from coming onto the claimant's land? Admittedly, in other tort cases, the courts tend not to inquire into whether the claimant had a right that the defendant not act as he did, or whether the defendant owed the claimant a duty not to act as he did. However, that is because if the defendant did what the claimant is alleging he did ('He hit me'; 'He unjustly slandered me'; 'He lied to me'; 'He sold his goods pretending they were made by me') it will be so obvious that the defendant violated the claimant's rights in acting as he did that the issue is not worth going into. In tort cases where there *is* an issue whether the defendant violated the claimant's rights even if he did what the claimant alleged he did, the courts *always* ask, as a precondition of awarding the claimant a remedy: If the defendant did what he is alleged to have done, did the defendant's actions violate the

claimant's rights/did the defendant breach a duty owed to the claimant? Of course, it is *possible* that all this talk of 'rights' and 'duties' in the tort cases is a fiction – a 'device' that the courts employ to achieve some goal that they would rather not tell everyone they are pursuing. But it is not *likely*.

2   *Outcomes.* The traditional view of tort law explains the *outcome* of tort cases far better than the modern view. Take, for example, this imaginary case.[13] Suppose that John is a stockbroker and he secretly hates Paul because he wishes he could go out with Paul's girlfriend, Mary. One day John finds out that Biocorp – a public company – is about to announce that it is insolvent. John sees his chance to do Paul down. He rings Paul up and says, 'Paul – don't tell anyone I've told you this, but I hear on the grapevine that a company called Biocorp is about to announce that it has discovered a vaccine for AIDS. Buy as many Biocorp shares as you possibly can – the price will rocket as soon as this news gets out.' Paul instantly rings Mary up to tell her the good news. As a result, Paul invests £50,000 in Biocorp, and Mary invests £10,000. They both lose all their money when it is announced that Biocorp is insolvent.

Now – anyone who knows anything about tort law will be able to tell you that Paul will be able to sue John in tort for compensation for the fact that he has lost his £50,000; and that Mary will *not* be able to sue John. This is not a matter of dispute: this is a very easy case.[14] The traditional view of tort law has no problem explaining this result. When John lied to Paul he violated Paul's rights, not Mary's. So Paul is entitled to a remedy in tort in this case – compensation for the loss that he suffered as a result of John's lying to him – but Mary is not. John did not violate Mary's rights in acting as he did, so tort law does nothing for her. On the modern view of tort law, the fact that Mary is not entitled to sue John for damages here is very hard to explain. John is a bad man, and the courts are not normally overly concerned to limit the liabilities of bad men. But here they do – they only allow Paul to sue John, not Mary. Why? At the very least, if the modern view of tort law

[13] Zipursky 1998a can claim the credit for being the first to point out the huge hole in the modern view of tort law that the law's treatment of this case creates.

[14] It is so easy that it is very hard to find a case to demonstrate that Mary cannot sue John here.

were correct, one would not expect this to be such an easy case for tort lawyers to resolve. One would expect some voices to be raised in the decided cases in favour of allowing Mary to sue John. But there is nothing – for tort lawyers, nothing could be more obvious than that Mary cannot sue John here. Only the traditional view of tort law explains why it is so obvious to tort lawyers that Mary has no claim in this situation.

So – the traditional view of tort law explains *both* the way tort cases are decided, *and* the outcome of those cases. The modern view of tort law finds it difficult to cope with either task. Only one conclusion can be drawn: the traditional view of tort law is correct; the modern view of tort law must be rejected as heresy. As the great physicist Richard Feynman would tell his students, 'It doesn't matter how beautiful your theory is, it doesn't matter how smart you are. If it doesn't agree with experiment, it's wrong.' In judging whether a particular view of tort law is correct it is irrelevant how popular or unpopular that view is. The truth is not a matter of majority vote. The *only* way to determine whether a given view of tort law is correct is to ask: is it consistent with the reality of what happens in tort cases? The traditional theory of tort law passes this test; the modern view of tort law does not. In the war that now prevails among tort academics over the nature of tort law, we are firmly on the side of those academics who endorse the traditional view of tort law, and have written this textbook on that basis.[15]

The relevance of public policy to tort law

While we unequivocally reject the modern view of tort law, we disagree with those who have taken their dislike of the modern view of tort law to such an extreme that they deny that considerations of public policy should have any role to play in the operation of the tort law system.[16] To explain: those who endorse the modern view of tort law take the view that if A has

---

[15] Readers who are interested in pursuing this debate are referred to the opening pages of Chapter 3 ('Tort Law and Its Critics'), as well as the Appendix to this book, where we deal with Professor Jane Stapleton's criticisms of the traditional view of tort law. Student readers who are coming to tort law for the first time are advised not to read these passages until they have at least read Chapters 1 and 2 of this book and gained a bit more knowledge of tort law and its terminology.
[16] See, in particular, Beever 2007; and, to some extent, Stevens 2007.

caused B to suffer some kind of loss, A should be held liable in tort to compensate B for that loss if, all things considered, it would be desirable to make A pay B such compensation. On this view, considerations of what is in the public interest – or, in other words, considerations of public policy – have a crucial role to play in determining whether A should be held liable in tort to compensate B for the loss that she has suffered. If it would be contrary to the public interest to make A liable to compensate B, then it is obvious that A should *not* be held liable in tort to pay such compensation to B. If it would be in the public interest to make A compensate B, then it is equally obvious that A *should* be held liable in tort to compensate B.

So on the modern view of tort law, the courts *must* take into account considerations of public policy in determining whether A should be held liable in tort to compensate B for some loss that he has caused her to suffer. Some academics who are hostile to the modern view of tort law would like to argue that this is *wholly* wrong: considerations of public policy should not be taken into account *at all* by the courts in determining whether A should be held liable in tort to compensate B. Now – we *agree* that the mere fact that it would be in the public interest to make A compensate B is not enough to justify making A liable in tort to compensate B. If B's rights have not been violated in the situation we are considering, then A cannot be held liable *in tort* to compensate B for the loss that she has suffered. However, we cannot accept that considerations of public policy should have no role at all to play in how tort law cases are decided:

1   *Determining whether someone's rights have been violated.* If B wants to argue that A violated her rights in acting in some way, it seems to us that one has to take into account considerations of public policy in determining whether B had a right that A not act in the way he did. For example, suppose that B argues: 'A said something offensive to me and that upset me a great deal. I have an ongoing right that A not do anything that might offend me, so A violated my rights in acting as he did.' In determining whether B has such a right against A,[17] it seems to us obvious that one has to take into account the impact on freedom of speech that recognising the existence of such a right would have, and that the adverse effect that recognising a 'right not to be offended'

---

[17] See, generally, Duff and Marshall 2006.

would have on freedom of speech is one of the most obvious reasons why no such right is recognised in English law.

2 *Granting a remedy in a case where a wrong has been committed.* Let's assume that A has violated B's rights and B has suffered some kind of loss as a result. B is allowed to sue A in tort for compensation for the loss that she has suffered. As we will explain in more detail in Chapter 3, it seems to us that the reason why the law allows B to sue A for compensation in this case is because it is in the public interest that wrongs should be remedied. In the words of Lord Bingham, 'the rule of *public policy* that has first claim on the loyalty of the law [is] that wrongs should be remedied.'[18]

3 *Denying a remedy in a case where a wrong has been committed.* Suppose that it is admitted that A violated B's rights in acting as he did. Let's assume, for example, that A hit B for no good reason. In this sort of case, there is a strong presumption that B should have some sort of remedy against A for his conduct. But it seems to us obvious that if it would be contrary to the public interest to allow B to sue A in this case, then no remedy should be granted to B. The Latin sentiment, 'Let justice be done, though the heavens fall'[19] is *not* one that appeals to us. As we will see – most obviously in Chapter 26 ('Limits on the Right to Sue') – English law frequently denies remedies to the victims of wrongs on the ground that it would be contrary to the public interest to allow such a remedy to be granted.

4 *Adding extra remedies onto the basic structure of tort law.* The basic rule that underlies tort law goes as follows: if A violates B's rights and B suffers loss as a result, then B will normally be entitled to sue A for compensation for that loss. However, as we will see, the law adds lots of extra rules to that basic rule, such as:

(i) If A violates B's rights and B dies as a result, and B's dependants suffer a consequent loss of support, B's dependants will normally be allowed to sue A for compensation for that loss of support.

---

[18] *D* v *East Berkshire Community NHS Trust* [2005] 2 AC 373, at [24]–[25] (emphasis added).
[19] '*Fiat justitia, ruat coelum*' (the statement is usually attributed to Julius Caesar's father-in-law, Lucius Calpurnius Piso Caesoninus).

(ii)   If A was acting in the course of his employment by C when he violated B's rights, then B will normally be entitled not only to sue A for compensation for the loss she suffered as a result of A's wrong; she will also be entitled to sue C for such compensation.

(iii) If A violates B's rights in such an outrageous manner that he deserves to be punished for his conduct, then B may be entitled to sue A not just for damages to compensate her for the loss she has suffered as a result of A's wrong, but for extra damages designed to bring A's total liability up to a level sufficient to punish him adequately for what he has done.

As we will see when we look at these rules in more detail, it seems obvious that the law gives effect to all these extra rules because it is in the public interest to do so.

So we would reject the extremist position that considerations of public policy should not be taken into account at all in deciding tort law cases. The courts frequently take such considerations into account, and we see nothing wrong with their doing so.

End Notes

○ Letter 1 Why Law?

Take the following passage, which I believe is representative of the sort of thing you might read if you did an English degree. The passage is from Marshall McLuhan, 'Pound, Eliot and the rhetoric of *The Waste Land*' (1979) 10 *New Literary History* 557, at 557.

The Gettysburg Address. Delivered by President Abraham Lincoln on November 19, 1863 at the dedication of the Soldiers' National Cemetery at Gettysburg, where four and a half months before the soldiers of the Union Army scored a decisive, but bloody victory (roughly 50,000 Americans were killed in three days of fighting) over the rebel Confederate forces. This is regarded as the definitive text of Lincoln's address:

> Four score and seven years ago our fathers brought forth on this continent, a new nation, conceived in Liberty, and dedicated to the proposition that all men are created equal.
>
> Now we are engaged in a great civil war, testing whether that nation, or any nation so conceived and so dedicated, can long endure. We are met on a great battlefield of that war. We have come to dedicate a portion of that field, as a final resting place for those who here gave their lives that that nation might live. It is altogether fitting and proper that we should do this.
>
> But, in a larger sense, we can not dedicate – we can not consecrate – we can not hallow – this ground. The brave men, living and dead, who struggled here, have consecrated it, far above our poor power to add
>
> >

or detract. The world will little note, nor long remember what we say here, but it can never forget what they did here. It is for us the living, rather, to be dedicated here to the unfinished work which they who fought here have thus far so nobly advanced. It is rather for us to be here dedicated to the great task remaining before us – that from these honored dead we take increased devotion to that cause for which they gave the last full measure of devotion – that we here highly resolve that these dead shall not have died in vain – that this nation, under God, shall have a new birth of freedom – and that government of the people, by the people, for the people, shall not perish from the earth.

Thomas Hobbes. In Thomas Hobbes' *Leviathan*, Hobbes describes the natural state of mankind (i.e. the state of mankind in a world without legal systems) as involving a 'warre of every man against every man'. In such a state, he explains:

there is no place for Industry; because the fruit thereof is uncertain; and consequently no Culture of the Earth; no Navigation, nor use of the commodities that may be imported by Sea; no commodious Building; no Instruments of moving, and removing such things as require much force; no Knowledge of the face of the Earth; no account of Time; no Arts; no Letters; no Society; and which is worst of all, continuall feare, and danger of violent death; And the life of man, solitary, poore, nasty, brutish, and short.

Roberto Mangabeira Unger. See *The Critical Legal Studies Movement* (Harvard University Press, 1983), p. 119. His quote was originally about legal academics.

Competition for law jobs. A report prepared for the Law Society in 2003 by Heather Rolfe and Tracy Anderson, from the National Institute of Economic and Social Research ('A firm decision: the recruitment of trainee solicitors') is illuminating as to the sort of things taken into account by law firms in choosing who to recruit from the universities. A summary of the report can be downloaded from the Internet. Go to:

www.niesr.ac.uk/pdf/law.pdf

Letter 2 The Right Stuff?

Sudoku puzzles. Sudoku puzzles are readily available for free online. Try:

http://www.sudokuoftheday.com

What do they of cricket know? . . . See C.L.R. James, *Beyond a Boundary* (Hutchinson, 1963), Preface.

Letter 3 Law Degree or GDL?

A recent survey. See Vera Bermingham and John Hodgson, 'Desiderata: What lawyers want from their recruits' (2001) 35 *Law Teacher* 1, 20–1.

Letter 4 Arguing Effectively (1): Logical Arguments

In writing this chapter, I was heavily influenced by Peter Kreeft's excellent *Socratic Logic* (St Augustine's Press, 2004).

Letter 5 Arguing Effectively (2): Speculative Arguments

Occam's Razor. Named after William of Ockham, who was a friar who lived in England in the fourteenth century and was interested in logic.

Peter Birks. See his *Unjust Enrichment* (Clarendon Law Series: 1st edn, 2003; 2nd edn 2005).

Letter 8 Some Traps to Avoid

Allan Bloom. See his *The Closing of the American Mind* (Simon & Schuster, 1987), 25.

We know the statement 'all truth is relative' cannot be absolutely true. Similarly, if a *Cretan* told you 'All Cretans lie, all the time', you would automatically know that that could not be true. If his statement *were* true, then he would be telling the truth, in which case it wouldn't be true to say that all Cretans lie all the time.

Roger Scruton. See his *Modern Philosophy* (Pimlico, 2004), 6. For a slightly different attack on the idea that 'all truth is relative' – and the desire to be open-minded – see G. K. Chesterton, *Heretics* (1905), chapter 20:

> The human brain is a machine for coming to conclusions; if it cannot come to conclusions it is rusty. When we hear of a man too clever to believe, we are hearing of something having almost the character of a contradiction in terms. It is like hearing of a nail that was too good to hold down a carpet; or a bolt that was too strong to keep a door shut . . . Man can be defined as an animal that makes dogmas. As he piles doctrine on doctrine and conclusion on conclusion in the formation of some tremendous scheme of philosophy and religion, he is . . . becoming more and more human. When he drops one doctrine after another in a refined scepticism, when he declines to tie himself to a system, when he says that he has outgrown definitions, when he says that he disbelieves in finality, when, in his own imagination, he sits as God, holding no form of creed but contemplating all, then he is by that very process sinking slowly backwards into the vagueness of the vagrant animals and the unconsciousness of the grass. Trees have no dogmas. Turnips are singularly broad-minded.

The Brothers Karamazov. Translation © Richard Pevear and Larissa Volokhonsky, North Point Press, 1990.

Ronald Dworkin. See Dworkin, 'Rights as trumps' in Jeremy Waldron (ed.), *Theories of Rights* (Oxford University Press, 1984).

● Letter 10 A Mini-Dictionary of Law

Condemnation of Terrorism (United Nations Measures) Order 2006. See *A, K, M, Q & G* v *H.M. Treasury* [2008] EWHC 869 (Admin).

Legislation. See further John Gardner, 'Some types of law' in Douglas Edlin (ed.), *Common Law Theory* (Cambridge University Press, 2008).

A provision in an Act of Parliament will not be given effect to by the courts if it is inconsistent with European Union law. See *Macarthys Ltd v Smith* [1979] 3 All ER 325, 329; *R v Secretary of State for Transport*, ex p *Factortame Ltd* [1990] 2 AC 85; and *Thoburn v Sunderland City Council* [2003] QB 151.

Parliament is free – within as yet unspecified limits – to pass legislation that will have the effect of changing the definition of what counts as an Act of Parliament. See *Regina (Jackson) v Attorney General* [2006] 1 AC 262. A very clear discussion of the *Jackson* case can be found in David Feldman's chapter on 'Constitutional Law' in Barnard, O'Sullivan and Virgo (eds), *What About Law?* (Hart Publishing, 2007).

Rule of law. For the first view of the rule of law, see Lon Fuller, *The Morality of Law* (New Haven, 1969), chapter 2; also Joseph Raz, 'The rule of law and its virtue' (1977) 93 *Law Quarterly Review* 195 (reprinted in Raz, *The Authority of Law* (Clarendon Press, 1979), chapter 11). For the second and third views of the rule of law see Friedrich Hayek, *The Constitution of Liberty* (Chicago, 1960).

Montesquieu. See his *The Spirit of the Laws*, Book XI, chapter 6 ('On the constitution of England'):

> When the legislative and executive powers are united in the same person, or in the same body of magistrates, there can be no liberty; because apprehensions may arise, lest the same monarch or senate should enact tyrannical laws, to execute them in a tyrannical manner.
>
> Again, there is no liberty, if the judiciary power be not separated from the legislative and the executive. Were it joined with the legislative, the life and liberty of the subject would be exposed to arbitrary control; for the judge would then be the legislator. Were it joined with the executive power, the judge might behave with violence and oppression.
>
> There would be an end of everything, were the same man or the same body, whether of the nobles or of the people, to exercise those three powers, that of enacting laws, that of executing the public resolutions, and of trying the causes of individuals.

◉ Letter 12 The General Approach

Question-driven approach to learning about a subject. This approach to studying a subject is not new. In fact it is as old as Western philosophy. A different name for this approach to learning about a subject might be the *Socratic method* – named after Socrates, the grandfather of Western philosophy, who used a question-driven approach to find out from other people what exactly they knew about the meaning of concepts such as justice or virtue or courage. We nowadays give the name *Socratic method* to a particular method of *teaching* – that is, teaching students by asking them questions. American law schools regularly use the Socratic method to teach their students law, much to the frustration of the students: see, for example, Atticus Falcon, *Planet Law School*, 2nd edn (Fine Print Press, 2003) or Scott Turow, *One L* (Warner, 1977). In fact, the Socratic method is very effective as a teaching device – but only if the teacher is prepared regularly to inject *new* information into the discussion. It would be interesting – though very hard work – to teach in a university where students were taught law through the Socratic method, properly applied. So instead of giving the students lectures and making them read textbooks, teachers would talk to the students *all day*, giving them new pieces of information about the law every five minutes (say) while constantly asking them questions all the time to test their developing understanding of the law. I suspect such a university would achieve far better results in law than can be achieved using the lecture-and-textbook method of teaching.

◉ Letter 14 Reading a Case

Consider the following (imaginary) case. Another imaginary case demonstrating a variety of different approaches to deciding a case is provided by Lon Fuller, 'The case of the Speluncean Explorers' (1949) 62 *Harvard Law Review* 616.

◉ Letter 16 Reading an Article

Article on libertarians and crack cocaine. The format of this (imaginary) article is modelled on Anthony Kronman's article, 'Contract law and distributive justice' (1980) 89 *Yale Law Journal* 473.

Letter 19 How to Write an Essay

Interfoto case. See *Interfoto Picture Library* v *Stiletto Visual Programmes* [1989] QB 433, CA.

Bruce McFarlane. Letter to Michael Wheeler-Booth, 18 September 1956. See Harriss (ed.), *Bruce McFarlane's Letters to Friends 1940–1966* (Magdalen College, Oxford, 1997).

Letter 20 A Sample Essay

The mens rea of murder. See *Hyam* v *DPP* [1975] AC 55; *R* v *Moloney* [1985] AC 905; *R* v *Hancock and Shankland* [1986] AC 455; *R* v *Nedrick* [1986] 1 WLR 1025; *R* v *Woollin* [1999] 1 AC 82; *Re A (children) (conjoined twins: medical treatment)* [2001] Fam 147; John Finnis, 'Intention and side effects' in Frey and Morris (eds), *Liability and Responsibility* (Cambridge University Press, 1991); Lord Goff, 'The mental element in murder' (1988) 104 *Law Quarterly Review* 30; Glanville Williams, 'Oblique intention' (1988) 47 *Cambridge Law Journal* 417; Glanville Williams, 'The *mens rea* for murder – leave it alone' (1989) 105 *Law Quarterly Review* 387; Law Commission Consultation Paper No. 177, *A New Homicide Act for England and Wales* (2005), Part 4.

Letter 24 Last Advice Before the Exams

Thomas Dixon. See his *How To Get A First* (Routledge, 2004), 145–146.

Letter 25 Moving On

What does it profit a man . . . Matthew 16:26; Mark 8:36.

Attitudes to work. See Dorothy L. Sayers, 'Why work?' in her *Creed or Chaos? and other Essays* (Methuen, 1947).

Index

LawExpress

Understand quickly. Revise effectively. Take exams with confidence.

CONSTITUTIONAL AND ADMINISTRATIVE LAW

CONTRACT LAW

LAND LAW

EMPLOYMENT LAW

BUSINESS LAW

COMPANY LAW

CRIMINAL LAW

EQUITY AND TRUSTS

FAMILY LAW

EU LAW

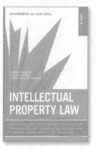
INTELLECTUAL PROPERTY LAW

TORT LAW

Other titles are available within the series.